ARISTOTLE'S
LAPTOP
The Discovery of our Informational Mind

Series on Machine Consciousness
ISSN: 2010-3158

Series Editor: Antonio Chella *(University of Palermo, Italy)*

Published

Series on Machine Consciousness – Vol. 1

ARISTOTLE'S LAPTOP

The Discovery of our Informational Mind

Igor Aleksander

Helen Morton

World Scientific

NEW JERSEY · LONDON · SINGAPORE · BEIJING · SHANGHAI · HONG KONG · TAIPEI · CHENNAI

Published by

World Scientific Publishing Co. Pte. Ltd.

5 Toh Tuck Link, Singapore 596224

USA office: 27 Warren Street, Suite 401-402, Hackensack, NJ 07601

UK office: 57 Shelton Street, Covent Garden, London WC2H 9HE

British Library Cataloguing-in-Publication Data
A catalogue record for this book is available from the British Library.

Series on Machine Consciousness — Vol. 1
ARISTOTLE'S LAPTOP
The Discovery of our Informational Mind

Copyright © 2012 by World Scientific Publishing Co. Pte. Ltd.

ISBN 978-981-4343-49-7

Typeset by Stallion Press
Email: enquiries@stallionpress.com

Printed in Singapore.

Contents

Contents

Foreword

Writing the first book in Antonio Chella's series on machine consciousness has been not only a pleasurable honor but also a daunting challenge. It was clear from the start that we should write about fundamentals rather than robots or algorithms. But what is fundamental about having a conscious mind? Applying the tenet of: "when in doubt consult Aristotle", the answer is clear in his *de Anima* (of the soul). For Aristotle, the fundamental nature of the mind is that it is a part of the soul and the soul is that which defines life in a human being. What can be more fundamental than that? From this perspective, no matter how smart a machine will be, it is not going to be alive and possess a conscious mind in the way of a living being. The point of this book is that the advent of information theory in the late 1940s, through the genius of US engineer Claude Shannon, totally changed the way one can think of machines. It became possible to ask and answer the question 'can a machine be conscious?' without treating the conscious mind as having the prerequisite of life. Instead of defining mind as a functional, thinking part of a living creature one can ask what constitutes the mind and how does it relate to what constitutes the brain. The answer we advocate is 'information'. Aristotle lived before 300 BC, when all known autonomous creatures for him were purposeful through the mind part of their 'soul' (defined as that which makes a body into a living object). Then the notion of information as a palpable, albeit immaterial, entity did not exist.

With this in our thoughts we follow two strands of scientific history — one in which the functioning of the living brain has been the subject of study through the conventional physical and biological sciences, and the other, that which Shannon suggests is transacted between communicating brains (real or artificial). The exciting part is the overlap between these two strands. So we directed this book at this overlap where we find brain and body which, we argue, is animated not by an Aristotelian soul but by Shannonian information. This idea has been increasingly accepted among theoreticians, particularly as a result of a paradigm called 'information integration' which is thought to be required by any physical system which can sustain consciousness, whether natural or artificial. Much of the book aims to explain the significance of this approach. We have chosen an essay style concentrating on the contributions of giants on whose shoulders the machine consciousness scientist, engineer or philosopher might stand. And, returning to Aristotle, we ask whether he might have relished an awareness of information theory in formulating his philosophy of the mind.

We are delighted to thank those who have helped us during the writing of the book. Antonio Chella has been most encouraging and has accepted our delays in delivering this manuscript with a cheerful mien. We would also like to thank Roz Davy for casting her professional psychoanalytic eye over chapter 9. We thank family and friends for putting up with "sorry, can't make it today – busy with the book". Finally we would like to thank our friends at the "Café de la Place" and the "Orange Bleue" in Octon, Languedoc, France, for plying us with coffee and the occasional glass of rosé and keeping us amused during the final editing stage of the book.

Igor and Helen, Roques
1 January 2012

Chapter 1

OVERVIEW: FROM ARISTOTLE TO THE BITS OF AN INFORMATIONAL MIND

All Things Informational

How can anything, let alone the mind, be informational? At the time of writing (January 2012), it is estimated that more than 300 million people in the world use laptops or personal computers, of which about 50 million use the internet to access virtual worlds where virtual creatures can exist.[1] While a scientist may regard this activity in the perspective of how well the technology works, philosophers may perceive it differently, by questioning how the 'existence' of a virtual object differs from, or is similar to, the existence of a real object in the real world. Some even take an enormous leap by saying that the way virtual objects 'exist' in a computer can throw some light on how the mind exists in the brain.[2] In contrast, in this book, we intend the computer to take a backseat in such discussions. We do argue, however, that virtual objects can exist as states of neural networks and that such objects can have just as vivid a character as any virtual creature in a virtual world created by an artist/programmer. However, neural network and the cells of a living brain have been in existence even before the advent of the programmed creature, some of these virtual objects are simply called the *thoughts* of the living organism. They are certainly not put there by a programmer but they arise through the attrition of living or, put in a less tortuous way, by the process of *building up experience by living*.

---

[1] See http://gigaom.com/2007/05/20/virtual-world-population-50-million-by-2011/.
[2] John Pollock, a philosopher at the University of Arizona, has written about this topic (see http://oscarhome.soc-sci.arizona.edu/ftp/PAPERS/Virtual-machines. pdf) as has the philosopher/computer scientist Aaron Sloman of the University of Birmingham in the UK (particularly 'Virtual Machines in Philosophy, Engineering & Biology' contributed to the 2008 Workshop on Philosophy and Engineering — See http://www.illigal.uiuc.edu/web/wpe/about/).

We are not the first to suggest that mind is a virtual object which emerges from a neural network.[3] But what are virtual objects? What are they made of? The inevitable, but not immediately comprehensible, answer is that a virtual machine is *informational.* This book is an attempt to unravel and explain this somewhat curious postulate. How can anything be made of information? How reassuring is it to know that our minds might be informational?

Aristotle appears in the title of this chapter because, with unequaled clarity and persuasiveness, he has shaped philosophy *and* science in a way that has remained influential right up to the present. As he would not have known what is meant by 'informational', the reflection of his ideas into modern philosophy of mind might be a factor that makes some philosophers reluctant to consider the possibility of the mind being informational.

It was only 2,500 years later that the so-called information sciences began to encroach scientifically on the human domain of communication. That communication can be assessed in terms of bits and bytes, computers can have memory and computers can even have malfunctions through electronic viruses are facts that are fairly well known to anyone who owns a laptop or a PC. And yet, looking for the 'mind' of an informational machine may still appear to be breaking some basic scientific rules. This book attempts, in the humblest possible way, to suggest that, had Aristotle possessed a laptop, he himself might have bridged the gap.

Sadly, scientists and philosophers have somewhat parted company on the validity of an informational approach to the mind. Much heated debate lies in scientific claims that philosophy brings nothing verifiable into our knowledge. Similarly, the philosopher does not like some elements of scientific certainty, seeing it as a form of arrogance. The basis of the informational style of argument is, however, scientific. The fact that it raises philosophical questions of existence and mind heralds a tiny glimpse of hope that philosophy and science may unite in an attempt to make progress. There is a problem of language. Expressions of the theory of information are mathematical and sometimes incomprehensible to those who do not naturally warm to the language of mathematics. This book aims to remove some of these barriers by tracing how some of the principles of information science have come about and how they might be expressed simply.

---

[3]Dennett, D. (1991). *Consciousness Explained* (Allen Lane, The Penguin Press).

The cast of characters in this story certainly includes Aristotle but also many others. Information is a young science and, in this first chapter, those who created it make their first appearance and then reappear later in the book. One aim of the book is to show that the true meaning of 'the age of information' is not, as some will have us believe, that we are a species driven by satellite navigation from computer workstation to digital television, while speaking to our virtual agents on mobile phones. The ambition is to be positive and suggest that the age of information is a future age in which our own minds will be better understood through a common interest among philosophers, scientists and computer experts in all things informational.

What is Information?

Remembering that we live in the 'information age' and asking ' what something is' drives the fingers in a rush to an internet search engine. Why not? In the case of 'What is information?' a number of definitions can be found. Here are some examples[4]:

> '*A message received and understood*'
> '*Knowledge acquired through study or experience or instruction*'
> '*A collection of facts from which conclusions may be drawn*'
> '*A numerical measure of the uncertainty of an outcome*'

The many answers are not a sign of differences of opinion among those who attempt a definition, but are more an indication that the word has multiple meanings. Floridi[5] calls 'information' 'a notoriously polymorphic phenomenon and a polysemantic concept', i.e., a word with many aspects and meanings. Floridi's philosophy analyses the multiplicity of these meanings by starting with a 'well-formed' *datum* which can have several characteristics: truth/falsehood, environmental (the height of a tree), instructional (being told how to do something) or factual (a state of affairs). Here we advocate for a more coherent analysis of the seeming diversity.

Taking the above list, consider 'A message received and understood'. The mention of a 'message' implies that there must be an entity who or which (not to exclude machines) wishes to send a message. There must be

---

[4]Available at http://wordnet.princeton.edu/perl/webwn?s=information.
[5]Floridi, G. (2010). *The Philosophy of Information* (Oxford University Press, Oxford).

a recipient of the message who or which does the *understanding*! But what is it to *understand* something? How quickly does the first attempt to find a simple definition of information bump into a huge philosophical problem. How are things understood? Here is what British philosopher John Locke (1632–1704), said in the first paragraph of his celebrated three-volume opus, 'An Essay Concerning Human Understanding'[6]:

> *...An inquiry into the understanding, pleasant and useful. — Since it is the understanding that sets man above the rest of sensible beings, and gives him all the advantage and dominion which he has over them; it is certainly a subject, even for its nobleness, worth our labour to inquire into...*

It is not the intention here to discuss Locke's philosophy, but to begin to appreciate that definitions of information naturally lead to matters of the mind. Indeed, words like 'knowledge', 'experience' and 'conclusions', in the other definitions, imply some mental effort. But the link is vague. An attempt to describe it in an unambiguous way needs to be taken in small steps.

It may seem odd, but a good place to start looking at information as a scientific idea is the most obscure of the above definitions: 'a numerical measure of the uncertainty of an outcome'. This definition refers to ideas which begin with the work in 1948 of a young engineer on the staff of the Bell Research Laboratories in the USA. He is Claude Elwood Shannon, (1916–2001).

Shannon and Crackly Telephone Lines and Minds

(Chapter 2. Shannon: The Reluctant Hero of the Information Age)

Claude Shannon is mostly associated with providing measurements and formulae that enable engineers to measure the efficiency of transmission media (telegraph lines, radio waves in space, etc.) But what has this to do with the mind? Shannon's efforts to measure information is based on surprise. 'The more one is surprised by a message or an experience, the

---

[6]First published in 1688, now available in the *Wordsworth Classics of World Literature* series.

more is the information gained'. We shall see that this fact alone allows us to suggest hypotheses as to how mind develops.

It was a quiet and subtle revolution: no headlines, no media presentations and no fuss. But, in 1948, Claude Shannon's formal definition of information made it possible, for the first time, to make information appear to be a utility like water or gas. *Amounts* of information became measurable in 'bits' as did the quality and capacity of transmission media such as telegraph wires, radio waves or just the air that transmits the pressure waves created by our voices. He made it possible to show why a crackly telephone line transmits less information than a good one.

According to Lord Kelvin, the ability to measure is to have a science[7]:

> ...*when you can measure what you are speaking about, and express it in numbers, you know something about it; but when you cannot measure it, ...you have scarcely in your thoughts advanced to the state of Science.*

Measuring information in bits or bytes (chunks of 8 bits) is second nature now: words like 'broadband', 'hi-fi' and 'megabytes per second' are familiar to anyone who owns a computer, a music system or a smart mobile phone. Even those who are not totally sure what such quantities mean are prepared to pay more for more 'megabytes per second' in their internet connection, knowing that it will enable them to download their movies more swiftly.

In defining a measurable quantity, information, Shannon has also spawned an underlying science called *Information Theory*. Engineers who design contemporary commodities such as the internet, cellular networks for mobile phones and global positioning systems (GPS) would be lost without this theory. But where does this leave the philosophical difficulties about 'understanding'? It is clear that Shannon found the idea of 'meaning' difficult, driving him to address deliberately the medium for carrying the meaning and not the actual message. Unless the medium has enough *carrier* capacity, the meaning will not be conveyed. So he wanted to measure amounts of information as a *carrier* for meaning for the purpose of transmitting as much of it as possible. Such capacity can be restricted by, for example, low 'fidelity' and interference from electrical 'noise' which are the chief enemies of good communication. He wrote clearly about concentrating

---

[7]Lord Kelvin (Sir William Thompson): *Popular Lectures and Addresses* (1891–1894, 3 volumes).

on the carrying medium and avoiding the (semantic) issues of the meaning of information in the second paragraph of his '*A Mathematical Theory of Communication*':

> *The fundamental problem of communication is that of reproducing at one point either exactly or approximately a message selected at another point. Frequently, the messages have meaning; that is they refer to or are correlated according to some system with certain physical or conceptual entities. These semantic aspects of communication are irrelevant to the engineering problem.*
>
> (Shannon, 1948).[8]

This statement led to some disagreement among communication engineers, some of whom *did* want to capture meaning in their system of measurement, and how this can be done is the subject of much of the book. But staying with *quantity* of information for now, Shannon's genius lies in his realization that no matter what information is being transmitted it can be measured in 'bits' (**binary units**). A bit is a choice of two values. Morse code is a good example: *dit* and *daat*, also called 'dot' and 'dash', being the two values. So *dit dit dit daat daat daat dit dit dit* is decoded by Morse coders as SOS — Save our Souls. Given enough time and a known code any message can be transmitted. So when that which is being transmitted is music it can be coded into groups of bits which, if transmitted fast enough, can be decoded to produce energy bursts that drive the earphones or the blaster loudspeakers that are now so familiar.

The enemies of efficient transmission of bits in a medium are the limited 'bandwidth' of the connection and the amount of 'noise' it contains. The idea of limited bandwidth is familiar to those who listen to recorded music — the higher frequencies of sounds and the very low frequencies tend not to come through as clearly as the middle range. This is true not only of sounds but of all media that transmit information and, for instance, applies also to radio waves that travel through free space and to other forms of transmission such as via cables. The bandwidth of a medium is the range of frequencies it can carry. Because particles rush about at random in these media, there is interference with the transmitted signals, called *noise*. So some of the bits or groups of bits of information traveling in these media can be corrupted by noise or hindered by the lack of bandwidth.

---

[8]Shannon, C. E. (1948). A mathematical theory of communication, *Bell Systems Technical Journal* **27**, 379–423, 623–696.

Shannon did one wonderful thing in the face of these deterrents to proper transmission. He developed a formula that allowed the designers of transmission systems to look around for codes that can get the maximum possible transmission of information across a medium despite a given unavoidable amount of noise and with a given limited bandwidth. But that is not the limit of his genius. He also showed how networks of switches may be analysed using the notation of propositional logic. This can be applied to networks of neurons too. More is said of this below. Here, it is important to nail down the appearance of Shannon information theories even at the level at which neurons transmit information to one another. We shall see (in Chapter 6) that this leads to hypotheses as to how and when consciousness might arise in a neural network.

Why Billions of Cells?

(Chapter 3. Billions of Brain Cells: Guesses and Models)

The study of the role that the material of our brains plays in our conscious sensations has had a rough historical ride. Aristotle assigned a 'minor importance' to the brain and wrote that the 'the seat of the soul ... and nervous function ... is to be sought in the heart'.[9] Notoriously, Descartes laid the foundations for dualism by appealing to the pineal gland as a link between ventricles — where the non-material matter of the mind resides — and the muscular behavior of the body. Now we know that the pineal gland secretes melotonin which helps us with jet lag and that the ventricles contain cerebrospinal fluid which cushions our brains against physical shock.

It was Schwann and Schleiden (1847)[10] who, noting that most growing biological objects were made of cells, identified a varied and dense cellular structure in the brain. But, rather than throwing light on how brains function, this created confusion by initiating a major division of opinion. There were the *reticularists*, who effectively said 'so what?' to the brain being cellular. The fact that the liver and one's big toe are cellular does not explain what they do and how they do it. Then there were the

---

[9] *De motu anima*, published in the fourth century BC.
[10] Schwann, T. and Schleiden, M. J. (1847). Microscopical researches into the accordance in the structure and growth of animals and plants (Printed for the Sydenham Society) London, C and J Adlard, 268 pp.

neuronists, who suspected that the cells (*neurons*, by then) were not passive, but contributed *en masse* to some complex function of the brain. The Nobel Prize committee felt that the cellular notion was important and awarded the 1837 Prize for Physiology and Medicine to neuronist Johannes Evangeliste Purkinje for his exquisite work on the cells and seemingly purposeful structure of the cerebellum. But then they hedged their bets in 1906 by awarding a shared prize to reticularist Camillo Golgi, for his most revealing staining techniques, and neuronist Santiago Ramón y Cajal for his detailed microscopic taxonomy of a variety of cell types and structures. By then, the neuronists were beginning to win, and the importance of discovering what the billions of cells in the brain are doing grew as evidenced by more Nobel prizes. In 1932, Charles Sherrington was given the prize for his discovery that the link between the output (axon) of one neuron and an input of another, the synapse, was not only variable, but also controllable by the chemical product (neuromodulator) of other neurons. And as recently as 1963, Lloyd Hodgkin and Andrew Huxley won the prize for discovering how the axon of a neuron generates pulse codes. By then, Shannon's theory of information had been well established and it became clear that the stuff that neurons trade between them is informational.

In the meantime, Warren McCulloch and Walter Pitts (1943) published their seminal paper on the logical nature of the neuron and its synapses, with an immediate link to Shannon's propositional logic formulation of switching circuits. Is the brain a massive switching circuit? Does something beyond the McCulloch and Pitts formulation emerge when spiking is included in models? While these questions were and still may be arduously debated, we feel that whatever the answers may be, they are incomplete without the next bit of history.

The Circles of the Mind

(Chapter 4. Imagination in the Circles of a Network)

With the model of a neuron as a decision element, the scientific world fell into a deep error. It jumped to the conclusions that the brain, being bombarded by sensory information, reacts to this through its progressive logical decision-making across intricate neural nets which adapt to provide the right responses. Known as the stimulus–response philosophy, this squeezes out the possibility of sustained thought and memory which we know can happen even without stimuli. Memory was thought to be somehow sited in the progress of the activity from stimulus to response. It was the US zoologist-turned-psychologist Karl Lashley who strove to destroy this notion since it did not quite agree with his observations that even severe lesions sometimes only cause *gradual* degradations in a person's ability to think, suggesting that some mass activity of neurons with some redundancy is at work.

Together with his student, Donald Hebb, he formulated the hypothesis that thought depends on inner, circular paths in neural tissue that might provide a potential home for the informational mind. In 1956, this gave impetus to what became called *automata studies*[11] by none other than Claude Shannon, with a young colleague called John McCarthy (yes, one of the grandfathers of artificial intelligence).[12] They organized a meeting which put in place some fundamental models and analyses of machines with automata. Some major figures contributed to the proceedings. S. C. Kleene (1909–1994)[13] advanced a theory of input events that would lead to an 'acceptor state' that indicated that some structural rules were obeyed by the sequence of events. This was particularly useful in the design of automata that check the parsing of languages. And E. F. Moore (1925–2003) introduced 'state structures' which represent the complete function of an automaton. This has a very useful graphical representation which is often used in the book.

In 1956, Shannon and McCarthy expressed the belief that an understanding of networks and machines with internal states, through a proper mathematical formulation, is crucial to an eventual understanding of the mind. This promise did not materialize, and state machines were only used in the odd program, sometimes for the parsing of language. When it comes to 'informational minds', we believe that an understanding and deployment of automata theory is crucial. But even given automata theory and state structures, something is still missing. The states of an informational mind do not inform only through having a state structure: being conscious demands that the states themselves be somehow 'felt' — they should be 'phenomenal', as overviewed next.

---

[11] An automaton is a system with an internal state that is a function not only of the current input but also of the past history of such inputs.

[12] It was during the writing of this book that we sadly heard of the death of John McCarthy on October 24, 2011.

[13] One of the pioneers of theoretical computer science, known for 'recursive functions'.

Phenomenal States

(Chapter 5. Phenomenal Information: The World and Neural States)

When our eyes are open, whatever mental states there might be are about what we would describe as 'that which we see'. But when we close our eyes, removing that which is being seen, our mental states continue to be about something. It cannot be denied that what is being seen in the 'mind's eye' is not only about things in the real world, but has an affinity with what was once seen. The 'aboutness' of mental states is the essential feature of a movement in philosophy: phenomenology. German philosopher Franz Brentano (1838–1917) called this aboutness 'intentionality'. His student Edmund Husserl (1859–1938) initiated the phenomenology movement which is a philosophy that starts with a reality based on what the inner sensations of the world are like, and recognizes that this can be the only reality for the thinker. While Husserl might not have had views on the neural support for such a reality, in our own work we have been intrigued by the question of how an automaton might have reality-based states which we call phenomenal. We note that for such states to be useful, this inner reality cannot be at odds with world reality — this would not be good for survival. Imagine if an apple in position X were to give rise to our seeing it in position Y, or if the trigger for our seeing an apple were to be a rock. The observer would be misled and would end up undernourished.

There is also the possibility that the inner state of an automaton could be a pattern that uniquely encodes the external event. We reject this possibility, since, when faced with the alternative of a *useful* internal state coding, that is, one that contains the information needed for the organism to behave in a purposeful way, it is unlikely that evolution would have chosen the former.

For some years, since 1968 to be precise, we have been experimenting with something called 'iconic learning', and a formal description of this was published.[14] Iconic learning is a simplified-world way of creating states that accord with input. Let there be a specific point (pixel) in the input image we label a. Iconic learning devotes a neuron to this point which at any moment learns to output the value of input a for an input vector which

---

[14] Aleksander, I. (1996). Iconic learning in networks of logical neurons, *Proc. ICES '96*, Springer Lecture Notes in Computer Science, 1259.

samples many points in the input image. The effect of this is for the state of the network to be a copy of its input image.

In this book, we describe a series of experiments with neural automata to show that phenomenal representations are not achieved 'by any old neural net', but require a subtle set of parameters (neuron size, with respect to net size, ratio of feedback versus input connections, etc.) in order for the phenomenal representations to be formed. This is as a background to the next, more recent, development in the saga of the informational mind.

Information Integration

(Chapter 6. Information Integration: The Key to Consciousness?)

The notion that phenomenal states, i.e., conscious states, may depend on subtle properties of neural networks came to the fore with a vengeance over the last decade or so years. Here is a quote from Tononi[15]

> ...*to the extent that a mechanism is capable of generating integrated information, no matter whether it is organic or not, whether it is built of neurons or silicon chips, and independent of its ability to report, it will have consciousness.*

This is a remarkable claim. Is it really true (as Tononi suggests) that the formal basis for the system support of consciousness has been tracked down to something called 'integrated' information? Later,[16] we explain two forms of this theory, one based on effective information transmitted across boundaries within the network, and the other based on the information involved in state transitions. A pleasing and useful element of this work is the introspective judgment that mental states are *unique*, in the sense that each generates information with respect to the others, and that they are also *indivisible*, which means that the nets that carry them must be capable of representing causal relationships within the state.

---

[15]Tononi, G. (2008). Consciousness as integrated information: A provisional manifesto, *Biological Bulletin* **215**, 216–242.

[16]Using the work of two colleagues, David Gamez and Michael Beaton funded by the Association for Information Technology Trust to look into the importance of this area.

This is a helpful way of characterizing a mental state. It bridges from the introspective hunch to a physical requirement of a network. These two properties spell out what is meant by integration, and Tononi defines a parameter Φ to indicate how well a network integrates. The higher the Φ of the network, the better the network is able to produce mental states. So the high Φ areas of the brain are where consciousness is likely to reside. Now comes the first problem. Even in very simple networks, it is very difficult to measure Φ. This is because it requires the use of all possible partitions and a calculation of Φ for each one of them. The worst offender, the partition with the lowest Φ, determines the Φ for the whole network. In the book we describe an alternative way of measuring the capacity for integration based on the 'liveliness' of neurons. Liveliness, in a few words, is the probability that a neuron will transmit a change from one of its synapses to the axon. This produces a faster assessment of a kind of integration — not the same as Tononi's but one that again indicates the ability of a network to have unique and indivisible states.

But there is a second problem. Information integration theory lacks a discussion of how states become related to reality. Tononi's suggestion is that qualia (the phenomenal nature of inner states) may be characterized by identifying a geometrical structure composed of vectors of informational transactions of progressively more complex groups of interacting neuron. While this provides interesting polyhedrons that Tononi suggests are a representation of the qualia of a network, we allow ourselves the luxury of disagreeing with this. We go on to take a closer look at how visual representations of the reality of the visual world might occur in a simplified model of the visual system. The support of qualia may be much more obvious than the sight of intricate polyhedrons.

The Joy of Seeing

(Chapter 7. The Joy of Seeing: Gathering Visual Information)

When tired of too much theorizing with abstract models, it is always healthy to touch ground with the elements of nature, in this case those that exhibit puzzling sensations such as mental images. In the book we review the meticulous work of Semir Zeki[17] in studying the anatomy of the visual system

---

[17]Zeki, S. (1993). *A Vision of the Brain* (Blackwell Science, Oxford).

and how its function depends on this anatomy. He particularly addresses the fact that a considerable amount of specialization occurs in different parts of the visual system. For example, changes in color in the visual world cause activity in one part of the visual cortex, while motion or changes in shape do so in another. This leaves Zeki and his readers intrigued by how this disparate activity leads to the 'precise spatiotemporal registration' that is associated with the joys of seeing. We draw on our own work[18] on 'depiction' to suggest an important integrating factor — muscular activity. We postulate that signals from the muscles serve to index the selection of neurons according to where in the world the attention is focused. We show with a simple model how the image from the fovea (a tiny central area of the retina) when combined with eye movement information can 'paint' a high acuity image of the world.

From this, we go on to speculate how not only motion and perceptual signals but also time might be integrated. We conclude that the state structure of the informational mind is an unending stream of unique and indivisible states which becomes lodged, but with a lesser precision than in the original perception, in what we call memory. We back this up with some simulation experiments which again show that the choice of network parameters (integration, indeed) strongly determines whether this mental state structure is a reasonable representation of our visual experience as aided by our ability to interact with and explore the world.

Some Don't Like This

(Chapter 8: The Informational Mind: Oxymoron or New Science?)

Not all modern thinkers who worry about the nature of mind feel reassured by or even in mild agreement with the assertion that the mind is somehow informational. We set out not to conduct an adversarial battle over this issue but to understand their objections and then allow such objections to drive us into being clearer about what we mean by 'an informational mind' and sharpen up the concept.

---

[18] Aleksander, I. and Dunmall, B. (2000). An extension to the hypothesis of the asynchrony of visual consciousness, *Proc. Royal Soc. B Biol. Sci.* **267**(1439), 197–200.

We review the contention by philosopher and gerontologist Raymond Tallis (2004)[19] that 'the mind is not a computer' and that the inclusion of information in discussions of brain and mind is responsible for creating a huge confusion in such discussions. But Tallis' real quarrel is with Patricia Churchland's 'neurophilosophy' (Churchland, 1986).[20] This was published in the early days of the revival of 'connectionism' and mainly concerned itself with multi-layer recognition of image-like data. Tallis is therefore quite right that the mind can neither be reduced to the base level of information processing in a computer (some might call it the 'machine level') nor to successive 'recognitions' in the neural layers of the brain. In our approach the mind is informational because of the nature of the internal states which are the result of a subtle dynamic behavior of the net in response to 'stimuli'.

Synapse expert Susan Greenfield objects to relying on information gleaned by someone using the internet. It concerns her that this could lead to a solipsism that curtails a young person's ability to *discover* information by social interaction and science (see Swain, 2011).[21] She fears that this will irrevocably alter the youngster's mind. We argue in the book that, whatever informational models there may be of *curiosity* (e.g. Kelly, 1955),[22] if youngsters are normal to start with, they are unlikely to show a malfunction because information happens to be easy to get.

Luciano Floridi (2010)[23] is a prime motivator in the *Philosophy of Information*. A classically trained philosopher, he promulgates *data* as the focus for informational science in an attempt to concentrate on semantic rather syntactic issues. This appears to have two characteristic inspirations: data as it is commonly processed in a computer, and the linguistic representation of world events. This contrasts with our approach which is driven by the way that information creates our minds, and may not be 'well-formed' like the

---

[19]Tallis, T. (2004). *Why the Mind is Not a Computer: A Pocket Lexicon of Neuromythology* (Imprint Academic, Exeter).
[20]Churchland, P. (1986). *Neurophilosophy, Towards a Unified Theory of the Mind/Brain* (MIT Press, Cambridge, MA).
[21]Swain, F. (2011). Susan Greenfield: Living online is changing our brains, *New Scientist*, 3 August.
[22]Kelly, G. A. (1955). The Psychology of Personal Constructs, Vols. I and II. Norton, New York (2nd printing: 1991, Routledge, London, New York).
[23]Floridi, G. (2010). *The Philosophy of Information* (Oxford University Press, Oxford).

data in a computer but may say something about the minds of living entities including those that do not use language. So perhaps Floridi's models
and our own do not contradict one another but merely represent information as formalized for machine processing in the former case, or as sculpted
by our neural apparatus in the latter.

Another skeptic is the recently deceased Theodore Roszak (1933–2011).
He flourished in the 1960s when looking at the threats to a sustainable social
culture in general and due to information in particular (Roszak, 1986).[24]
He was concerned by the amount of power the word 'information' added
to phrases such as 'the information economy' or 'the information society'.
His concern, which is easy to share, was that 'information' as it is crunched
by a computer may be mistaken for the 'ideas' with which humans live in
the world. Even more frightening is the thought that large corporations
see themselves as controlling information sources and methods of dissem-
ination. This, he felt, would degrade the value of ideas with respect to
information simply because the latter have greater economic potential in
corporations and the military than the former. An aim of this book has
been to show that ideas are not excluded by a scientific understanding of
the mind, nor are they likely to be missing from artificial machinery with
mind-like properties.

A contemporary philosopher with a truly questioning outlook on information is Riccardo Manzotti of the Free University of Language and Communication in Milan. Sometimes he expresses himself in self-drawn cartoons,
one of which is called 'Where and when is information?'[25] Using the example of a the message 'help' written on a piece of paper, put into a bottle
and tossed from a desert island to be picked up by someone unknown, he
concludes as follows. Information is a process spread in time and space: it
is with the sender of the bottle, the sea, the bottle, the paper and, later,
with some recipient. 'Informational minds' could indeed be seen as parts of
a process which forms bridges between many such minds and the elements
of an external world. If one takes any one of these items in isolation it will
not reveal a compete model of the entire process. Much more work needs
to be done on this inspiration. So the material in the book could be seen

---

[24]Roszak, T. (1986). *The Cult of Information: The Folklore of Computers and the
True Art of Thinking* (Pantheon Books, New York).
[25]To be published in the APA newsletter on Philosophy and Computers — details
to be announced. Manzotti can be contacted at ⟨Riccardo.manzotti@iulm.it⟩

as asking how it is that a neutrally supported mind can take part in such a widespread process.

The Dark Submerged Layers of the Mind

(Chapter 9. The Unconscious Mind: Freud's Influential Vision)

Here we have suggested that a mathematical treatment of the informational mind yields a structure of iconic states that exist by virtue of their accessibility. That is, if the world presents sensory stimuli to an individual, new states are created, but also old ones can be evoked. This structure forms our memory which is at work both during perception and in the absence of it. But historically, the mind was a dark and inaccessible place: a possible home for the spirits of madness, the humors of malevolence or the infestations of evils. Could such horrors be generated by the processes of iconic creation of mental state structures? We will explore how the iconic method can, indeed, create inaccessible states in the state structure. That is, states can be created which, with further growth of the state structure, can lose their links to the rest of the structure. Sometimes this is due just to lack of usage but at other times it may be because entry into those states has had an adverse effect and was purposefully avoided. It is intriguing to realize how close Sigmund Freud's ideas of unconscious areas of the mind and the role of repression are to the isolation of states that can occur during the growth of the state structures of an automaton. In the book we examine theses similarities and discuss the process of psychoanalysis that Freud used to restore access to the hidden states.

And Now For Aristotle

(Chapter 10. Aristotle's Living Soul)

We end the book by taking a closer look at Aristotle's *De Anima* — his scheme for defining the 'form' of the matter of the body as that which causes 'being alive'. Written by a mature Aristotle with as much wisdom as he could muster, he found considering this 'soul' to be 'one of the most difficult things in the world'. Such form defines the 'livingness' of living creatures. It contains a perception of the world, the capacity for nourishment and the mind. The mind of humans is particularly able as it can 'understand' the form of other minds.

The key mystery is how the mind of an individual can be sensitive to the 'form' of another, which it clearly is. This is the basis for believing that the sciences, concerned as they are with the 'matter' of a living organism, will not be successful in addressing 'form' and an interaction between forms. Explaining the mind in terms of science is for Aristotle as fruitless as trying to use physics to explain what properties of bronze make a bronze statue of Hermes capable of honoring the god. How familiar this all sounds, and how powerful a proof is '*de Anima*' of the influence of Aristotle on basic philosophical beliefs which one finds today not only among philosophers, but also as part of general culture. Such an inheritance not only concerns Aristotle's clear explanations, but also some of his perplexity, which makes him declare that this is the most difficult of topics. We review how in this book we have tried to reduce some of this perplexity by introducing the science of information which, we argue, has much more to do with form than with matter. We imagine meeting Aristotle in an attempt to introduce him to the information sciences, but only find him in his dying moments. Are we too late?

Chapter 2
SHANNON: THE RELUCTANT HERO
OF THE INFORMATION AGE

Brief prologue: The exemplary engineer

Claude Elwood Shannon (1916–2001) grew up in Gaylord, Michigan, in much the same way that many young American men might have done. Taught at the local public school, he was good at maths and science, while at home he built radio-controlled model planes, boats and a telegraph link to his friend's house, down the road.[1] How, then, did this unassuming young man become someone whom veteran engineer Solomon W. Golomb calls "the father of the information age" and who rates his intellectual achievement as "one of the greatest of the twentieth century"[2]? Bearing in mind that this was the century of Einstein, Marconi, Sartre, Freud, Madame Curie and many other great intellectuals, Golomb's assertion is of considerable importance.

So it is somewhat surprising that many will not have heard of Claude Shannon. This is partly due to the fact that he was a reserved and unassuming person who shunned publicity. And it is because he was an engineer, and engineers are not supposed to hit the headlines. There is a myth abroad that the scientist does the intellectual work of discovery and the engineer turns this into usable products. Shannon is proof that this is a fallacy. His passionate fascination of working with systems that use information led him to understand and express for others that information has an essence

---

[1]A brief biography of Shannon by Sloane and Wyner may be found at http://www.research.att.com/~njas/doc/shannonbio.html and in: Sloane N. J. A. and Wyner A. D. (1993). *Claude Elwood Shannon: Collected Papers* (IEEE Press, Piscataway, NJ). These references were invaluable in guiding the historical parts of this essay.
[2]Solomon Golomb is an eminent professor at the University of Southern California. He wrote a retrospective article on Shannon in *Notices of the American Mathematical Society*, **49**(1), 8–10.

that is every bit (!) as challenging as the molecular structure of matter or the cosmological makeup of the universe. This is an intellectual *tour-de-force* indeed. Why was it that the telegraph line to his friend down the road messed up some of the messages? In fact, the title 'Father of the Information Age' came from the discovery that the essence of information is such that it can be measured and that systems for transmitting it can be designed so as to mess up the least number of messages. The enemies of accurate transmission are interference ('noise', in technical terms) and the fidelity ('bandwidth') and these, Shannon showed, can be fought by understanding them mathematically.

All this appeared in "A Mathematical Theory of Communication",[3] a seminal paper published in 1948 when Shannon was 32 years old. It might be quite normal in the career of a budding engineer to write a significant paper at that age. But Shannon was much ahead of his time, and by this age, he had already discovered how to make machines that use information for calculations and how information can be used for the control of machines. Here, these discoveries are treated chronologically so as to capture some of the pace of Shannon's life, his thinking and his incisive insights.

From Michigan to juggling machines

A quiet corner of Gaylord, Michigan

Gaylord, Michigan, even today sports only just over 3000 inhabitants. It sees itself as an Alpine village where skiing and snowmobiling are attractions in the winter. There is now in Gaylord a pleasant area called Shannon Park. Its central attraction is a bronze statue of a pensive Shannon that was cast in the year 2000 bearing the inscription shown below:

> ### Claude Elwood Shannon Father of Information Theory
>
> Electrical engineer, mathematician, and native son of Gaylord. His creation of information theory, the mathematical theory of communication, in the 1940s and 1950s, inspired the revolutionary advances in digital communications and information storage that have shaped the modern world.

(Continued)

---

[3]Shannon C. E. (1948). A mathematical theory of communication, *Bell Sys. Tech. J.* **27**, 379–423, 623–696.

(Continued)

This statue was donated by the Information Theory Society of the Institute of Electrical and Electronics Engineers, whose members follow gratefully in his footsteps. Dedicated October 6, 2000 Eugene Daub, Sculptor

Claude Shannon was borne in Petoskey, Michigan, but lived in nearby Gaylord during his early years. His father was a businessman and judge and mother a teacher and, for a time, principal of Gaylord High School. This is the very school where Claude graduated aged 16, with a distinct ability in mathematics and an interest in making things work. He followed his bent and obtained dual Bachelor degrees in both Electrical Engineering and Mathematics at the University of Michigan. This mix of creating and analysing complex systems has been the hallmark of Shannon's genius throughout his life. After retirement at the age of 62, Shannon amused himself with inventing seemingly impossible gadgets such as a juggling machine made from the puppet of celebrated comedian W. C. Fields.[4] This bore yet another hallmark of his character: a kindly sense of humor that went with the twinkle in his eye.

Impact at MIT

After graduating from the University of Michigan, Shannon entered the Massachusetts Institute of Technology. For the 20-year old graduate, this was the ideal institution: it had an aura of advancing both the theoretical and the practical intricacies of the most advanced engineering systems. He was accepted as a research assistant by the charismatic and audacious inventor of many calculating machines, Vannevar Bush.[5] This was a way in which Shannon could overcome the problem of having to find the fees to

---

[4] A valuable record that includes Claude Shannon's commentary may be found at http://www.flickr.com/photos/jeanbaptisteparis/2410723674

[5] Vannevar Bush was not only an adventurous and far-sighted engineer, but was able to persuade politicians to support what was otherwise seen as a fanciful idea: mechanized computation. Bush became the Director of the Office of Scientific Research and Development which, among other things, oversaw the Manhattan Project under which the atomic bomb was developed.

study at MIT. Working with Bush allowed him to register as a part-time graduate student while helping his mentor with his latest invention, the Differential Analyzer (DA). The main task for this machine was to solve mathematical equations by representing numbers as rotational positions of cylinders and gearwheels (a bit like a speedometer in a car). The machine also needed to be controlled by motors that turn the cylinders and these had to be turned on and off. It is here that Shannon made his first lasting impact in defining systems that are driven by information. He was conscious of the fact that experienced engineers were designing circuits of electromagnetic relays (switches that can be turned on and off by an electric current rather than a finger on a button). But they were doing this using their intuition and experience. Under the guidance of F. L. Hitchcock, a seasoned mathematician in the mathematics faculty, Shannon was determined to show that there must be a mathematical way of not only analyzing relay circuits but also synthesising them for best performance. The stroke of genius came when he realized that an algebra of truth and falsehood values proposed almost 100 years earlier by George Boole was just the required theory. Shannon presented these ideas in a Master of Science (MS) thesis within one year of arriving at MIT. This has been hailed by several commentators on the history of science (for example, H. H. Goldstine[6] and Howard Gardner[7]) as the most important MS thesis ever written. In 1940 it was awarded the American Alfred Noble prize by the joint engineering societies of the USA — a significant achievement for a 20-year old.

Dr Shannon — Mathematician?

In the many biographies that exist of Shannon, there is a notable lack of comment on his doctoral thesis entitled 'An Algebra for Theoretical Genetics'. It sounds important and fundamental, so what might have happened? This 74-page thesis is available for all to read and reveals a relentlessly mathematical style in its writing. But there is none of the handy touching of ground with engineering examples as appeared in his MS thesis. The mathematician in him had written it, but what happened to the engineer? It may have been Vannevar Bush's fault. Impressed with Shannon's use of algebra

---

[6]Goldstine H. H. (1980). *The Computer from Pascal to von Neumann* (Princeton University Press, Princeton, NJ).
[7]Gardner H. (1987). *The Mind's New Science* (Basic Books).

in the analysis of switching, he suggested first that Shannon might be happier in the Mathematics department where his MS supervisor was sited. Second, as Bush himself was leaving MIT to become President of the Carnegie Institute in Washington, he became aware that one of the Institute's branches (The Cold Spring Harbor Laboratories in New York State) would welcome a rigorous look at the organization of genetic knowledge. This soon sparked an interest in Shannon, who spent part of 1939 getting acquainted with what needed to be done by working with the experienced geneticist, Dr Barbara Burks, and completing his Doctoral thesis in 1940. Now being treated as a mathematician, Shannon might have felt that what was needed is the creation of an algebra that would describe results already known informally in genetics. But whether this was too abstract or too remote from the mathematical abilities of the geneticists of the time is not clear. The thesis remained unpublished. Interviewed in 1987, Shannon remembered somewhat wistfully his work on the process of population evolution[8]:

> "I set up an algebra which described this complicated process. One could calculate, if one wanted to (although not many people have wanted to in spite of my work), the kind of population you would have after a number of generations".

The note of regret might explain Shannon's return to his favored haunt: the optimizing of some complex engineering system through the use of mathematics. Nevertheless, he obtained his PhD in Mathematics for the genetic work, interestingly in the same year as his MS for the analysis of switching circuits.

The Bell Telephone Laboratories

Advanced research in engineering was not only done in universities. Bell Labs was an enterprise jointly set up in 1925 by two industrial telephone giants: the American Telephone and Telegraph Company and the Western Electric Company. The intention was to attract the world's best engineers and scientists, give them largely a free hand with only slight nudges that innovation in communication systems was the business of the laboratories. This was a successful formula and led to several major inventions and Nobel Prizes. For example, this is where John Bardeen, Walter Brittain and

---

[8]Sloane N. J. A. and Wyner A. D. (1993). *Claude Elwood Shannon Collected Papers.* (IEEE Press, Piscataway, NJ), p. xxvii.

William Shockley invented the *transistor*, the tiny semiconductor building brick that most computing and communication systems contain in millions. This work merited a Nobel Prize for Physics, one among the seven obtained by this laboratory. Sadly this involvement in basic research has recently been discontinued.[9]

For Shannon, Bell Labs was the ideal place to work. He went there for a spell in the summer of 1940, immediately after completing his doctorate. He returned to his MS topic of switching circuits and found a design procedure that used his algebra to reduce the cost of switching systems. This became a fundamental method for the design of the kinds of circuit that all digital systems rely on today.[10] By the beginning of the 1940-1 academic session, Shannon was awarded a prestigious National Research Fellowship at the Institute of Advanced Studies at Princeton. This too was a place of study where some of the greatest minds in science had pursued their interests. Einstein was among these, and it is said that once, when Shannon was lecturing at the Institute, Einstein came in, listened a while and then whispered something in a student's ear before leaving. Excited by this, wondering what the great man had to say about his lecture, Shannon asked the student. It turned out that Einstein was looking for the men's room![11] At Princeton, Shannon worked with pure mathematician Hermann Weyl, who was happy to encourage the 24-year-old to follow a new passion: the need to formalize information transfers in communication systems so as to make them as good as possible.

As war was beginning to rage in Europe in 1941, Shannon was invited to join Bell Labs to work on anti-aircraft machines that would calculate the aiming direction of guns given the current speed and direction of an aeroplane. He remained affiliated with Bell Labs for the next 31 years although his links with MIT were never severed. In 1958, he became a permanent member of the MIT faculty while still associated with Bell Labs. It was from Bell Labs, in 1948, that Shannon wrote *A Mathematical Theory of*

---

[9]Over the years, large companies have tended to pull out of basic research and Bell Labs, under the parent company Alcatel-Lucent, announced its redirection of basic research towards marketable products in 2008.

[10]Shannon C. E. (1949). The synthesis of two-terminal switching circuits, *Bell Sys. Tech. J.* **28**, pp. 59–98.

[11]See the personal appreciation of Shannon by Arthur Lewbel (Economics professor at Boston College and fellow juggler) at http://www2.bc.edu/~lewbel/Shannon.html.

Communication — the 'Magna Carta' of the information age (so described by Sloane and Wyner in footnote 1). Why was this so important?

The need for an information theory

The eulogies are not hard to find: we've already mentioned 'Magna Carta' as already well as 'The Father of the Digital Age' and 'the greatest achievement of the century'. But how did Shannon himself rate his insights? Was there a moment of blinding insight? In a recent essay on the great engineer, Erico Guizzo stresses that Shannon himself has always played down the idea of a moment of sudden insight.[12] He was aware that powerful theories were already known, but they had drawbacks and he set out to do something about it. Shannon acknowledges the earlier work of Nyquist and Hartley as having laid down the foundations of theories on which his own were founded. Harry Nyquist was a senior colleague of Shannon's also working at Bell Labs. The history of telecommunications has two distinct roots: telephony and telegraphy. The encoding of voice patterns as voltages (i.e., analog signals) characterize the first, while Morse-encoded information is the familiar example of the second. But in the late 1920s, the distinction between the two became blurred. By taking samples of voltages of voice patterns these could be encoded into pulse patterns (known as pulse code modulation or PCM). Nyquist had related the ability of a cable to transmit voice signals directly to the number of pulses it might also transmit.[13] Hartley, another senior engineer at Bell Labs, had also recognized the limiting nature of the fidelity or bandwidth of transmission lines.[14] So how was one to design transmission, coding and decoding equipment that would do the very best with the limited line? In 1948 he found the answer. He opens his 1948 paper by pointing to the need for a general theory of communication:

> *The recent development of various methods of modulation such as PCM and PPM (Pulse Position Modulation) which exchange bandwidth for signal-to-noise ratio has intensified interest in a general theory of communication.*

---

[12] Guizzo E. M. (2003). The Essential Message: Claude Shannon and the Making of Information Theory, Masters in Science Thesis, MIT. Available at: http://dspace.mit.edu/bitstream/handle/1721.1/39429/54526133.pdf?sequence=1.

[13] Nyquist H. (1928). Certain topics in telegraph transmission theory, *Trans. AIEE* **47**, 617–644.

[14] Hartley R. V. L. (1928). Transmission of information, *Bell Sys. Tech. J.* **7**(3), 535–563

Shannon's quest was to enable engineers to design these pulse systems so as to maximize the amount of information transmitted across a line with given deficits. Leaving aside the details for the time being, the key steps were the definition of a measure of information (the celebrated 'bit') and a method of calculating how many bits could be transmitted in a given time for signals coded in any way that engineers had already invented or might yet invent. The brilliance of Shannon's theory was the translation of the measurable characteristics of noise and bandwidth limitations into a maximum value for the channel capacity of a system that could not be exceeded no matter how one encoded the information. Importantly, this unleashed a search for the efficient designs that make best use of this maximum and this has made possible today's communication systems: the internet, satellites and the handheld phone/computer devices, all of which make efficient use of limited capacities.

As a purely intuitive impression, Shannon's insight into information capacity limitations of a line no matter how coded, is reminiscent of Einstein's insight into the speed of light as a limit for the velocity to which a particle could be accelerated, no matter what its mass might be. The similarity does not lie in the science but in the original thinking that was necessary for both.

Fun and games

Not long after the publication of the communication theory papers, Shannon shifted his target to a topic that had little to do with the analysis of information channels. He liked playing chess and he had experience of computers from the time when he was working with Vannevar Bush. It was inevitable that he should ask the question of whether a computer could be made to play chess.[15] In 1949 this was an outrageously fanciful suggestion. Not so much because chess was seen as evidence of human intelligence, but because computers at that time were conceived and perceived as calculating machines. What has calculation to do with chess? First of all, a board position can be represented by a whole lot of numbers: each piece can be numbered as can its position on the board. The movement rules for each piece can be expressed as mathematical formulae that generate all the

---

[15]Shannon C. E. (1950). Programming a computer for playing chess, *Philos. Mag.* Series 7, **41**(314).

possible 'next' positions for each piece. What's more, an expert chess player can assign a numerical value to key board positions in terms of whether they lead to a win. So much for the mechanics. But how does the machine make decisions about what to do next?

Shannon was struck by the fact that some numerical calculating programs have what are called 'branches'. For example, if the result of a calculation is a negative number, the ensuing calculation may need to be different from what it might be had the result been a positive number. This requires the computer to be equipped with machinery that executes '*if* X *then* Y' commands. To play chess, these were just the kind of actions Shannon required. *If* the board state is X then the computer can calculate P, Q, R, . . . , that is, the set of all possible moves it could take. But more than this, for each move the computerized player can take, the machine can work out the moves the opponent can take and so on, many moves ahead.

Anyone who plays chess will immediately recognize that the number of moves that needs to be evaluated explodes enormously as more steps ahead are considered. And yet, good players can predict roughly what will happen seven or eight moves ahead. Shannon decided that the most important thing to be done to program a computer to play chess efficiently was to prune these searches through astronomical numbers of positions in order to limit the number of calculations involved. Shannon's algorithms are still used in most chess-playing programs available at the time of writing.

The broader significance of Shannon's chess work is far greater than the fact that chess-playing machines now beat most average players. Chess is a logical rather than a numerical process. The capacity for chess turned the perception of the computer from a competent number processor to that of a device that could solve logical problems. This unleashed an entirely new field of endeavor: Artificial Intelligence (AI), defined as doing on a computer that which if done by humans would be said to require intelligence. The subsequent history of AI is one of amazing promises, spectacular failures and vacillating enthusiasms. Perhaps its practitioners should have read Shannon's assessment of his own chess program toward the end of his paper:

> *It is not being suggested that we should design the strategy in our own image. Rather it should be matched to the capacities and weakness of the computer. The computer is strong in speed and accuracy and weak in analytical abilities and recognition. Hence, it should make more use of brutal calculation than humans.* (see footnote 15.)

In contrast with major philosophical confusions that have surrounded AI during the last 60 or so years, Shannon's clear headedness is to be admired. In his paper, he stresses that *'it is hoped that a satisfactory solution of this problem will act as a wedge in attacking other problems of a similar nature and of greater significance.'* By 'other problems' he had in mind machines that would help engineers with designing communication systems, an endeavor that could be seen as being repetitive and uninteresting. Interestingly, he also mentions machines for language translation, military strategy development and orchestrating a melody. Even if these turned out to be harder than Shannon might have imagined, they underscored that the development of practical machines was the driving force in his thinking. This contrasts with the mistaken ambitions of some of his successors that machines could be made smarter than people without understanding what makes people smart in the first place.

The years that followed: life-like machines

In 1949, here was this young 33-year-old engineer who had laid down the foundations for designing switching circuits, brought new insights into the nature and practice of communications and changed the perception of what computers can do. What was left for him to do? One happy step was for Shannon to marry Betty Moore, a mathematician and computer analyst at Bell Labs. They had three children, Robert, Andrew and Margarita. In his professional life at Bell Labs, he was given the freedom to take communication theory whichever way he felt fit. This included the publication of older work on cryptography, previously kept under wraps due to its implications in defence equipment. He also produced new ideas on making systems of switches more reliable through the use of multiple versions of critical parts of a circuit. These methods and their later variants underpin schemes where reliability is paramount: from the passenger safety required in control systems for aeroplanes, to the reliable connections between computers needed by those who use the internet.

But as time went by, another side of the brilliant engineer began to emerge: the love for the curious and the zany. A favorite is his design of a small box with nothing but a switch on its front panel. There's only one thing to do — throw the switch. An eerie buzz is heard from the inside of the box. The lid opens, a mechanical hand emerges, moves towards the switch, turns it off, returns into the box allowing the lid to close. Then all is quiet. The box does no more than this, but descriptions from those who observed it were usually something anthropomorphic like "the thing inside does not want to be disturbed". Explicitly or not, Shannon recognized that movement is perceived as a sign of life. In pre-Socratic Greece, Thales of Miletus (624–545 BC) was thought to have equated autonomous motion with the presence of minds. Such mechanical 'life' must have been the fascination that led Shannon to build a maze-traversing mouse he called Theseus. Its relay computer 'brain' was actually under the surface of the maze driving the mouse using a magnet. This was in the early 1950s. In the intervening years many organizations started running mouse maze-solving competitions with Theseus as the patron saint of robot mice.

Returning to academia and bowing out

In 1956, Shannon returned to a joint visiting appointment in electrical engineering and mathematics at MIT. This became a full Professorship in 1958 bearing the title of Donner Professor of Science. Robert Gallagher, Emeritus Professor in Electrical Engineering at MIT, was a graduate student at MIT when Shannon returned. He writes: '... students and younger faculty members viewed Shannon as an idol.'[16] Apparently he did not supervise graduate students but encouraged young researchers to stand back from the details of their work and look for new formulations of their problem. Many of those he influenced went on to become engineering leaders in the digital *tsunami* that hit industry and academic research in communications in recent times.

Most published histories of Claude Shannon will stress his passion for unicycling and juggling which, on occasions he would do at the same time. He even produced a formula for a three-ball juggling action which some jugglers wear with pride, printed on their T-shirts. This analysis helped him to build a juggling robot for which he somewhat curiously adapted a model of the revered comedian W. C. Fields.[17] Visitors to his home would be shown to a 'toy room' — a kind of Santa's Grotto where, among much else, were his rocket-powered frisbees, gasoline-powered pogo sticks and a computer that worked in Roman numerals. This was a measure of his joy at what nowadays might be called 'lateral thinking'. Here was a shy man,

---

[16]Gallagher R. (2002). Shannon at MIT, in *Claude Elwood Shannon (1916–2001) Notices of the AMS*, **49**, 1.

[17]See http://alum.mit.edu/pages/sliceofmit/2011/08/15/claude-shannon/.

but one who could think inventively better than most. For this he was given many major accolades, including being elected to the Royal Society of London, the American Philosophical Society and the US National Academy of Sciences.

Shannon died at the age of 84 on February 24, 2001. He had been suffering from Alzheimer's disease and little has been recorded of his last few years. But it is one of the ironies of human existence that a man who had done so much to aid human communication, would perish through an insidious deprivation of this ability.

Communication according to Shannon

(*This section is intended for those meeting Shannon's ideas for the first time, indeed those who would like to know what* entropy, binary codes *and* channel capacity *are.*)

The Bit

Histories of communication at a distance abound with stories of smoke signals, drums and semaphores before going on to radio, telephone and telegraph. The point that puzzled Shannon was that, while clearly the telegraph is more convenient than smoke signals, there was as yet no way to define this difference precisely and to measure it? Could there be such a definition and specifically what units should be used to measure amounts of information transmitted?

A glance at the first page of that historical paper 'A Mathematical Theory of Communication' (see footnote 1) reveals the following:

> "*The significant aspect [of communication] is that the actual message is one* selected from a set *of possible messages.*"

Say there are eight horses in a race. Andy is at the race and he promised to let his friend Bob know the number of the winner by phoning at exactly 4 p.m. So as not to incur costs, Bob would not answer the phone and Andy would let it ring the number of times that corresponds to the number of the winning horse. With one horse in the race, Bob could predict the result with total accuracy and the information gained from the result would always be zero. To guess is not so easy with eight horses and would be even harder with more than eight. Shannon's view was that the greater is the uncertainty resolved by a message, the more information it contains. So should the measure of information be just the number of messages among which a choice is to be made? Shannon thought not. To see why, imagine that the message has to be held on switches so that, instead of Andy phoning, the ringing can be done by some machine (details of how such a machine might work are not important). To store each of the eight messages corresponding to the eight horses, eight switches might be used. But there are ways of using fewer switches. Only three switches can provide eight messages through clever coding. One way of doing this is 000, 001, 010, 011, 100, 101, 110, 111 (where 0 = switch off, and 1 = switch on). Were one to pay money for the switches, the 3-switch version is clearly more frugal than the 8-switch code. To measure the amount of information for a communication that involves an uncertainty among a number of alternatives, knowing the fewest number of switches that are needed is a useful start.

Instead of using the word *switches*, Shannon suggested that they be called *binary unit* because any manifestation of a 'yes/no' state will do: it does not have to be a physical switch. A hole in a paper tape (as in ancient computers) is just as good at representing a binary unit as a clunky switch. The birth of the word *bit* was due to a suggestion by an eminent visitor to Bell Labs from Princeton University: John W. Tukey, who himself went on to make major contributions to what is now called *signal processing*.[18] Shannon acted as midwife to the word by publishing it for the first time in 'A Mathematical Theory...' (see footnote 3).

To be formal, the *bit* is defined as the unit with which one measures the information gained through the resolution of a question with 2 equally probable answers.

That is, if the question is something like 'how has the coin landed?' the answer, as there are only two alternatives, contains 'one bit'. But if the question is 'who won the 8-horse race?', assuming that all the horses are equally likely to win, the answer contains 3 bits of information. But what of numbers other than one and eight? Is there a general way of calculating amounts of information?

First we note that $8 = 2 \times 2 \times 2$ and is written as 2^3 and is read as 'two to the power three'. The number of bits is the power of 2 which gives the number of alternatives. For the two-message (head/tail) case where the

---

[18]This is not the only word that John Tukey brought into common usage, *software* is another.

number of bits is 2, the 2 may be written as 2^1, which corresponds to one bit. And for 16 it would be 2^4. But what if there is some general variable number of alternatives X for which we want to find the number of bits j? This would be written as

$$X = 2^j$$

Luckily, this can be turned around to give j when X is known.

$$j = \log_2 X \qquad (2.1)$$

At school we learned that logs ('logarithms') can be looked up in tables and usually these were using the decimal system, i.e., in the form

$$k = \log_{10} Y \quad \text{where } Y = 10^k$$

For some of us, computers replace log tables and any spreadsheet program will evaluate Equation (2.1). Putting aside how to do this, the important fact is that the number of bits required for any number of equal choices can be worked out. For example $\log_2 8 = 3$ for the 8-horse race, or even, for 294 raffle tickets sold, the winning number carries about 8.2 bits of information ($\log_2 294 = 8.199622\ldots$ — thank you, computer). (So for 8.2 bits of information you would need 9 switches.)

What is entropy and why does it matter in communications?

The simple definition of the bit was a big step, but it raised many questions in Shannon's mind which would need to be answered in order to have a coherent theory of communication. For example, what if the coin is biased and has a greater probability of falling one way than the other? What if some horses in the race are better than others as is usually the case? How can the idea of a reduction of uncertainty be then associated with such systems?

Shannon found that a mathematical property called *entropy*, existing in the physics of interacting particles, indicates how far a system is from settling down to some rest state. Entropy is highest at rest (e.g., tea when it has cooled down to room temperature) and cannot decrease without the input of energy. It needs to be stressed that Shannon did not equate information to particle physics, he merely spotted the convenience of the mathematical formulation. Entropy usually has the letter H and is given the formulation

$$H = -\sum_{i=1}^{n} p_i \log_2 p_i \qquad (2.2)^{19}$$

While this may look somewhat complicated it can be unraveled, as will be seen, and then it can be evaluated on a computer. So all that is needed to calculate H, is to know the probability p_i of each of the possible events then H is the information conveyed by the occurrence of one of the events.

To begin to see how this works, we look at the biased coin. There are two possible events, heads or tails. Normally, p_i for each of these is 0.5. But for a biased coin, say that the probability for heads (say, p_1) is 0.6. As there are two possible events only, their probabilities must add to 1, so the probability of tails (say, p_2) is 0.4. Plugging these values into Equation (2.2), and using the trusty spreadsheet, H works out at about 0.97 bits. This indicates that the information content of tossing a biased coin is less than were the coin true (i.e., when the two probabilities are both 0.5 and H evaluates as 1). As the probabilities move away from 0.5, H decreases, falling to 0 when the probabilities are 0 and 1 (or 1 and 0), that is when the result is totally certain.

So the crux of Shannon's inventiveness was spotting that the entropy function provides a usable measure of the information content of sets of messages. His next target was to show how this measure can be used in designing efficient systems for transmitting information.

Communication at a distance

Shannon showed that even the most complex of communication systems can be reduced to three components: the information source, the channel and the destination. The *information source* is often a human being, either speaking or using a machine such as a Morse key or a computer keyboard. It could be a computer or some other machine that generates information by answering a question or giving the result of a computation. At the other end of the system is the *destination*, which could be a person or a machine for whom, or for which, the message is intended. As these elements could

---

[19] $\log_2 X$ is the power of 2 that gives us X. This works out as follows, for $X = 2$ it is 1, $X = 4$ it is 2 and for $X = 12$ it is 3.58. . . .

be distant in space, there is a need for some medium for transmitting the information. This is called a *channel*. The channel is the villain of the piece for two reasons. First, it can confuse the transmitted information due to the presence of random events termed 'noise' by engineers, because it can sound like a hiss or a crackle on a telephone. Second, there are rapidly changing signals it just cannot transmit (bandwidth). Hi-fi enthusiasts know all about that: a cheap amplifier will just not transmit all the subtlety of the highest notes of a violin. All this needs explaining.

How much information can a channel transmit?

First, a little more about what *bandwidth* (given the symbol B) is, and what is meant by *noise* 'N'. A pure note on a violin is an undulating pressure wave created in air by the vibrating string. It can be heard because it induces a corresponding vibration in the eardrum, which stimulates parts of the brain and which we then report as 'hearing'. The *frequency* of the note is the number of times that the wave is repeated in each second. A high note on the violin has a *frequency* of about 2,000 wave repetitions (cycles) per second.[20] Hi-fi enthusiasts know that their amplifiers can only reproduce a limited set of frequencies although they usually cope quite well with high violin sounds. But what happens when one is not dealing with clean violin sounds?

The world of communication owes a great deal to the work of French mathematician Jean-Baptiste Joseph Fourier for discovering that any sound or repetitive 'waveform' (such as speech or music in general) could be broken down into a whole lot of clean waves (mathematically, *sine* waves, the set of frequencies present at any moment being called a frequency *spectrum*). The sounds of speech are anything but single clean waves. What matters is whether the entire spectrum for a sound is transmitted or not. For example, even telephone designers of the early 20th century knew that total frequencies appearing in the human voice lay between 300 and 3,400 Hz (see footnote 19) so the bandwidth of lines and equipment had to deliver this and were set at about 4,000 Hz.

Noise in a line is that hiss and crackle that prevents you from hearing the transmitting voice very clearly and may cause confusion between words such

---

[20]x cycles per second are also called x Hertz, honouring the 19th century physicist, Heinrich Hertz.

as "sat" and "fat". What matters tremendously in determining whether the right signal is received, is the relative power of the signal compared to the power of the noise.

Shannon asked a question both simple and very general: given that a source generates information at some rate of R bits per second, will the channel, limited as it is by noise and bandwidth, be capable of transmitting this information without interfering with it? It is in this context that Shannon derived his second major equation (the first being 2.2 above).

$$C = B \log_2(1 + S/N) \qquad (2.3)$$

In English, this equation tells us that the channel's maximum capacity C (measured in bits per second) can be calculated by taking the bandwidth of the line B (measured in Cycles Per Second, or Hertz) and multiplying it by the logarithm (base 2) of 1 plus the ratio of signal power S divided by the noise power N. The general derivation of this equation to cover all kinds of channel is quite tricky, but inspired. Here it is enough to work out why the equation makes sense rather than try to reproduce Shannon's mathematical reasoning.

The little group $(1 + S/N)$ may be explained as follows. Assume that information is being transmitted as electrical impulses and the bandwidth is such to allow W such impulses to be transmitted every second. Say that the number of messages in the pulse is indicated by the number of power units it contains, say S. To make sure that the presence of just one power unit is not to be confused with noise, it must be a little greater than N. The expression, $\text{Log}_2 (1 + S/N)$, usefully turns out to have the value 1 when $S = N$. This is the case where the presence or absence of a single power unit is barely detected, which, correctly, is evaluated as being one bit of information. To give another example, say that the S is 3 and N is 1, then the presence of 2 bits is detected.

So if the signal pulse is transmitted B times each second, the channel capacity in bits per second, C, is given by Equation (2.3).

Channel capacity and the digital age?

In the present day, most communication at a distance is done digitally and this is largely due to the insights gleaned from Equation (2.3). For example, the waveform generated by speech can be sampled, that is, measured over a very short period of time, but done very often. How often? Here too there is a Shannonian answer. Shannon, using some work done earlier by

Harry Nyquist,[21] proved that sampling should happen at the rate of twice for every cycle of the highest significant frequency in the signal. This has become known as the Shannon–Nyquist sampling theorem. For speech, it was said above, the highest significant frequency is 4,000 Hz, and so, this requires 8,000 samples per second. From Equation (2.3), S/N in telephone lines is usually better than about 300. This makes Log_2 $(1 + S/N)$ about 8 bits so 8 bits are made available for the encoding of the samples into one of 256 messages. So, digitized speech generates information at the rate of 8000×8, i.e., 56,000 bits per second.

Those using the internet just before the turn of the millennium will remember the 56 kilobit *modem* with which one can 'dial up' the internet via the telephone network. Indeed the 'modem' is also a result of the remaining two elements foreseen by Shannon for a complete communication system. 'Modem' stands for Modulator–Demodulator. These are devices which respectively code the speech signal for efficient transmission and then decode it into speech at the other end. The *coder* and *decoder* were seen by Shannon as parts of a communication system that are essential to match the *line* to the *source* and the *destination* for transmitting information as close to the channel capacity of the line as possible. Figure 2.1 shows a structure that Shannon saw as applying to all communication systems.

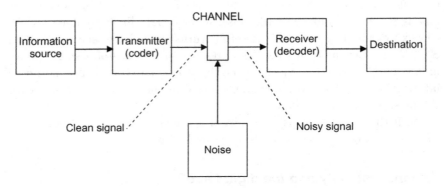

Fig. 2.1.   Shannon's concept of a general communications system.

---

[21]Nyquist H. (1928). Certain topics in telegraph transmission theory, *Trans. AIEE* **47**, 617–644.

Of course, a complete system would have two of the structures in Fig. 2.1, one going from one user to another and the other doing the reverse.

Shannon and the internet

Most computer users are connected to the internet through telephone lines using some 'broadband' system of communication. This fits perfectly into the breakdown of Shannon's general model of Fig. 2.1. The *source* is a computer controlled by the Internet Service Provider, which is like a telephone exchange which selects a page of information from one of all the computers on the internet for connecting to its *transmitter/coder*. The *receiver* is the user's computer. The *coder* uses a technology such as Asymmetric Digital Subscriber Line (ASDL) which is based on the following idea. A telephone line has a great deal more *bandwidth* than is required for voice signals. For example, a common standard is a total *bandwidth* of 1,104,000 Hz (1,104 kilo Hz or kHz) of which only 4.0 kHz is required by the voice signal. But how can this spare bandwidth be utilized?

First, the frequencies between 0 and 4 kHz are transmitted as direct voice signals. Then a gap is left until 26 kHz so that users can be provided with filters that separate out the higher frequencies that will be used for the internet. These are familiar little boxes that are delivered with the *modem* equipment which arrives when purchasing the broadband service from a provider. In ADSL, the next band between 26 kHz and 138 kHz (112 kHz) is allowed for uploading information from the user while the larger *bandwidth* 138 kHz to 1104 kHz (1066 kHz) is used for downloading data to the user. Without overcomplicating the description, to use this bandwidth, the *coder* transmits a pattern of 256 tones each at a slightly different frequency, 'peppering' the available bandwidth. The binary pattern consists of the presence or absence of these tones. Various tricks implemented in the *coder* and *decoder* are used to make the best use of these available bandwidths.

However, applying Equation (2.3), Shannon suggests the download speed (given a realistic $1 + S/N = 16$ for the average ADSL line) might be of the order of 4000 kb/s. The ADSL serving the computer on which this text is being written has a measured speed of 1600 kb/s. So the designers of encoders and decoders have some scope for competition. Indeed, broadband suppliers are vying with one another, by managing noise levels and increasing the use of bandwidth, to offer download rates of over 20,000 kb. So Shannon not only developed a theory of communication but also created a technical terminology which has become part of everyday language for the majority of those who live and work in industrial countries.

Shannon and the informational mind

The impact of information theory went way beyond the communications industry. It found applications in almost every field of endeavor. Examples are not only physics,[22] genetics,[23] sociology[24] and psychology[25] but also many others, even including divinity.[26] There is, however, a significance of Shannon's work which is deeper than its functional application. It is the continuing proof that concepts in nature which might have been seen by Aristotle as outside the mathematical domain may be better understood through formal analysis and the building of working models. In this, Shannon could be said to be a *cybernetician*, i.e., someone who looks for explanatory principles that machines may have in common with living humans. Other cyberneticians like Warren McCullogh and Norbert Wiener rose to greater celebrity status. However, in delving into many forbidding issues in the informational nature of the mind, it is the curiosity and the humility of the young lad from Gaylord, Michigan, that continues to remain an inspiration.

---

[22]Harmuth H. F. (1993). *Information Theory Applied to Space-Time Physics* (WSPC, Singapore).
[23]Shimbel A. (1965). Information theory and genetics, *Bull. Math. Biol.* **27**(1), 177–181.
[24]Soest J. L. (1955). A contribution of information to sociology, *Synthese* **9**(1), 265–273.
[25]Attneave F. (1959). *Applications of Information Theory to Psychology: A Summary of Basic Concepts, Methods, and Results* (Holt, New York).
[26]See the work of Prof. David Ford at Cambridge University (www.divinity.cam.ac.uk).

Chapter 3

BILLIONS OF BRAIN CELLS: GUESSES AND MODELS

Not neural networks 101

This chapter is not intended to be a primer on neural networks although neural networks are its main topic. Here we will track the gradual progress in the understanding of the machine that produces 'mind' from an early mistaken model located in the heart, to a sophisticated and structured network in the brain. We now take this notion almost for granted, but for those on whose insights this acceptance rests, it was an arduous journey of guesses and insightful theories. To follow this, some elementary explanations known by many who have studied neural networks are given. Experts can skip these: our aim is to follow this road to understand the historical building bricks on which a contemporary model of an informational mind is built.

Where is the mind?

What physical organs give the living organism its power of thought that is, its 'mind'? This is something that Aristotle got totally wrong. He wrote about 'the seat of the soul' — the Aristotelian 'soul' contains what we might now call the 'mind'.

> The seat of the soul and the control of voluntary movement — in fact, of nervous functions in general, — are to be sought in the heart. The brain is an organ of minor importance. (from *De motu animalium*, 4th century B.C.)

This error is particularly odd in the face of the belief of his predecessors that the brain was responsible for thought. In an insightful article, the distinguished psychologist Charles Gross of the University of Princeton[1] writes of this apparent aberration. He puts it down to the fact that, despite his brilliance as a thinker and an observer of nature, Aristotle was not a physician. Those who believed that the brain was the control center of the body at the time of Aristotle or before (for example, Alcmaeon of Crotona and Hippocrates) were physicians and anatomists. Although they had virtually no persuasive experimental evidence for their hunch, their motivation to cure disease got them closer to the truth. While Aristotle did his fair share of dissection, he favored the heart as generating the physical energy necessary for the intelligent motion of the body. Among other observations, he noted that the beat of the heart could be affected by emotion and that the blood was needed by sensory organs which are supplied from the heart. Gross relates how this uncertainty continued into the middle-ages in Europe and the Arab world, despite the influential work of Galen (129–200 AD). Galen too was a physician who, through meticulously conducted experiments, showed that nerves emanating from the brain were responsible for actuating muscles.[2]

Here speculative minds turn to the possibility that a proper way of understanding that 'conveying' control to the muscles is not only a matter of supplying energy, it also requires the supply of information. So if Aristotle had been aware of the need to look for informational channels in human anatomy, might the brain have been understood to be the competent controller it is earlier in the history of medicine?

The history of progress in the understanding of the brain may be traced through many encyclopaedias both on paper and the web (e.g., http://faculty.washington.edu/chudler/hist.html).

This turns out to be an intriguing mix of fable and anatomy. A long-standing belief known as the 'pre-cerebral view of mind' located the elements of thought in three different places in the body. Desires were to be found in the liver, vital forces in the heart and rationality, and 'animal spirit' in hollow ventricles in the head. It fell to René Descartes in 1649[3]

---

[1]Gross C. G. (1995). Aristotle on the brain, *The Neuroscientist,* **1**(4), 245–250. Available at: http://www.princeton.edu/~cggross/Neuroscientist_95-1.pdf.

[2]Nutton V. (1998). Galen. *Encyclopaedia Britannica.*

[3]Descartes R. (1649). *Les Passions de l'âme* (Henry le Gras, Paris).

(one year before he died) to recognize that part of the brain was the source of information for driving the muscles. He did not put it that way, of course. He imagined that nerves conducted pressures that caused the muscles to inflate and deflate like balloons. However, this was only a responsive motor, where the control of this engine, that is, its rationality, was still to be found in immaterial spirits of the ventricles. And possibly the most quoted supposition in the history of neurology is Descartes' linking of the immaterial to the material through the notorious pineal gland. But pineal gland or not, the mind had shifted from the heart of Aristotle to the brain of Descartes. It only took 2,000 years.

Descartes' view of the importance of the brain was corroborated by the English physician Thomas Willis, who was collecting real pathological evidence that certain disturbances of thought could be localized in the brain. Willis' major weapon was his knowledge of chemistry.[4] Willis, though, had no time for the pineal gland. He devoted his strenuous efforts in dissecting humans and animals to the localization of the differing aspects of mind. In particular, he identified some chemical features of mental maladies. We know that what is now called Parkinson's disease is due to a shortage of dopamine, a chemical with interesting information transmission properties. More of these 'neurotransmitters' later, for one could speculate that were it not for Willis, we might still be blaming evil spirits for mental deficits instead of looking for medication through chemistry.

Willis died in 1675, having positioned the mind firmly in the brain and having coined the word *neurology*, the medical specialization of matters related to the brain and its nervous system. He had shown that chemistry was important and that different parts of the brain served different purposes. This was the state of affairs for most of the 18th century. In the 19th and 20th century, the big questions about how these areas of the brain did what they did became the major focus of exceptionally imaginative scientific research.

The fine grain of the brain

What was this grey porridge-like organ made of? Clearly those who followed Thomas Willis, armed with ever-improving microscopy, became aware of

---

[4]See http://science.jrank.org/pages/10242/Mind-Thomas-Willis-Birth-Neurology.html.

anatomic structures of seemingly purposeful shapes without having a clear knowledge of how these structures were constituted. The discovery that all living matter was made of cells began with the observations by the German Botanist Matthias Schleiden. In 1838, he found cells in plants, and this was extended a year later by physiologist Theodor Schwannwho had observed cellular structures in the organs of animals (including humans). So 'Cell Theory' was born: all living materials whether in plants or animals are composed of cells.[5] But are the cells of the brain just a way of creating a fused structure or is there something the cells of the brain did which was different from the cells of, say, the leaf of a poplar tree? These two possibilities gave rise to a debate among researchers of the organization of the brain that raged for the best part of 40 years.

On one hand were the reticularists, who believed that the cells of the brain formed a fused structure that functions as a whole in much the same way as a leaf acts as a solar energy convertor. Opposing this were the neuronists, who believed that brain function could be traced to the activity of the cells themselves, that is, the *neurons* (or *neurones*). Central to the quest to resolve this issue was the ability to stain tissue so that it shows up better under ever-improving microscopes.

One anatomist to make a profound difference in weighting neurology towards the neuronist position was the Bohemian anatomist, Johannes Evangelista Purkinje (1787–1869). Working as a professor at the University of Prague, he led a varied scientific life. Not only did he study visual perception, he also produced the thinnest known slices of nervous tissue using a *microtome*.[6] With this, in 1837, he discovered the cellular structure of the cerebellum, a fist-like part of brain that rests at the back of the skull and which is now known to be involved in the refinement of the control of limb movements. He described and drew the structure of some large neurons now known as Purkinje cells. He called them *corpuscles* and speculated that they performed a specific task: collection, generation and distribution. This indeed, was a neuronist suggestion which significantly began to undermine the reticular doctrine.[7] Neural shapes were also published (posthumously)

---

[5]Schwann T. and Schleiden M. J. (1847). *Microscopical Researches into the Accordance in the Structure and Growth of Animals and Plants.* (Printed for the Sydenham Society, London).

[6]An exceedingly sharp knife for slicing organic material: a bit like a salami slicer for exceedingly thin slices of salami.

[7]See en.wikipedia.org/wiki/Purkinje_cell. (last accessed June 9th 2012.)

Billions of Brain Cells: Guesses and Models   **43**

in 1865 in paper by Otto Dieters (1834–1863), who noted that an outgoing 'axis cylinder' (now called an *axon*) had some connective relationship to incoming 'protoplasmic processes' (now called *dendrites*). While the axis cylinder supported the discrete neuronic description, the protoplasmic process could still appear joined by anastomosis[8] and so form part of a tissue.

Probably the most influential character in this period of rapid discovery was Camillo Golgi (1843–1926).[9] As an eminent but self-effacing Italian histologist, he discovered a method of staining nervous tissue using silver nitrate, which brought to the microscope the most exquisite, previously unseen fibres in nervous tissue, and which clearly outlined the structure of neurons. For this he became a Nobel laureate in 1906. Despite being able to describe nervous tissue in greater detail than before, he nevertheless continued to believe that his findings supported reticular theories as his stain revealed beautiful network-like structures of many neurons. While his method suggested the modular nature of the neuron, he remained a confirmed reticularist.

Cajal (1852–1934)

It was the work of Santiago Ramón y Cajal that led to the identification of neurons as the building bricks of the brain and the ultimate recognition that the neuronist doctrine was useful in advancing the understanding of the brain. He shared the 1906 Nobel Prize with Golgi, which was an even-handed way for the prize committee to deal with reticulum–neuron controversy. Born in a small village in Spain (Petilla de Aragon in the Navarre province), young Santiago did not take well to early schooling and developed a rebellious attitude, which caused him to change school several times.[10] His interests lay in painting and art, but his physician father exerted pressure for him to study medicine at the University of Zaragoza. But could it have been his love of art and his artistic skills that drove him towards histology? His drawings of neural tissue are still among the most impressive results in the history of neuroscience. Based on the use of the Golgi stain and Cajal's own improvements, these figures are still the images

---

[8] A natural or surgical joining of parts or branches of tubular structures so as to make or become continuous <wordnetweb.princeton.edu/perl/webwn>.

[9] See http://nobelprize.org/nobel_prizes/medicine/laureates/1906/golgi-bio.html.

[10] See http://en.wikipedia.org/wiki/Santiago_Ram%C3%B3n_y_Cajal.

first met by neurology students — they are the icons of the shape of neurons that remain in the mind.

After studies of many areas of the brain, Cajal developed the fundamental insight that dendrites were conduits to the axons, which in turn connected to terminals on the dendrites of other neurons. That identified the neuron as a single element with a one-way function. It is now recognized that this flow was informational in nature.[11] But if the neural doctrine is to declare the neuron as a building brick of the brain, there still needs to be interaction between the neurons to allow a network of neurons to develop a cooperative function. This idea shaped research in neurology during the last decade of the 19th century.

The electrochemical neuron

Another historical strand in the understanding of the functioning of the nervous system is the discovery by the Italian physician Luigi Galvani (1737–1798) that an electric spark can move the leg of a dead frog. This opened the possibility that the brain communicates with muscles through electrical signals and this was confirmed by many studies right into the 20th century. A salient figure was the noted London-born physiologist and 1932 Nobel Prize winner, Charles (later Sir Charles) Sherrington (1857–1952). He studied the way that axons make contact with nerves. He named the contact point a *synapse*, from the Greek roots of συν (*syn*: together) and χαπταω (*haptao*: grasp). This turned out to be a complex junction that uses chemicals called *neurotransmitters* to influence the behavior of the receiving neuron. While Sherrington's discovery of the synapse was a huge stimulus toward the definition of what a neuron does, the next discovery by Alan Lloyd Hodgkin and Andrew Huxley in 1952 showed how an axon initiates a polarity reversal which travels down the axon fibre and causes neurotransmitter action at the synapse at the end of the fibre.[12] Yes, they too earned the Nobel Prize in 1963. Also, with the discovery that the neuron has the capacity to link with other neurons, it became possible to

---

[11]See   http://neurophilosophy.wordpress.com / 2006/08/29/the-discovery-of-the-neuron/.

[12]Hodgkin A. L., and Huxley A. F. (1952). A quantitative description of ion currents and its applications to conduction and excitation in nerve membranes, *J. Physiol. (Lond.)* **117**, 500–544.

think of the nervous system as a network of cells that encode and transmit *information* not only from brain to muscle, but also within the brain itself.

With this, the perspective on what neurons do changes dramatically: it now becomes intriguing to attempt to apply this kind of analysis not only to the behaving part of the brain but also to the thinking part of the brain.

A Logical Calculus of nervous activity

The thread of the analysis of neural networks for their contribution to thought pre-dates the work of Huxley and Hodgkin by nearly 10 years. The work was mathematical, with the purpose of creating a model of the neuron with which mathematical statements might be made about mind and thought. In 1943, Warren McCulloch, a physician, and Walter Pitts, a mathematician, published a paper called "A Logical Calculus of the Ideas Immanent in Nervous Activity".[13] Before looking at the contribution of this seminal paper, we ask, who are Warren McCulloch and Walter Pitts?

Warren McCulloch

'Unconventional, fiercely knowledgeable and sophisticated' are probably the words that most who have met Warren Sturgis McCulloch would have used. McCulloch, in giving the 1960 Korzybsky Memorial Lecture[14] recounted a discussion with his college principal. The college was Haverford, a Quaker institution, and the principal was Rufus Jones, a highly influential Quaker philosopher.

> *"Warren," said he, "what is thee going to be?"*
> *And I said, "I don't know."*
> *"And what is thee going to do?"*
> *And again I said, "I have no idea; but there is one question I would like to answer: What is a number, that a man may know it, and a man that he may know a number?"*
> *He smiled and said, "Friend, thee will be busy as long as thee lives..."*

---

[13] *Bull. Math. Biophys.* **5**, 115–133.
[14] First published in 1960 in *General Semantics Bulletin,* 26–27, 7–18.

Indeed, McCulloch's working life was devoted to the discovery of what it might be in the physiological makeup of a living creature that allows that creature to have knowledge. At Haverford, he studied psychology and philosophy, but, wishing to join the Naval Reserve, he transferred to Yale and saw active service at the end of the First World War. He graduated in 1921 with a BA in Philosophy and a minor in Psychology. He felt the need to deepen his knowledge of *"what is a man ..."* and obtained an MA in Psychology in 1923. But he needed to know more 'from the inside' and so joined the College of Physicians and Surgeons in New York, where he qualified as a medical doctor. After several internships during which he became interested in schizophrenics and psychopaths, he encountered philosopher Eilhard von Domarus, who was attempting to express the difficulties experienced in these diseases as logical terms. That is, given that a normal human 'understands' logical form as a matter of course, in sufferers of mental diseases this sense fails, and he thought that this failure may be monitored.

In 1934, McCulloch returned to Yale's Laboratory of Neurophysiology, where with psychiatrist Dusser de Barenne he started calling their interests 'experimental epistemology'. As Margaret Boden points out,[15] this seems a contradiction in terms but is not. Philosophers use the word epistemology to mean a normative theory of knowledge. McCulloch was interested in finding ways that the nervous system could mediate the having of any knowledge at all. Indeed, it was his ambition throughout his working life to show that mathematical analysis and modeling clarify and facilitate philosophical discussion.

It was in 1941 that McCulloch became a Professor of Psychiatry at the University of Chicago and it was there that he met Walter Pitts, to form a partnership of enormous scientific importance of which more later. McCulloch joined the Electronics Laboratory at MIT in 1952. While this may seem a strange abandonment of the medical world, the attraction is clear. MIT was the cauldron where Cybernetics, 'the science of communication and control in man and machine', was brewed. Norbert Wiener, MIT mathematician and founder of Cybernetics, had gathered a small group of friends to discuss in some depth mathematical laws that apply both to living organisms and designed systems. Among these friends

---

[15]Boden M. (2006). *Mind as Machine: a History of Cognitive Science, Vol 1.* (Oxford University Press, Oxford).

were Mexican physiologist Arturo Rosenblueth and MIT computer pioneer Julian Bigelow. Their collaboration resulted in a brief essay entitled *Behavior, Purpose and Teleology* published in *Philosophy of Science*[16] in 1943. This paper addressed the philosophical notion of *Teleology* (the study of purpose and causes in nature). A tiny excerpt is:

> *Teleological behaviour thus becomes synonymous with behavior controlled by negative feedback, and gains therefore in precision by a sufficiently restricted connotation.*

Right or wrong, it is clear that this is precisely the kind of thinking that would have appealed to McCulloch. Indeed McCulloch was a founder of a broader discussion group called 'The Macy Conferences', the purpose of which was to set the foundations for a *general science of the workings of the human mind*. All was set for a massive attack on the mind using formally stated theories of information and control. Indeed, over the years, these formal approaches not only clarified some issues in the philosophy of mind and the nature of behavior, but also underlined some of the enormous difficulties that such an ambition entails.

Sadly, McCulloch and Wiener parted company in about 1963 for scientific and personal reasons,[17] leaving a distinction in Cybernetics between the mathematical approaches independent of physiology (NW), and approaches based on formalizations of the neural networks of the brain (WSMcC). This theme reappears in other parts of this book. McCulloch continued working actively at MIT (partly on models of the frog's visual system) until his death at the age of 70. His thoughts are best encompassed in his book of essays entitled 'Embodiments of Mind'.[18]

Walter Pitts (1923–1969)

Were one to search for someone who was the exact opposite of Warren McCulloch, Walter Pitts could not have been a better fit. Where McCulloch studied at prestigious US universities, Pitts had no university education

---

[16]Rosenblueth A. Wiener N. and Bigelow J. (1943). Behavior: Purpose and teleology, *Philosophy of Science* **10**, S18–S24.

[17]Andrew A. M. (2005). Dark hero of the information age: In search of Norbert Wiener, the Father of Cybernetics, *Kybernetes,* **34**(7–8), 1284–1289.

[18]McCulloch W. S. (1988). *Embodiments of Mind* (MIT Press, Cambridge, MA), 2nd printing.

at all. Where McCulloch was extrovert and ebullient, Pitts was shy and shunned social occasions. Where McCulloch's scientific knowledge spanned the widest spaces of philosophy, psychology and medicine, Pitts was fiercely and brilliantly focused on logic. As a scientific duo they were the ideal complement for one another. Attempts to reconstruct Walter Pitts' life suggest a difficult trajectory with a dismal ending. There are very few sources. Many simply repeat the same facts. Here we try to distil what is known to understand Pitt's role in 'A logical calculus ...' (see footnote 13).

There are two main sources, one by Jerry Lettvin, a long-standing friend of Pitts' who worked with McCulloch and Pitts on the frog visual system at MIT.[19] The other is by science author Pamela McCorduck through her influential book, 'Machines Who Think'.[20] We gather that Pitts had a lonely and difficult youth. At the age of twelve, he once sought solace from roughnecks by spending days and nights in a library reading Russell and Whitehead's Principia Mathemetica. Reportedly he wrote to Russell pointing out some problems he had found. Russell replied with an appreciative letter which persuaded the young Pitts that he wished to become a logician. His father disapproved, wanting Walter to work and earn money. At the age of 15, Walter dropped out of school and ran away to Chicago to attend lectures at the university where, among others, he was able to listen to those given by Bertrand Russell.

Apparently, Russell suggested that Pitts should read 'The Logical Structure of the World', the latest book by the logician and philosopher Rudolf Carnap, who had recently arrived in Chicago University as a refugee from Europe. Having discovered passages that did not appear to be correct, Pitts reportedly marched into Carnap's room and handed him an annotated, corrected, copy of the book. Thereafter, Carnap, after some searching for this anonymous person, offered him insignificant employment which just enabled him to survive. It was McCulloch's arrival at the university in 1942 which caused a major change in Walter Pitts' life. McCulloch invited the destitute 19-year old logician and his friend Jerry Lettvin to live in his house. It is here that the discussions which culminated in the 'logical calculus' paper (see footnote 13) started their fermentation. In his 1960 Korzybsky

---

[19]Lettvin J. Y. (1998). [Interview with J.A. Anderson and E. Rosenfeld]. In J. A. Anderson & E. Rosenfeld (Eds.), Talking Nets: An Oral History of Neural Networks (MIT Press, Cambridge, MA) pp. 1–21.

[20]McCorduck P. (1979). Machines Who Think: A Personal Inquiry into the History and Prospects of Artificial Intelligence (W.H. Freeman, San Francisco).

Memorial Lecture (footnote 14) McCulloch spoke of meeting Pitts in Chicago:

> ... *I met Walter Pitts, then in his teens, who promptly set me right in matters of theory. It is to him that I am principally indebted for all subsequent success.*

Pitts followed McCulloch to MIT and continued the collaboration while doing odd theoretical work with Norbert Wiener and an atomic energy project. But the polemic between Wiener and McCulloch caused the former to send a demoralizing letter to Walter Pitts, questioning his abilities and informing him that his services would no longer be required. It is said that this launched Pitts into a downward spiral of desperation. He died a few years later, in 1969 at the age of 46, a few months before McCulloch. Some say it was a disease related to alcohol abuse and others say it was suicide. Whatever the case, this was a sad end for one of the brightest logicians of the 20th century!

The logical calculus

In most systems made of many components, there is a complex relationship between what the system does and how the components are connected. This is sometimes called 'the function/structure' problem. In philosophy and physiology, it is called the 'mind/body' problem. The reason it is a problem is that structure is often not a good indicator of function. Think of lifting the lid off a computer, there is no way that even the most detailed knowledge of how the chips are connected will indicate whether the machine is doing e-mail or calculating the laws of the universe. And yet, the tradition in the study of the human body is to learn vast amounts about structure and to try to infer function from this the structure.

As a physician, McCulloch was well aware of the discoveries of Ramón y Cajal and Charles Sherrington. The single neuron had been identified as a physical entity forming a system through synaptic connections to other similar units to form networks so the structure side was being ever better explored. But on the function side, mental rationality, wisdom and the rest, somehow emerge from this system of interconnected neurons. But how and why? This was the question McCulloch had resolved to answer. It must be said that to this day this remains one of the major question of science. Answers do come at a rather leisurely pace, largely from the distortions in function that occur as a result of disease or accident. Computer scientists are fond of pursuing the lifting-the-lid argument above, by saying that the circuits are general and any rationality is instilled by the programmer. But in 1943, it is perhaps fortunate that this argument did not yet exist as it distorts the discourse into equating the brain to a general purpose computer which it certainly is not.

Again, in his reminiscent Korzybsky Lecture (footnote 14), McCulloch tells of his definition of and quest for a 'psychon',[21] an elemental event of mentality which he had postulated in 1923. In this way of thinking, mental events such as envy or recognition of a face would be made up of the activity of ever-differing collections of psychons. In 1929, he began to think of the all-or-none 'firing' of the axon postulated by Cajal as a candidate for his idea of a psychon. But the major part of the calculus fell into place in discussion with Walter Pitts through the realization that a neuron could receive a positive encouragement to fire (excitation) at some synapses and a negative discouragement from firing (inhibition) at others. This means that, in firing, the neuron has performed a computation (or a *calculus* in the vocabulary of the 1940s) in weighing up the information provided to the neuron through its synapses by other neurons. A little example might help at this stage.

While Fig. 3.1 must be totally familiar to anyone who has ever studied neural networks, here we use it to illustrate the realization that went into the

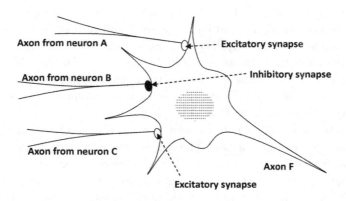

Fig. 3.1.   Sketch of a neuron with axon F.

---

[21]Not to be confused with the name of the planet in the British TV series of the late 1970s: 'Space 1999'.

writing of the 'Logical Calculus' paper (see footnote 13). The question on the table was, given that connections between neurons had been discovered and that informational impulses could travel from axon to synapse, what was the nature of these informational transactions? To answer this, consider the entire set of possible firing patterns on A, B and C. Say that firing is given the numerical value of 1 and not firing, 0. It then becomes possible to work out the effect of all the incoming patterns of firing on the neuron, once the effect of the synapses has been taken into account. Say that an inhibitory synapse (as at B) negates the input, that is, it inputs −1 to the body of the neuron if its input is firing where an excitatory one simply transmits 1 if its input is firing. The total of what all the synapses are doing to the body of the neuron is called an activation.

For example, the incoming pattern $ABC = 111$ the activation is $1 - 1 + 1 = 1$. By contrast, $ABC = 101$ causes an activation of 2, which is the highest that can be achieved with the neuron in Fig. 3.1. But what does the body of the neuron do? It fires at its axon if the activation is high enough. It therefore applies a *threshold* to the activation. The exact chemical processes of the functioning of neurons are still being studied today, but what matters is that McCulloch and Pitts wished to assess this in mathematical rather than chemical terms. To do this a table of all activities that the neuron could be doing is shown in Table 3.1. (The threshold is interpreted as 'equal-to-or-greater-than'.)

Table 3.1.   This is the function table for the neuron of Fig. 3.1.

ABC	Activation	F(thresh => 0)	F(thresh => 1)	F(thresh => 2)
000	0	1	0	0
001	1	1	1	0
010	−1	0	0	0
011	0	1	0	0
100	1	1	1	0
101	2	1	1	1
110	0	1	0	0
111	1	1	1	0

Note: The first column shows the total activation for all the possible binary patterns of firing. The other columns then show the actual output of the neuron for different threshold settings. In line 1 it is only a threshold of 0 that generates a 1 as the activation is equal to the threshold.

The key realization driven by looking at such tables is that the appropriate mathematics for describing what the neuron is doing is the kind of logic that Shannon used for switching circuits: the calculus of propositions. For example, it is now possible to write:

$$F(thresh => 0) = (A' \bullet B \bullet C')'$$
$$F(thresh => 1) = (A \bullet B') \cup (A \bullet C) \cup (B' \bullet C)$$
$$F(thresh => 2) = A \bullet B' \bullet C$$

Where, A' reads (***not*** A),

$A \bullet B$ reads A ***and*** B

$A \cup B$ reads A ***or*** B

It may not be obvious to all how these logical statements are derived. This does not matter. What matters is that the question "what does a neuron do?" can be answered by "it performs a logical calculus on the firing patterns of its afferent (incoming) neurons".

The Consequences

As will be seen, the field of 'neural networks' is currently well established as an alternative to conventional algorithms and is often described as being 'more like the brain'. But this is not the way that McCulloch and Pitts saw it. They recognized in their calculus a potential basis for universal computation. Turing's paper, describing his famed model of a universal machine, had been published in 1936,[22] seven years prior to the 'logical calculus'. John Von Neumann had not yet published his report on the EDVAC, which was to establish the quasi-universal basis for all we have called 'a computer' to this day.[23] In the Korzybsky Lecture (footnote 14), McCulloch felt the need to summarize the "logical importance" of the calculus. This referred to the universality of their neuron and the networks they could create. A neuron as shown in Fig. 3.1, with a threshold of ≥ 2 picks out (or recognizes) just one pattern of inputs (101). Synapse polarity can be chosen so that *any* single pattern of inputs can be recognized. Given that a logical function can always be represented by a truth table (e.g., Table 3.1), McCulloch

---

[22]Turing A.M. (1936). On computable numbers, with an application to the Entscheidungs problem. *Proc. London Math. Soc. 2* **42**, 230–265.
[23]Available at http://qss.stanford.edu/~godfrey/vonNeumann/vnedvac.pdf.

showed that (with a slight modification of the neuron as will be seen later) circuits with arbitrary truth tables can always be built. He also pointed out that John von Neumann was using neurons to teach people how to build computing machines. He asserted that this entirely logical argument had shown that machines that perform a universal set of computations could be built or "begotten". Even though his claims to universal computation were questioned,[24] the broader conclusion was fundamental: the brain was a machine that could be understood through the laws of logic.

Learning and adaptation

Contrary to the later acclaim of neural networks as the 'alternative' form of computing based on learning rather than programming, the McCulloch and Pitts calculus was not about learning. Their concern with logic and computation drove them down the theoretical path of showing that there exist configurations of neurons that perform a very large set of computational functions. However, the potential for learning attracted some of the leading exponents of artificial neural networks. It begins with the modeling of the plasticity, known to be a property of synapses, that leads to modifications of neuron function. Making this modification purposeful in some way is the objective of the contributions which we briefly examine below.

Bernard Widrow

The Connecticut-born electrical engineer Bernard Widrow was one of those who throughout his life believed that learning and adaptation have an important role to play in the design of electronic systems. A graduate of the MIT Electrical Engineering Department, at age 23 he was pursuing a PhD when McCulloch and Pitts came to MIT in 1952. In an interview with Andrew Goldstein recorded in 1997, Widrow reminisced[25]:

> ... *McCullough and Pitts were in a different building. They were active at MIT at the same time that I was working on the beginnings of adaptive*

---

[24]Kleene S. (1956). Representation of events in nerve nets and finite automata, in Shannon, C. and McCarthy J. (Eds.), *Automata Studies* (Princeton University Press, Princeton, NJ), pp. 3–42.
[25]See http://www.ieeeghn.org/wiki/index.php/Oral-History:Bernard_Widrow# Stanford.3B_adapting_neural_elements.

filters. There was nothing in [the ideas of] McCullough and Pitts that had anything to do with changing the coefficients to allow this thing to learn. ... ... Pretty soon I began to be interested in adapting neural elements. Let's say you have a truth table. You say, "Well, I'd like a piece of logic that can implement this truth table. ... ... My thinking was, that if you could put in a set of inputs into the weights, you could then adjust the weights to cause the correct output decision for that set of inputs. I was taking a flexible piece of logic and teaching it. ...

In 1956, Widrow became an Assistant Professor at MIT before moving to Stanford where, together with 'Ted' Hoff, he developed further his ideas on adaptation. In Widrow's model, the synapses become variable multipliers of the input which are systematically adjusted to remove the error in the activation and achieve the correct axonal output. He called this model the *Adaline* (ADAptive LInear NEuron) and systems of such neurons *Madeline* (*Multiple adaline*) systems.[26] While at MIT, Widrow was surrounded by, and fascinated by, wild, early talk of artificial intelligence. In the interview with Andrew Goldstein (footnote 26) he said:

... I began thinking about thinking, and I began thinking about how do you make a machine that can do it. I came to the conclusion that it would be about twenty years before anything of any consequence in engineering would come from an attempt to build a machine that thinks. I knew enough. I was pretty naive, but I knew enough to know that if one were interested in an academic career in engineering then one could not do something that would have a potential payoff only after twenty-five years.

How right he was. Thinking about thinking and building machines that do it, is still (in 2012) a target rather than an achievement. But certainly more is known about the nature of the challenge and Widrow's simple model of neural adaptation was an important piece of the jigsaw that forms our informational mind.

Frank Rosenblatt (1928–1971) and his detractors

Frank Rosenblatt was an enthusiastic pioneer of neural networks, exploring them mainly for their adaptive powers of pattern recognition. As a Professor at Cornell University, he ran a popular interdisciplinary course on 'Theory of Brain Mechanisms'. His book *'The Principles of Neurodynamics:*

---

[26]Widrow B., and Hoff M. (1960). Adaptive switching circuits. *Institute of Radio Engineers* (now IEEE) *Western Electronic Show and Convention* **4**, 96–104.

Perceptrons and the Theory of Brain Mechanisms', published in 1962 (Spartan Books), was the work that caused many young researchers to turn their heads towards neural networks. Sadly, Rosenblatt died in a boating accident on his 43rd birthday, depriving science of one of the few researchers who were providing a foundation for neural modeling. He had defined the word 'perceptron' which uses both fixed and learning versions of the McCulloch and Pitts neuron. The key feature came from Rosenblatt's desire to classify large patterns. So he used many fixed neurons with arbitrarily selected weights connected at random to some interface that held the pattern to be recognized. The classification came from a learning McCulloch and Pitts neuron connected to the output of the random neurons, which was trained to respond with a 0 or a 1.

His neurodynamics book is full of examples of pattern sets that could be discriminated by the perceptron (simulated on an IBM 704 computer). Clearly there were patterns that could not be discriminated, but if they could, his weight-adapting method was guaranteed to find the appropriate classification. Rosenblatt, in his writing and in interviews, often claimed that the rules that drive brain mechanisms were being discovered. This frequently gained him the attention of the press for having built a 'brain-like' machine. According to Widrow,[27] this type of attention infuriated colleagues who would have preferred to see speculations properly assessed in scientific journals.

Was it the fury of colleagues or a genuine desire for a truly scientific assessment that caused Seymour Papert and Marvin Minsky at MIT to launch an explicit attack on Perceptron-like systems[28]? There are stories of rivalry between Minsky and Rosenblatt: they had been to the same school in the Bronx. But the Minsky and Papert book is an elegant analysis of the very reasons that some structures cannot discriminate certain pattern characteristics. The conclusions drawn by Minsky and Papert were that some simple properties of patterns such a 'connectedness' between two black areas on a white background cannot be distinguished from 'non connectedness'. Their typical example is shown in Fig. 3.2.

---

[27]Widrow B. (1998). [Interview with J.A. Anderson and E. Rosenfeld]. In J. A. Anderson and E. Rosenfeld (Eds.), *Talking Nets: An Oral History of Neural Networks* (MIT Press, Cambridge, MA).

[28]Minsky M. and Papert S. (1969). *Perceptrons, Introduction to Computational Geometry* (MIT Press, Cambridge, MA).

Fig. 3.2. 'Connectedness': The image on the left is of one continuous object whereas the one on the right consists of two disconnected objects.

Minsky and Papert showed that no finite-sized perceptron could perform the task that distinguishes connected from not connected patterns. Clearly a very simple computational algorithm exists which can do this.[29] The impact of Minsky and Papert's book was astounding. Work on neural nets in the US came to a complete halt for about 10 years. But here is an important point. This disruption occurred *not* because the book demonstrated that neural network investigations did not provide the furthering of an understanding of the brain (where Rosenblatt's enthusiasm and press descriptions were criticized by colleagues) but for not providing a means for doing the kind of algorithmic computation done on conventional computers. In fact, if a human being attempts to distinguish between the two images in Fig. 3.2, this is well nigh impossible without getting a pencil out and tracing out the paths. In other words, the Minsky and Papert argument leads one to ask what it is in the informational human mind that causes the human to grab hold of a pencil.

But this point was not recognized. However, in some way, a true search for an informational assessment of what neurons in the brain do had just begun.

---

[29]Something like: assuming a rectangular grid, pick on a black square and turn it to white moving onto a neighboring black square to repeat the process. If the algorithm cannot continue as there are no neighboring black squares but there are other black squares in the image, then the image is disconnected.

Closed paths and other escapes from objections

Books on the history of neural networks will declare that the exit from
the dark ages of neural network research in the US was led by California
Institute of Technology's John Hopfield. He showed that, taking a network in which the inputs of each neuron were connected to the outputs
of all other neurons the network would "fall" into one particular pattern
of neural firing. In this work, pattern recognition was no longer of central
interest. Rather, since at any moment, the output of the neurons may be
taken together to form a *state*, the interest centers on what are the moment-
to-moment changes in the state and learning is such that the net may be
made to remain stable in preferred states. The net "exhibits knowledge" of
such states by entering them and remaining stable in them particularly if
the net is started in a pattern similar to one of the training patterns.[30] Hopfield used the metaphor of the energy of a ball falling into a hole to explain
the falling into these knowledge states in terms of energy. The study of this
behavior is crucial in attempts to understand mind-creating informational
activity in neural networks. The Hopfield network (as it is now known) was
an embodiment of an idea that had previously intrigued McCulloch and
others. Quoting McCulloch again from the Korzybsky Memorial Lecture
(note 14):

> *In looking into circuits composed of closed paths of neurons wherein cir-
> cuits could reverberate we had set up a* theory of memory. *(our under-
> lining)*

It is likely that neural nets that allow information to circulate and thereby
create what are known as 'sequential automata' are the most important
aspect of linking the function of neurons to the emergence of the informational mind. This will be examined in the next chapter, as will be the work
of psychologists Karl Lashley and Donald Hebb, who were the pioneers of
the realization that conscious thought may be due to 'reverberations' in
neural networks that have closed loops.

A second strand of work escaping from the Minsky and Papert cen-
sure came in 1986 with the publication of two volumes of advancing

---

[30]Hopfield J. J. (1982). Neural networks and physical systems with emergent
collective computational abilities, *PNAS* **79**(8), 2554–2558.

neural network science under the heading of Parallel Distributed Processing (PDP).[31,32] Led by psychologists Jay McLelland and David Rumelhart, a group of 10 enthusiasts set out to show how neural modeling can be extended beyond the Minsky and Papert analysis. Here the key advance was the demonstration that multi-layered networks (which they chose to call 'multi-layer perceptrons') can achieve this provided that a training scheme can be devised. This was the celebrated 'error back-propagation' algorithm based on the 1974 Harvard PhD thesis by National Science Foundation scientist Paul Werbos.[33] In a nutshell, this is a way of distributing the error measured at the output of a net backward through the net, and then using this to adjust the weights of intermediate layers to get rid of the output error. This opened the way for using neural networks (or simulations of neural networks) to solve a variety of practical pattern recognition problems. However there is another aspect of PDP which, importantly, impinges on the theme of this book: informational mental events. The group closely analyzed the stable states of a neural network which Hopfield had analyzed earlier (footnote 31) and found that some were more stable than others. That is, were the entire network subjected to noise it could be dislodged from these partly stable states. So the net could fall from less stable to more stable states until it would no longer be dislodged.[34] In much of this book, we link network states to experienced mental states. The phenomenon of finding ever more stable states may link to the feelings that arise when one is trying to put a name to a face. Is it George...? No, is it Harry...? No, it's David! David is clearly the most stable of the experienced sequence of states. So, is it possible that noise does not always have a destructive effect in a system? Does it help the brain to think? We return to this in the next chapter.

---

[31]Rumelhart D. E., McClelland J. L. and the PDP Research Group (1986). *Parallel Distributed Processing: Explorations in the Microstructure of Cognition. Volume 1: Foundations* (MIT Press, Cambridge, MA).
[32]McClelland J. L., Rumelhart D. E. and the PDP Research Group (1986). *Parallel Distributed Processing: Explorations in the Microstructure of Cognition. Volume 2: Psychological and Biological Models* (MIT Press, Cambridge, MA).
[33]Werbos P. J. *The Roots of Backpropagation: From Ordered Derivatives to Neural Networks and Political Forecasting* (Wiley, 1994).
[34]In Chapter 7 of the PDP books, Hinton and Sejnowski defined a 'Boltzmann' machine.

Spiking neurons

Since the early part of this century, neural network researchers have become concerned with achieving greater biological realism in the operation of the neuron. Adopting the Hodgkin and Huxley model of the neuron (see footnote 12), where the input activity to the neuron is integrated as a membrane potential until some threshold is reached and the neuron spikes before going into a refractory period when it is virtually out of action, gives rise to varied and rich patterns of spike generation and synchronization between neurons in a group. On the whole this means that a neuron can transmit a richer assessment of its incoming information than the fire/not fire decision. Eugene Izhikevich of the Neurosciences Institute in San Diego gives an insightful account of such a neuron.[35] Here we take the view that spiking does not alter the logical role of a neural network, it merely enriches the modes of transmitting information from one neuron to others in response to a combination of spiking inputs. Work using spiking neurons identifies interesting patterns of coherence among neurons in an interconnected network.

In current neural network studies, one finds research that focuses on more accurate models of the biological neuron but this does not always add to an understanding of the capacity of systems with architectures composed of a variety of neural network modules. Understanding this capacity of these systems is an objective of this book, so we conclude this chapter by discussing a neuron that is *less* like living neurons in detail. However, this contains the essential logical function of a neuron which, we suggest, provides insights into the global informational properties of brain-like architectures. Of course, these ideas might need revising if it comes to light that neurons have as yet undiscovered logical properties.

Weightless neurons

Here we introduce a neuron that has resulted from our own modeling work.[36] We took seriously the McCulloch and Pitts suggestion that the

---

[35]Izhikevich E. M. (2003). Simple model of spiking neurons, *IEEE Transact. Neural Networks* **14**(6).

[36]A recent review of this methodology may be found in Aleksander I., De Gregorio M., França F.M.G., Lima P.M.V. and Morton H. (2009). A brief introduction to Weightless Neural Systems, *Proc. ESANN'2009, European Symposium on Artificial Neural Networks — Advances in Computational Intelligence and Learning*, Bruges, Belgium, 22–24 April.

neuron primarily performs a logical function and we departed from the weight-adjusting mode of learning in order to make the learning itself a logical process. Since its first formulation in 1966,[37] the weightless neuron underwent several modifications. Here we describe its most recent and most general form and use this in our continued story. We refer to this version as the *Logical Neuron* or LN.

The essence of the LN is that it should (i) *learn* to respond to information at its synaptic inputs, and (ii) generalize by being insensitive to small departures from the learned examples. As seen above, 'conventional' neuron models achieve (i) through synaptic weight changes, and they achieve (ii) through the summing arrangements which are insensitive to small changes in the input information. We describe the LN formally below, illustrate it with an example and comment on these two tasks.

Let each LN have n binary inputs so that $X^k = \{\mathbf{x}_1^k, \mathbf{x}_2^k \ldots \mathbf{x}_{2^n}^k\}$ is the set of all the n-bit messages that the kth neuron can receive. Say that each LN has a single binary output z^k.[38]

Learning in the LN is a matter of associating a subset of X^k with values of z^k. Therefore, the training set is a set of pairs

$$T = \left(\mathbf{x}_p^k, z_p^k\right), \left(\mathbf{x}_q^k, z_q^k\right) \ldots$$

These pairs are stored in the neuron.

'Recall' in the LN refers to an input $\mathbf{x}_u^k$, an unknown (i.e., possibly not in the training set) element of X^k. The output is computed as follows: in X^k, find the 'nearest neighbor' of $\mathbf{x}_u^k$. This is the stored input message that has most bits in common with $\mathbf{x}_u^k$. In other words, the pattern with the minimum *Hamming Distance* is selected.[39] Say that this is message $\mathbf{x}_j^k$. The output of the neuron is then z_j^k. However, if several stored messages are at the same least *Hamming Distance*, and they are paired with different values of z^k then the output is a value of z^k picked *at random*. If all the stored values of the nearest patterns are the same z_j^k, then this is the generated output of the neuron.

---

[37] Aleksander I. (1966. Self-adaptive universal logic circuit, *IEE Electron. Lett.* **2**, 321.

[38] If a neuron with a richer communication needs to be modeled, m LNs can be used in parallel providing an output set of 2^m messages.

[39] The number of positions at which the corresponding symbols d between two binary messages of equal length are different, is called *Hamming* distance (named after the US mathematician, Richard Wesley Hamming, 1915–1998).

In sum, LN (i) learns by storing input/output pairs and recalls the output of the stored input closest in Hamming distance to the unknown input. The LN *generalizes* by virtue of the Hamming distance choice, which achieves a result for small differences between unknown and stored inputs. The neuron can also say "I don't know", i.e., when it outputs a sequence of output values at random.

Example

An LN has $n = 4$ and therefore its total set X^k contains $2^n = 16$ messages. We choose a training set of six messages:

$x_1x_2x_3x_4$	Training output z^k
1 1 1 1	1
1 1 0 0	1
1 1 0 1	1
0 0 1 0	0
0 1 1 1	0
1 0 0 1	0

Here is the response of the neuron to some unknown messages (nearest neighbors and neuron outputs are shown **bold italic**).

Training	HD for 1110	HD for 1000	HD for 0011
1 1 1 1	*1*	3	2
1 1 0 0	*1*	*1*	4
1 1 0 1	2	2	3
0 0 1 0	2	2	*1*
0 1 1 1	2	4	*1*
1 0 0 1	3	*1*	*1*
Output	*1*	*d*	*0*

The neuron makes definite decisions for messages 1110 and 0011 as the nearest neighbors agree, but 'says': *I don't know* for 1000 where the nearest neighbors disagree.

Looking back in this chapter: Mind and the science of the day

The historical path of understanding the mechanisms of mind reflects, without much choice, the scientific philosophies and methods of the day. For w, the heart as the energizing organ of the body and its motion was thought also to provide the thinking power for that body. But physicians noticed that malfunctions in the brain correlated with disaffections of thought. The 'science of the day' from Aristotle to Descartes, had little to say about the brain and attempts of understanding relied on fable or religious belief. Descartes lived in an age where the power of steam and hydraulics was becoming harnessed, and this is likely to have influenced his understanding of how muscles are moved by thought. So in his view, the pineal gland had to translate the "immaterial spirits of the ventricles" into pressures in hydraulic pipes that expand or contract the muscles.

Both Sherrington and Cajal were in their twenties when Thomas Edison, in the USA, founded the Edison Light Co. The wondrous ability of distributing energy across cities and nations must have influenced the idea that control of brain on muscles used conduction in some way akin to the way that electrical cables service a widely spread population. But a lesser known science was the controlling power of logic published by Shannon in 1940 (see Chapter 2) as part of his explorations in information. This was understood and appreciated by McCulloch and Pitts, who saw logic as the explanation of what the neural circuits of the brain do.

So, is it the fate of theories about brain and mind that they derive from the latest ideas in in the natural sciences or technology?[40] We believe that informational sciences actually bring something new into this arena. An aim of this book is to show that the deepening of understanding of information of the 1940s has produced models more appropriate for the study of the brain/mind relationship than any other in the history of science. But the story has only just begun. Now we find a shift from the dynamics of power in electricity distribution networks to the logic of neural networks.

---

[40]This trend was continued by Sir Roger Penrose a physicist of the 'quantum age', who argued that an explanation can be found in the quantum domain: see Penrose R. (1989). *The Emperor's New Mind* (Oxford University Press, Oxford). This position is often opposed: Tegmark, M. (2000). The importance of quantum decoherence in brain processes, *Phys. Rev. E.* **61**, 4194–4206.

Chapter 4

IMAGINATION IN THE CIRCLES OF A NETWORK

Logic will get you from A to B. Imagination will take you everywhere.

Albert Einstein

... as the images unwind,
like the circles that you find
in the windmills of your mind

Alan and Marilyn Bergman and Michel Legrand, theme for 'The Thomas Crown Affair'

Neural thought: A target for this Chapter — State Structures, Not 'Cat' or 'Dog' Cells

In the story set out in Chapter 3, neurology as interpreted by mathematics provides a very general statement of what the atomic unit of the brain, the neuron, does. In the language of information, this statement suggests that a neuron transmits one of a limited set of messages to many other neurons. It also receives messages within this set from a large number of neurons. It then learns to recognize some of the co-occurrences of certain messages at its inputs and signals this by issuing its own message or saying 'I don't know' by outputting a random sequence of messages. It would be quite easy to jump to the mistaken conclusion that the neural nets of the brain principally accept masses of sensory information which they somehow 'recognize', that is 'label'. If, for example, a person is looking at an animal which is either at a cat or a dog, many of his or her neurons are sampling the masses of messages at some sensory interface like the eye retina. We could hypothesize that these neurons pass their messages to a smaller number of neurons and so on until just one neuron issues the message 'cat', 'dog' or 'something else'. Our aim in this chapter is to show that it is very unlikely that an informational brain operates in this way. A much more likely occurrence is that sensory input is a stimulus to neural activity that changes with time and constitutes the path of 'thought' in time. Even closing one's eyes leads to a cornucopia of mental images and thoughts which could not be described as 'recognitions' of sensory input. There are recognitions by individual neurons, but these are of what other neurons are doing. This leads to a flow of neural states in time, a flow that is the physical basis of thought. In this chapter we seek to clarify this idea.

Again, the idea that the dynamic action of a neural assembly is a correlate of thought does not come out of the blue — there is a history of those who have grappled with trying to understand these relationships. This helps to set a human background to the otherwise stark nature of the theoretical ideas.

Lashley, the Iconoclast of ancient connectionism

Karl Lashley (1890–1958) was described in 1961 in the biographical memoirs of the (US) National Academy of Sciences as "... one of the greatest psychologists of our time ..." despite having "... no earned degree in psychology ...".[1] So who was Karl Spencer Lashley?

Born in Davis, West Virginia, to a father involved in merchandizing and a mother with a deep respect for literature and education, his early education was turbulent. It included an excursion by his parents to Alaska in search of gold. Despite interrupted schooling, he reached the University of West Virginia, where he encountered zoology at the age of 16, deciding to make this his life's work. After getting his Bachelor's degree, he first met psychology while at the University of Pittsburgh where he elected to do undergraduate laboratory work in experimental psychology while working for his Masters' degree in Zoology. A move to Johns Hopkins University and a thesis on *Hydra*, a tiny fresh-water animal known for asexual reproduction, led to the PhD degree. Again, zoology was the theme, but soon

---

[1]Beach, F.A. (1961). *Karl Spencer Lashley. Biographical Memoir* (National Academy of Sciences, Washington).

after qualifying, he not only worked on learning behaviors in birds but also on the acquisition of human motor skills: an clear foray into psychology.

His interest in the neurology of learning combined with later work on brain-injured patients brought Lashley to his pioneering work on the effect of brain lesions on learning with which he is said to have begun the 'ground attack on connectionism'. It should be explained that in the 1920s 'connectionism' had quite a different meaning from that used in the 1980s. The latter refers to the computational properties, analyses and applications of neural networks, post 1986.[2] The earlier meaning referred to the strengths of supposed connections between stimulus and response as learning takes place. The work of Edward Thorndike during the early 20th century is typical of this *behaviorist* stance.[3]

As Lashley's reputation grew, he was sought by several universities. First as assistant professor at the University of Minnesota, then to the University of Chicago where he became a full professor at the age of 39. A few years later, in 1935, the University of Harvard decided to create its first professor of psychology by appointing the "best psychology professor in the world". The search committee selected the then 45-year-old Lashley. His title became that of 'Professor in Neuropsychology' and, later, 'Director of the Yerkes Laboratories of Primate Biology'. He retained this position until his retirement in 1955.

His most substantial publication was *Brain Mechanisms and Intelligence*, published by the Chicago University Press in 1929. This contained the salient part of his experimentation which conclusively destroyed the stimulus–response connectionism popular at the time. Lashley's experiments were to show that progressive lesions of cortical areas resulted in a gradual decrease in learning ability in animals. Early connectionism predicted that drastic rather than progressive impairments would be discovered. Lashley introduced three new concepts which the connectionist fraternity found to be contentious. The first of these is 'mass action'. Were there to be specific neural structures that ensure the recall of particular items of learning, lesion experiments would have created the loss of specific memories. Instead in rats the extent of the deterioration of their ability to recall paths through mazes appeared to be related only to the amount of

---

[2]Following the publication of the Parallel Distributed Processing books by Rumelhart and McLelland (MIT Press).

[3]Thorndike, E. L. (1911). *Animal Intelligence* (Macmillan).

cortical tissue that was destroyed rather than the location of the destruction. Therefore the 'mass action' of neurons was seen to be at work.

The second concept was dubbed the principle of 'equipotentiality' and related to results of experiments on the ability of rats to distinguish between simple drawings such as triangles and circles. Lashley again progressively lesioned parts of the primary visual cortex (also known as 'striate' or V1) and found that the memory was retained equally, irrespective of which sections were removed, that is, all areas were 'equipotential'. Indeed 90% of the primary visual cortex could be removed without impairing the ability to discriminate. Of course, in retrospect, it is now considered doubtful that V1 is involved in conscious memory tasks, so Lashley's conclusions are no longer seen as being significant. But at the time, this was seen as evidence of distribution rather than connectionism.

The 'engram' was the third concept. It is a compendium of the other two concepts. The engram refers to the supposed physical change in some part of the neural structure of the brain which seems necessary to encode new memories. It seems evident that there should be some change, and at the age of 60, looking back on his career, Lashley reported a failure in not being able to find this change in a paper entitled 'In search of the Engram'.[4] In part, he concludes:

> *The series of experiments has yielded a good bit of information about what and where the memory trace is not.*

This is not a negative result. We now know that the engram is not easily discernable at the level of physical structure. It is true that any learning that takes place does cause physical changes in neurons, but patterns of firing across large networks are now thought to represent what has been learned and these are created by subtle and possibly not discernable changes in the function of neurons. In the rest of this chapter we shall see how this happens. But for now we applaud one of Lashley's insightful conclusions (also found in footnote 4):

> *The learning process must consist of the attunement of the elements of a complex system in such a way that a particular combination or pattern of cells responds more readily than before the experience. The particular mechanism by which this is brought about remains unknown*

---

[4] *Physiological Mechanisms in Animal Behaviour.* Symp. for the Soc. For Exp. Biol. No IV, 1950 pp. 454–482.

While more is now known about the mechanisms that determine the 'pattern of cells', this still remains controversial and continues to be a topic for investigation.

Donald Hebb: Nailing mind to brain

When Lashley moved from Chicago to Yale, he brought with him a 31-year-old Canadian doctoral student called Donald Olding Hebb. Hebb had an indirect path to being a psychology student. After a rebellious life at school, he graduated in Arts from Dalhousie University. Intending to be a novelist, he taught in schools before entering McGill University in Montreal to obtain an MA in Psychology.[5] Depressed by the death of his first wife in a car accident, and the limitations of his school teaching he recognized that his enthusiasm lay in physiological psychology and decided to leave Canada. Advised by his McGill mentor Boris Babkin, he joined Lashley in Chicago and traveled with him to Yale, completing his PhD in Spatial Orientation in 1936.

After teaching at Queens' University and then collaborating with Lashley again at the Yerkes Laboratory, Hebb returned to McGill in 1947 as a Professor of Psychology, later becoming the Department Chair. He remained at McGill for the rest of his working life. In 1949, he published '*Organisation of Behaviour*', a brilliant and influential text that took forward from Lashley the theory of cooperative neural action in the brain.[6] Most of our discussion of Hebb's work is based on the content of this book.

His theory, like Lashley's, is driven by the discovery that removal of cortical material does not impede effective thought, casting doubt on theories of learning based on connection changes between stimulus and response. He goes on to note that 'attention' is a mechanism that cannot easily be denied. That is, between a stimulus and a response, a choice can be made among several possible responses. The dominant theory of the time was that of arch-behaviorist B.F.Skinner,[7] that there was no inner activity in the brain

---

[5]http://en.wikipedia.org/wiki/Donald_O._Hebb. (accessed date 29th July 2012.)
[6]Hebb, D. O. (1949, 2009). *Organization of Behaviour* (John Wiley, New York (original) and Mahwah N.J. Lawrence Earlbaum e-Library).
[7]Skinner, B. F. (1938). *The Behavior of Organisms: An Experimental Analysis* (Appleton Century, New York).

except that which links stimulus to response, but it was clear to Hebb that there was sufficient evidence against these ideas. On this proposition of Skinner's Hebb pronounced:

> *The present book is written in profound disagreement with such a program for psychology*

Hebb's contribution to psychology is often stated as the formulation of two principles: first he sees learning as an increase in the efficacy of firing links between neurons and second he posits the creation of meaningful cell assemblies which sustain 'thought' as reverberations. Hebb's book marks one of the most significant turning points in the history of psychology: from behaviorism that plays down the mental state, to the centrality of the mental state as the basis of behavior. It is also quite remarkable how the book addresses many contemporary issues on the informational nature of the mental state — how neural complexes may be formed and how they relate to reality is material that populates current discussions about consciousness as we shall see.

Neural (Hebbian) learning

Recalling (from Chapter 3) the model of a neuron as having a synapse that lies between the axon of one neuron and the body of another (see Fig. 3.1 in Chapter 3), Hebb's rule states:

> *When the axon of cell A is near enough to excite B repeatedly, or persistently takes part in firing it, some growth process takes place in one or both cells such as A's efficiency, as one of the cells firing B, is increased.*

In the language of synaptic weights in the McCulloch and Pitts model, the weight between A and B is increased when A and B fire at the same time. This method of causing a network to learn to recognize input patterns is still much used in practical applications of artificial neural networks.

Cell assemblies

Hebb suggested that the way in which a network represents the external world in inner 'thought' is through sustained sequences of firing patterns in 'cell assemblies'.

The state of play after Hebb

The sea change from behaviorism to some form of acceptance of mental states has already been mentioned. However, Hebb's suggestions opened a set of important questions. How is a mental state created? How does it become meaningful? How does it influence behavior? Interestingly, McCulloch and Pitts had, since 1943, identified the need for theory on these questions by referring to the existence of 'circles' (closed loops) in neural networks[8]:

> ... *activity may be set up in a circuit and continue reverberating around it for an indefinite period of time ... [it] ... may involve reference to past events of an indefinite degree of remoteness.*

They were clearly talking about sustained sequences of firing patterns in cell assemblies. While Hebb refers to McCulloch's work, he sees it as exercises in mathematics 'which simplify the psychological problem almost out of existence'. The problem was not so much with mathematics, but with a lack of a rigorous way of dealing with these closed loops. How this was addressed, now follows.

Automata studies

So far in this story, the characters came from differing backgrounds: Physiology (McCulloch and Lashley), Logic (Pitts) and Psychology (Hebb). In 1956, a new specialization was added to the list: computational theory. At a meeting organized at Princeton University in 1956 by Claude Shannon and John McCarthy, the theme was *Automata Studies* and the meeting served to define the field of *Automata Theory* through several papers related to the internal states of neural structures.

The lead paper, 'Representation of Events in Nerve Nets' was by Steven Cole Kleene (1909–1994), who was destined to be among those hailed as pioneers of the use of mathematics to discover what could and what could not be computed. In the 1956 'Automata Studies', he set out a system of

---

[8]McCulloch W. S. and Pitts W. H. A logical calculus of the ideas immanent in nervous activity, *Bull. Math. Biophys.* **5**, 115–133.

mathematics that indicated what could and what could not be represented by neural networks that both did and did not include 'closed loops'.[9]

The McCulloch and Pitts formulation of neural networks was time-based in the sense that from the creation of an input to the neuron to the moment that it would respond there was assumed to be a unit time delay. This means that even nets without closed loops are sensitive to the time sequences of their inputs. Figure 4.1 shows the way in which Kleene presented a neural network.

The way Kleene analyses neural networks (or *nerve nets*) is shown in Fig. 4.1. Accepting that the input to a neuron at time t determines its output at time $t + 1$, and using the notation $X(t)$ as reading 'the value of the output of neuron X at time t', we can write the logical function for this net as:

$$P(t + 2) = A(t + 1) \; \textit{or} \; [[\textbf{\textit{not}} \; B(t)] \, \textit{and} \; C(t)].$$

Kleene encourages us to think in terms of an *event* that leads to a firing of the output P, and this is expressed as a table set out as (inputs ABC)×(time steps t, $t+1$). For the above example the following event leads

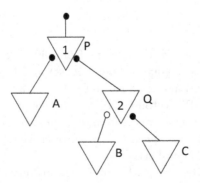

Fig. 4.1.   A nerve net as presented by Kleene: A, B, C are *input* neurons, P and Q are *inner* neurons, the number is the threshold of the neuron, full circles are excitatory synapses, empty ones are inhibitory.

---

[9]S. C. Kleene (1956). Representation of events in nerve nets and finite automata, in C.E. Shannon and J. McCarthy (Eds.), *Automata Studies* (Princeton University Press).

to the firing of P at time $t + 2$, (that is $P(t + 2) = 1$):

	A	B	C
$t + 1$	1	0	0
t	0	0	1

To explain, if at time t, ABC are 001, due to the action of Q, Q will be 1 at $t + 1$. If then A is 1 both inputs to P will be active and P will fire at $t + 2$. For that matter, P would also fire if A was 0. This is said to be a *positive definite* event which leads to the firing of the output. A *non-positive definite event* is a similar table which does not lead to the firing of the output — it could be:

	A	B	C
t+1	1	0	1
t	0	1	1

The key point made by Kleene (echoing a similar result of McCulloch and Pitts) is that for all positive (or non-positive) definite events there exists a neural network which represents the event by firing (or not firing). Clearly, to get a view of what it is that supports the 'mental state' in the neurological brain, Kleene's analysis argues that there are vast areas of 'inner neurons' that contribute our mentality without evoking 'closed loops'. But closed loops (circles) there are, and Kleene argues that McCulloch and Pitts' assessment of these was "obscure" and so he proceeded "independently".

The outcome of this independent process is that Kleene identified the class of neural nets with closed loops with the class of *finite automata*.

Finite automata

As in the example above, interest focuses on how the state of the inner neurons can be affected by sequences of states on the input neurons. Above, such sequences were called 'definite'. We now look at one specific network with a closed loop and inspect the sequences that lead to its inner states.

The question Kleene asked was how events at A and B that lead to different states of L and M differ from 'definite events' This can be gleaned by using Table 4.1.

Assuming that L M at time t is 0 0, then any sequence of inputs A B=0 0 will leave L M at 0 0. If A B remains at 0 0 at time $t + 1$, L M will stay at 0 0. The same will be true no matter how long these sequences of inputs

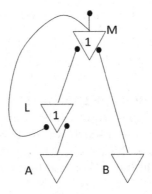

Fig. 4.2.   A neural network with a closed loop connecting inner neurons L and M. A and B are input neurons. Again, full circles are excitatory synapses.

Table 4.1.   This shows the inner state (L M) at time t+1 for an input at (A B) and state (L M) at time t

			A B at t		
L M a t t + 1		00	01	10	11
L M at t	00	00	01	10	11
	01	10	11	10	11
	10	01	01	11	11
	11	11	11	11	11

remain A B = 0 0. Even more spectacular is the application of A B=1 1 which causes the net to enter L M=1 1 from which it cannot escape. In other words, state L M=1 1 means that input 1 1 has occurred at least once in the past history of the net. These kinds of inputs are not 'definite' events as the size of the input table is not determined. But they are what Kleene called *regular events* — these differ from 'definite' events as they allow undefined numbers of repetitions of the input.

As an example in Table 4.1 the following input sequences (A B) will take the state (L M)from 00 to 11

(11) or

(01)(01) (which reads (01) followed by (01)) or

(00)*(11)(11)* (where (*00*)* reads 'input message *00*' is repeated zero or any number of times) and similarly (*11*)* reads ' input message *11*' is repeated zero or any number of times.)

These sequences are called 'regular expressions'. We also note that there is another helpful way in which the same information as in Table 4.1 can be represented. This is called the *state diagram* or *state structure*. This is shown in Fig. 4.3.

The 'regular expression' that is 'accepted' by the net going from state 00 to state 11 is obtained by considering all paths that lead between the two. In these expressions, one can also use the link **'or'**. Then with considerable effort we can show the complete regular expression that takes the state from 00 to 11:

(00)* (11) gets us to (11) directly.

But (01)(01 **or** 11) also gets us there. But this has neglected the fact that from(01) the sequence (00 **or** 10)(00 **or** 01) could happen on the way to (11) so this second path is written

(01)((00 **or** 10)(00 **or** 01))*(01 **or** 11)

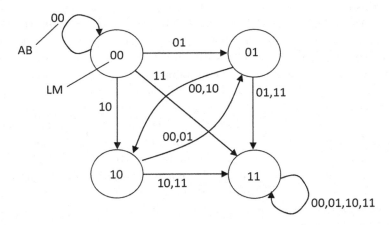

Fig. 4.3. The state structure of the circuit in Fig. 4.2. This contains the same information as Table 4.1. Given any state of LM (drawn as a circle) at time t, an arrow labeled with an input message (AB) from that circle to another, the other circle represents the state at $t + 1$. Some states have arrows leading back to themselves, and these too are labeled with the AB inputs which cause this re-entry.

Similarly the third path is

(10)((00 **or** 01)(00 **or**10))*(10 **or** 11)

Putting it all together, starting in 00 and ending in 11 the net is said to 'accept' the complete regular expression:

(00)*((11) **or** ((01)((00 **or** 10)(00 **or** 01))*(01 **or** 11)) **or** ((10)((00 **or** 01)(00 **or** 10))*(10 **or** 11))(11)*

This expression is neither readable nor very meaningful. But Kleene's definition of regular expressions had a more profound effect in computational theories than identifying the difference that 'circles' make in nerve nets. Regular expressions can be described as a 'grammar' of a language. Kleene's work led programmers to design 'parsing' automata that check a program for correct syntax. There are some excellent textbooks in this area[10] that not only deal with automata with a finite number of states as visited in this section but also with automata that are given infinite memory (such as a Turing Machine that use an infinite recording tape) and which can parse languages that are more sophisticated than the 'regular' variety mentioned here.

In this section, we have described Kleene's recognition that neural networks with circles (i.e., closed loops) *are* finite state automata. But the story is beginning to drift away a little from its aim to discover the informational dimension of the mind into computational theory. Historically, how the very important property of memory due to loops in neural networks was not followed up in terms of how this memory could actively represent some sort of experience. Note how Fig. 4.2 indicates a too-enduring memory of the fact that AB=11 has occurred at some time by causing the net to get stuck in state LM=11. In terms of value to a living entity this may not be all that useful. Clearly the neural networks of the brain have states that provide all that we call memory and that which we sometimes describe as our 'inner conscious life'. But surprisingly little has been said over the years about the *coding* of states that might have a correlation with what we sense and describe as our consciousness.

---

[10]Hopcroft J. E., Motwani R., and Ullman J. D. (2000). *Introduction to Automata Theory, Languages and Computation,* 2nd Edn. (Pearson Education, Harlow, UK).

More automata studies: The beginnings of major controversies

Outside of Kleene's concise mathematical analysis of the computational character of neural networks, the 1956 *Automata Studies* meeting brought together researchers with different opinions about the way that the new breed of computer theorists could help neurologists to make sense of the informational function of the brain. In the introduction to the proceedings, the then 29-year-old John McCarthy[11] and the more mature 40-year-old Claude Shannon pointed out that the extraordinary contemporary power and potential future power of the digital computer primarily allowed complex models of the physiological brain to be tested.[12]

The beginnings of a controversy could be seen in the three major sections of the proceedings. The first section (which contains Kleene's paper) is on mathematical formulations of neuron and network models proposed by neurophysiologists. They attempt to analyze the informational properties of structures actually found in the brain or simplifications thereof. The quest is to identify and describe through mathematics the capacity for such structures to act in 'intelligent' ways. Discoveries of pattern recognition properties and memory were encouraging. The second section is about Turing machines. Of course, at the time of the *Automata Studies* meeting, Turing's work on universal computation (1936)[13] and his discourse on whether machines could think (1950)[14] had already been influential in this community. The main contributions in this section addressed universal computation while in the preface, the editors were minded to dwell on giving precise definition to the word "thinking" and point to Turing's work on the imitation game.[15] They then point to the fact that this could be a trivial exercise as a large number of responses could be stored and some

---

[11] This is the McCarthy who is the Stanford professor who is said to have coined the term 'Artificial Intelligence' and became the 'guru' of those working in AI.

[12] It is with great sadness that, during the writing of this book in November 2011, we heard of John McCarthy's death.

[13] Turing A.M. (1936). On computable numbers, with an application to the Entscheidungsproblem, *Proc. London Math. Soc.* 2 **42**, 230–265.

[14] Turing A. M. (1950). Computing machinery and intelligence, *Mind* **59**, 433–460.

[15] They phrase it as "... a machine is termed capable of thinking if it can, under certain prescribed conditions, imitate a human being by answering questions sufficiently well to deceive a human questioner for a reasonable period of time."

interlocutors could be fooled. In this book, we have not dwelled on Turing's work. Clearly Turing was one of the giants of the mathematical analysis of computers and what could be achieved through computation. However, here we have left the algorithmic approach to one side, preferring to pursue 'mind' as a property of cellular systems. This does not mean that we do not value the last sixty or more years of classical artificial intelligence (AI) which Turing helped to spawn.

This controversy as to whether one attempts to understand intelligence as a product of neural structure or as being evidenced by the behavior of a machine no matter how this is achieved, persists to the present day as is discussed in the chapters which follow. We have not forgotten the third section of the proceedings of 'Automata Studies 1956'. This is on what in contemporary language might be called 'constructivism': achieving an understanding by synthesis. This method is also championed among many contemporary researchers who create informational structures that claim to model conscious processes as is seen in the rest of this chapter. For now, we recognize that *Automata Studies* brought together a group of thinkers who had recognized that 'information' was a vital ingredient of the essential character of mind.

Neural automata theory simplified

Staying with '*Automata studies*' one finds a seminal contribution on finite automata by Edward Moore, a mathematician working at the Bell Laboratories. The phrase he used instead of *finite automata* was '*finite-state machines*'. While he describes his work as having an 'experimental' character, he means by this the examination of what it is that one can discover about the inner states of a machine by carrying out experiments on its external terminals. In fact, he sees these not as laboratory experiments but describes them as 'thought' or '*gedanken*' experiments.[16] That is, these are conceptual experiments designed to discover the limitations of what external measurements can reveal about internal states. This consideration is vital when the machine in question is the brain and information is sought about the internal structure of the mind. Of course no mention of brain and

---

[16]Moore E. F. (1956). Gedanken experiments on sequential machines, in C.E. Shannon and J. McCarthy (Eds.), *Automata Studies* (Princeton University Press, Princeton).

mind can be found in Moore's paper, but some of the fundamental ideas he developed are highly significant and are worth repeating here.

Moore defined a finite automaton as having five elements:

i) A set I containing a number a of input messages, represented as symbols $I = \{i_1, i_2 \ldots i_a\}$

ii) A set Z containing a number b of output messages represented as symbols $Z = \{z_1, z_2 \ldots z_b\}$

iii) A set Q containing a number c of internal states represented as symbols $Q = \{q_1, q_2 \ldots q_c\}$

iv) A rule W which specifies the 'next' state (i.e., at time $t + 1$) from set Q for every pair comprising one element from states Q (at time t) and another from inputs I (at time p). This is written as

$$W : (I \times Q)_p \to Q_{p+1}$$

Note that the sign '$\times$' here reads as 'the set of all pairs of elements one taken from I and the other from Q

v) A rule Y which specifies the output associated with every state. This is written as

$$Y : Q \to Z$$

For a book that's meant to be maths free, the above seems not to be helpful. An example should cut through this notation which in the end really does help. We take the automaton with the state structure in Fig. 4.3. We note that this figure shows the coding of the specific neural circuit, while the Moore formulation is expressed so as to distinguish with symbols the different input, output and state messages that could occur. In the example, we let

the inputs AB = 00, 01 10, 11 be described as

$$I = \{i_1, i_2, i_3, i_4\}.$$

Similarly states LM = 00, 01 10, 11 be described as

$$Q = \{q_1, q_2, q_3, q_4\}.$$

But what of the output Z? Let us say that we are only interested in whether a specific set of states has been reached or not. This only requires two messages, that is,

$$Z = \{z_1, z_2\}.$$

To work out W it is best to create a table that represents all possible input/state pairs imagined at time p and shows the resulting state at time $p + 1$.

The reader may have the feeling that this is the same information that has already been seen in Table 4.1. There is, however, one vital difference: Table 4.2 leaves open the coding for the states and indicates an inner behavior that is independent of coding. But what of the output rule? In Table 4.3 there is an arbitrarily chosen suggestion:

In this case W and Y describe the behavior of some kind of booby trap! Started in any state (but not q_4) with any input (but not i_4) the machine will undergo state changes outputting z_1 until input i_4 occurs at which point the circuit enters state q_4 and output z_2:a somewhat mild model of an explosion, characterized by the fact that no input can cause an exit from this state.

Table 4.2. The rule W for the machine of Fig. 4.3.

Q_{p+1}	i_1	i_2	i_3	i_4
q_1	q_1	q_2	q_3	q_4
q_2	q_3	q_4	q_3	q_4
q_3	q_1	q_1	q_4	q_4
q_4	q_4	q_4	q_4	q_4

Table 4.3. A Y output rule for the machine in Table 4.2.

q_1	$\rightarrow$	z_1
q_2	$\rightarrow$	z_1
q_3	$\rightarrow$	z_1
q_4	$\rightarrow$	z_2

Lessons from Moore's work

We recall that the thrust of Moore's work is to assess how much of the state structure of an automaton can be gleaned by observing its behavior in response to an input sequence selected by an experimenter. The first result of Moore's *gedanken* experiments comes from the following realization.

> **State Coding:** *The behavior of an automaton is fully specified by the group* $\{I, Q, Z, W, Y\}$. *While I and Z can be observed as coded messages by an experimenter, no such knowledge of Q can be obtained.*

In other words, the coding of Q can only be discovered by taking internal measurements. There is a loose parallel here to what can be inferred about a particular mind through the external art of psychoanalysis (that is, nil about what the neurons are doing) and through neurological measurements of what the neurons are doing (this is, in general, very hard to do).

A second lesson can be understood by looking at the state structure shown in Fig. 4.4.

> **Multiple machines:** *Whatever external tests are done on an automaton, at any time during the experimentation many automata would fit the results.*

Engineers sometimes look for the simplest (least number of states) automaton that fits the experimentation if they wish to build an equivalent system that does not cost too much. The overall effect of Moore's analysis in the chase for an informational mind is that coming to conclusions from an observation of external behavior only is fraught with difficulty. Nevertheless throughout the history of AI, the Turing view has been taken that if a system appears outwardly to have a mind — then it has one. In many parts of this book, we will indicate how much we dissent from this point of view. Having a mind has to do with creating internal states that represent aspects of the external world rather than arbitrarily coded ones.

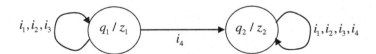

Fig. 4.4. Automation equivalent in outward behaviour to the automation of Tables 4.2 and 4.3.

Finding inner states

In the revival of interest in neural networks in the 1980s, networks with internal connections were certainly considered, but it is by no means evident that coding representing aspects of the external world was of central interest. The revival brought new pioneers to the fore. Revealing biographies of these neural innovators have been written in a valuable book by James Anderson and Edward Rosenfeld.[17] Here we briefly mention those who were most interested in networks with internal states. The work of Hopfield, Hinton and Werbos on the analysis of networks with feedback was reviewed in the last chapter. Here we introduce a few more of the actors on the stage where the play focuses on the search for the informational mind.

Meanwhile . . . outside the US: Eduardo Caianiello

The Minsky and Papert upheaval had a greater restraining effect in the US than in the rest of the world. Outside the US, many scientists and engineers, continued to be intrigued by the findings of McCulloch and Pitts and the enthusiasm of Frank Rosenblatt. They pursued in a major way the understanding of the neural machinery in our brains. In Italy, for example, there was a highly regarded physicist, Eduardo Caianiello (1921–1993), who turned to neural networks in 1961.[18,19] Caianiello strongly supported Norbert Wiener's enthusiastic definition of the new science of cybernetics as the study of information and control in the animal and the machine under the same institutional roof. With an early career that spanned Italy and the US, he was appointed to the prestigious chair in Theoretical Physics at the University of Naples at the age of 34. In 1968, he founded the Institute of Cybernetics of the Italian National Research Council, which became one of the premier centers for the study of cybernetics in Europe. Sadly, hampered by financial difficulties in the National Research Council, Caianiello

---

[17] Anderson J. A. and Rosenfeld E. (Eds.) (1998). *Talking Nets: An Oral History of Neural Networks* (MIT Press, Cambridge).

[18] Caianiello E. (1961). Outline of a theory of thought processes and thinking machines. *J. Theor. Biol.* **2**, 204–235.

[19] Paul Cull, a computer scientist at Oregon State University, gives an informative posthumous account of Caianiello's contribution to neural modeling: Caianiello and neural nets, in S. Termini (Ed.) *Imagination and Rigor: Essays on Caianiello's Heritage, 10 Years After His Death* (Italian Institute of Philosophy and Science, Milan, Springer, Berlin).

had to oversee the closure of the Institute in 1977. He moved to the University of Salerno where, with characteristic flair, he founded a new science faculty where computing science and engineering were taught alongside the more traditional topics. During these years, he also founded the International Institute for Advanced Scientific Studies in Vietri sul Mare. After his death, this continued to run as the 'Caianiello School on Neural Networks' under the direction of his successor, Professor of Theoretical Physics, Maria Marinaro.

Caianiello's contribution to understanding the internal state structures of neural networks 'with loops' (currently, preferably called 'recursive' or 'dynamic') was to separate short-term and long-term dynamics. In the short term, one can assume that the external influence on a neural circuit remains constant. This means that whatever the state of the net, there can be only one 'next state'. So the state sequence must eventually return to a previously visited state forming a cycle. There are therefore states that belong to cycles and some that don't. Those that don't are either 'transient', meaning that there are states that lead in to them, or 'initial' which means that no states lead to them. A little illustration relating back to the machine in Table 4.2 might help.

Figure 4.5 shows four so-called *autonomous* automata (that is, automata that operate on their own with unchanging input), one for each possible constant input state. That is one for each column of a table such as in Table 4.2. The first (i_1 constant) shows two separate single-state cycles and

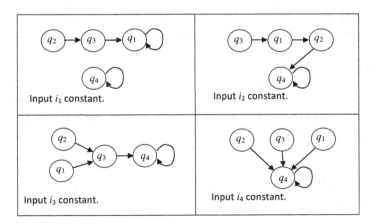

Fig. 4.5. Four different state structures can be found for the machine in Table 4.2: one for each possible constant input.

we note that there is no way of getting from one to the other. Such distinct groupings are generally called 'confluents'. Examples of transient states are q_1 for i_2 constant and q_3 for i_3 constant. q_2 is an initial state in all except (i_2 constant). Caianiello drew attention to the fact that the language of state structures (How many confluents? How many single-state cycles? How long are the cycles? How long are the transients?) expresses the informational character of the inner response to an external stimulus, or just internal 'contemplation'. In other words, it calls for mathematical technique that relates the physics of the net to its state structure, that is, its body to its informational mind.

Referring to the study of networks with frozen function as being determined by *neuronic equations*, he proposes a second strand of investigation based on function changes that might take place while the net is 'running'. He called these *mnemonic equations*. Here, he allowed the weights to change in much the same way as Hebb did. While the resulting equations are hard to solve, they do point to question about the development of useful state structure in learning neural nets and this still requires research at the present day.

Meanwhile . . . Outside the US: Teuvo Kohonen

Teuvo Kohonen (1934–) is an eminent Finnish engineer, and, at the time of writing, an Emeritus Professor at the Helsinki University of Technology, where he spawned one of the world's most appreciated neural network teams. This is well known for the 'self-organizing map' which is described briefly below. In his interview with James Anderson and Edward Rosenthal (see footnote 16), he describes how his interest in neural networks developed during a visit to the University of Washington during 1968 and 1969. These were the 'dark years' for neural networks, and Kohonen recounts the swift rejections he had for attempted publications at that time. Since those days he has published a series of influential papers and books culminating in the third edition of '*Self Organising Maps*'.[20] So what is a self-organizing map?

A conventional arrangement consists of a two-dimensional (2D) array of neurons, all of which are connected to an n-input interface. All neurons are connected to the n inputs. The task of the array is to distinguish in

---

[20]Kohonen T. (2001). *Self-Organising Maps* (Springer Verlag, Berlin).

the 2D space the different patterns at the n inputs. Say that the patterns representing the numbers 56 and 92 are learned as being different targets, a neuron responds to the first and another to the second. Then Kohonen's algorithm works so that numbers in the vicinity of each (e.g., 55 and 57 on the one hand and 91 and 93 on the other) respond to physically close neurons. At the end of the process, the map separates in space patterns that are different and coagulates those that are similar. Applied to the recognition of speech, say, the map may position the phonemes (basic sounds of speech) in this 2D space and utterances then form trajectories in the 2D space, which are more easily distinguished than sequences of the original $n-$bit data. Kohonen and his colleagues built successful speech recognition systems using this scheme.

Back in the US . . . Stephen Grossberg

A US scientist who was active in the years between the Minsky and Papert pessimism and the revival of the 1980s is Steven Grossberg (1939–), often publishing with Gail Carpenter. Also interviewed by James Anderson and Edward Rosenfeld (see footnote 16), he describes his passion for linking mind to brain from an early age and throughout his scientific career. He and his wife Gail Carpenter are internationally appreciated for an ingenious model which demonstrates their Adaptive Resonance Theory, known as the ART model, which has had a series of progressive characterizations. Grossberg describes the way that ART structures stimulate thinking in the understanding of cortical dynamics in general, in a classical book published in 1992.[21] A sketch of the basic ART structure is shown in Fig. 4.6.

In the world of dynamic neural networks, there are two ways in which the internal state can be represented: distributed and localized. The distributed version involves the entire network and could then be an immediately obvious encoding of something meaningful (e.g., a picture of a cat, dog ...) or some state that is unique for the perceived item, but not similar to it (such as a number, or a particular distribution of on and off bits). Localized representation uses one or very few neurons to represent a meaningful object. The Kohonen neural network described earlier has a localized representation. Grossberg's ART uses both. Net 1 in Fig. 4.6 is a distributed

---

[21]Grossberg S. (1992) *Neural Networks and Natural Intelligence* (MIT Classic Series, Boston).

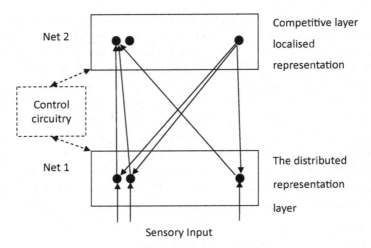

Fig. 4.6.　A highly simplified sketch to show the relationship between a (net 1) capable of a distributed representation and another (net 2), capable of localized representation.

representation of some sensory data, while net 2 contains individual neurons that respond to specific patterns in net 1. Furthermore, net 2 works in a competitive way. The neuron that is most driven in net 2 inhibits the others — this is known as 'winner take all' operation. This winner then broadcasts back to net 1 the pattern that most stimulates the winning neuron. Grossberg and his colleagues have made a major contribution to the explanation of a wide variety of thought-like behaviors in the functional brain by virtue of the fact that a knowledge of the real world (imagination) is retained in the internal and even autonomous states of the ART model. The reader can follow this work as it is well accessible through the internet.

So how do neurons think?

Should there be a moral to the story told in this chapter it is that the neural assemblies that inhabit our brains have a subtle relationship between the way their inner states change, the way that sensory contact with the world creates and then controls such state changes, the way that such states might acquire meaning and the way that some of these states lead to action in the world through muscular motor action. We met Karl Lashley, who drew attention to the fact that mass action of neurons, that is, a 'state', is vital rather than previously postulated localized 'recognitions' of world events. His student Donald Hebb showed how persistent activity in neural structures creates states that can be sustained even in the absence of external stimulation. We introduced Steven Kleene's and Edward Moore's idea of an automaton, which is a useful and simple (mathematical, if you like) way of talking about states, sensory influences and behavior as well as the way these link to neural structures. The work of Caianiello in separating out state structures that result from constant inputs shows how cyclic activity in a network may be seen as a characteristic of 'thought'. In contrast, Kohonen's work stresses that localization of activity is a way that a network can decipher world events and track their changes. Grossberg's ART, which combines localized and distributed representations, completes the discussion of features which distinguish different modeling techniques.

But this is just the beginning. What has been described above merely indicates that the state structures of automata relate to a way that one can think about thought. But most of the models need further consideration as to how they might capture thought. Rather than trying to relate the existing work found in several laboratories on the question of content, in the next chapter some very specific techniques studied in the author's laboratory are discussed. This involves the transfer of sensory information about the world into state structure that reflects that world.

Chapter 5

PHENOMENAL INFORMATION: THE WORLD AND NEURAL STATES

Is this a dagger which I see before me,
The handle toward my hand? Come, let me clutch thee.
I have thee not, and yet I see thee still.
Art thou not, fatal vision, sensible
To feeling as to sight? or art thou but
A dagger of the mind, a false creation,
Proceeding from the heat-oppressed brain?

Macbeth Act 2 Scene 1: (Spoken by Macbeth)

The Inner Eye

Towards the end of Chapter 4, a major division came to light: local versus distributed representation. Macbeth's wonderings, being a hallucination, suggest that it was not the world (that is, the dagger in the sheath on his belt) that beckoned him to commit murder, but something that materialized in his brain. Although we do not hallucinate often (that is, we are not often confused as to whether an object is external or mental) the experience of mental objects is an entirely commonplace event. In fact, it has been suggested that our visual perception is accompanied by mental images that complete the feeling of having seen an object even before the eye has had an opportunity to have a proper look at its target.[1]

An interest in the way that mental states relate to the real world gave rise to a movement in philosophy called 'phenomenology'. In analytic work with neural nets too, those which have inner states that depict the world are called phenomenological systems. Others which encode events in the world as a single cell firing for a single event are not phenomenological.

---

[1]Gregory R. L. (1970). *The Intelligent Eye* (Weidenfeld and Nicolson, London).

We discuss this below but stress now that it is hard to see how localised representation can sustain memory-like experiences.

Phenomenology

A common way to think of how we might 'know' about the world is to believe that the world is reality and the brain represents it somehow. Under the influence of computer technology, reality could be thought to be encoded internally in sequences of 0s and 1s as labels for each perception. Alternatively the codes could be neural firing patterns that represent reality directly — say as a picture made by firing neurons. Our behavior is then seen as being based on whatever this internal coding might be. The outlook that the detail of internal coding is unimportant as long as it leads to some seemingly rational behavior, generally goes under the heading of 'functionalism'. Phenomenology,[2] on the other hand, is a study of the first-person nature of a mental state, that is the way the mental state seems to the entity which experiences it. So when someone thinks of their dog and is asked to describe their thought, they are unlikely to respond with some sort of number code. We shall see that phenomenology is linked to another philosophical term: 'intentionality'. This kind of discussion centers on a mental state being about or being directed at objects that only exist in the mind and this becomes the reality for the owner of the mental state. Brentano[3] made a strong point about the 'inexistence' of such reality in the real world, leaving the relationship between the two to be worked out. Such phenomenal states will probably contain some more or less vivid images of things that exist in the world, such as contents of the fridge for breakfast, underground trains, heaps of scripts for marking or the image of a person with whom one is to have lunch. Arbitrary neural states, while they could be uniquely tied to the above experienced phenomena, would have to be re-coded into some phenomenal code, making their arbitrary version redundant. This is a discussion that starts with first-person reality. We take a look at those who defined this movement and spell out how their ideas lead to a search for phenomenal representations in the neural brain and

---

[2]The word 'phenomenon' is defined in English dictionaries as a direct object of perception.

[3]Brentano F. (1995). *Psychology from an Empirical Standpoint*, (Eds.) L. L. McAlister (Routledge, London), p. 88–89.

to informational models through the inclusion of meaning in the states of neural automata. In fact, if consciousness were to be the target of studies with computational machinery, contrary to the view prevalent in the world of Artificial Intelligence (AI), it is now increasingly believed that this must be based on the presence of meaningful mental objects hence patterns in the states of the neural network.[4]

Franz Clemens Horatio Hermann Brentano (1838–1917)

In philosophical literature, Brentano is famed for having asked what a mental state is about. This 'aboutness' is given the philosophical title of 'intentionality'. Brentano was born into a scholastic family living in the Rhine valley in Germany. He studied an astonishing variety of subjects (mathematics, poetry, philosophy and theology in Munich, Würzburg and Berlin).[5] His early philosophy involved interpretations of Aristotle,[6] who was clearly a philosopher who spoke forcefully to Brentano about how substance features in our perceptions:

> *We have seen that, according to Aristotle, the concept of substance is given directly in our perceptions, ... Thus the existence of substances is not a hypothetical assumption but secured through immediate evidence.* (*Aristotle and his World View*, p. 43).

For nine years (1864–1873), Brentano had been an ordained Catholic Priest, and became a Full Professor at Wurtzburg in 1874, followed by a move to Vienna and the publication of a seminal book on psychology — a very young discipline at the time. Scholars and students competed to study with Franz Brentano, and among his students were Sigmund Freud and Edmund Husserl.[7] We shall look closely at Freud's ideas in Chapter 9, while Husserl

---

[4]David Gamez in his PhD thesis (University of Essex, 2008) states:'*Consciousness is the presence of a phenomenal world.*' (emphasis added) — a statement which he goes on to justify.

[5]From a lucid essay on Brentano's life and work by Wolfgang Huemer in the *Stanford Encyclopaedia of Philosophy.* (http://plato.stanford.edu/entries/brentano/)

[6]Brentano F. (1911). *Aristotle and his World View.* Transl. in English by R. George and R. M. Chisolm. (University of California Press, Berkeley).

[7]He also mentored Thomas Masaryk, who was not known for being a philosopher but for being the founder and first president of Czechoslovakia.

is central to a study of phenomenology and is discussed next, albeit rather briefly.

Edmund Gustav Albrecht Husserl (1859–1938)

Were proof ever needed that a formal background in mathematics makes for good philosophy, Edmund Husserl is a fine example. Born to a Jewish family in Prossniz, Moravia (then part of the Austro-Hungarian Empire, now in the Czech Republic) Husserl studied astronomy at the University of Leipzig from the age of 16 to 18. Influenced by Thomas Masaryk (see footnote 6), he was able to hear some lectures given on philosophy by the pioneer of psychology, Wilhelm Wundt.[8] He went on to study mathematics in Berlin under the tutelage of two of the leading mathematicians of the time, Leopold Kronecker and Carl Weierstrass. But he was attracted to go to Vienna where, at the age of 24 he completed his doctorate on the theory of variations, the area of mathematics in which Weierstrass made a fundamental contribution.[9] The striking part of this story is that this was an advanced area of mathematics in which Husserl proved himself to be sufficiently competent among the masters of the field to make a career out of mathematics. Indeed, Weierstrass invited Husserl to Berlin to be his assistant, and it was when Weierstrass became ill, Masaryk arranged for Husserl to study with Brentano, which led to the development of Husserl's ideas of analyzing the aboutness of the mind as a first-person phenomenon. How could this be approached formally? Working with one of Brentano's former students, Carl Stumph, he wrote a habilitation thesis[10] which was published as a book under the title *Philosophy of Arithmetic*. Here the experienced mental state (the 'first person') featured as a psychological limitation of the number of objects that can occur in a conscious thought. This led to an accusation by Gottlob Frege (an early exponent of logic as a central discipline in mathematics) of using 'psychologisms' rather than

---

[8]Our main source for this biography is a 2007 article by Christian Beyer in the *Stanford Encyclopaedia of Philosophy*.
[9]This relates to 'functions of functions' and the way these reach maxima and minima.
[10]A tradition in some European countries of writing a thesis of a higher level than that required for a doctorate, usually necessary were one intending to enter the university world as a professor.

formal reasoning in attempting to understand the nature of arithmetic. Hurt by this, Husserl determined to operate strictly through accepted logical methods from which arose his philosophy of phenomenology.

In the simplest terms, phenomenology is a study of consciousness that reflects on the nature of experience. Given an individual observing an apple on the table, a phenomenologist would encourage us to focus a study on the nature of the experience of seeing the apple. A version of this experience continues to exist even if someone has removed the apple. Such an experience is the phenomenon of having encountered the apple. The phenomenon can occur as a perception or a memory. Referring to the 'informational mind' is closely aligned with the phenomenological stance. That is a mental state is about something which is informative to the organism. We return to this theme on several occasions in this book.

Other Phenomenologists

At the turn of the 20th century, the influence of Brentano and Husserl was such that many talented philosophers began contributing to the field of phenomenology, and several of these can be seen as speaking to the notion of an informational mind. Among these was the controversial figure of Martin Heidegger (1889–1976). The controversy was political and not philosophical: Heidegger had belonged to the Nazi party and had proclaimed allegiance to Hitler.[11] His major philosophical contribution had been made before this in a book called '*Being and Time*'[12] and relates to Heidegger's view that mental states can have a quality of *being* in the world (*Dasein*).[13] We return to this as an informational issue later in this chapter. Husserl's junior by 30 years, Heidegger's main quest was to elucidate the nature of

---

[11] After the war, Heidegger argued that his closeness to the Nazi party was not due to political conviction but due to a pragmatism borne of a need to survive and operate as a philosopher under the Nazi regime.

[12] Heidegger M. (1927). *Sein und Zeit at Max Niemeyer Verlag*, English translation: *Being and Time*, by J. Mcquarrie and E. Robinson (London: SCM Press).

[13] In our own work, we felt a need to consider 'being' as part of the mental state that was to be captured even in artificial systems. We refer to this as the Axiom 1 of consciousness: "*I feel as if I am in the middle of an* **out-there world**" See Aleksander I. (2005). *The World In My Mind, My Mind In The World: Key Mechanisms of Consciousness In Humans, Animals and Machines* (Exeter, Imprint Academic). This is discussed later in this chapter.

'being' and it took him some years of reading Husserl and discussing his ideas with him to determine that the phenomenological approach had some merit in his quest. But this collaboration came to an end, leaving Heidegger with an adaptation of the phenomenological approach to 'being' which Husserl described as a 'betrayal'.[14] There may, however, have been a difference of ideology rather than philosophy between the two. More of this, later in this chapter, when a logical analysis of Husserl and Heidegger's version of phenomenology is attempted.

An avid reader of Karl Marx but nonetheless influenced by Heidegger, (and Husserl, indeed) Maurice Merleau-Ponty (1908–1961) was another major figure in the shaping of phenomenological philosophy. In his influential work *Phenomenology of Perception*,[15] he clarifies Heidegger's *being* in the world by stressing the role of the body in doing this. He points out that perceptual phenomena are not passive events, but rely on the observer getting out there and controlling the *acquisition* of perceptual sensation. So such phenomena include the bodily sensations that control the flow of the coming into consciousness of the intentions ('directedness') of the observer toward the world. Again we shall return to this as Merleau-Ponty points the way to an informational analysis of this situation. For the moment we note that Merleau-Ponty was sceptical of efforts in science to explain phenomenal sensation as he feared that science would focus on trying to find the 'molecules of the phenomenal sensation'. This is clearly the same mistake as looking for the molecules of beauty in a sunset. Information analyses offer a science that is based on the bits of a sensation. But this approach too can be criticized through the patent failure of methods in artificial intelligence where the bits are like the bits of a digital photograph rather than bits that are part of a dynamic and evolving pattern of activity of neural networks. In the next chapter we draw a strong distinction between a digital photograph and a neural mental state.

---

[14]See the introduction Sheehan T. and Palmer R. E. (Eds.) (1997). Edmund Husserl, *Psychological and Transcendental Phenomenology, and the Confrontation with Heidegger*, translated by T. Sheehan and R. E. Palmer, *Edmund Husserl: Collected Works*, (Kluwer Academic Publishers, Dordrecht, Boston, London).

[15]Merleau-Ponty M. (1945). *Phénoménologie de la perception* (Gallimard, Paris). Trans. in English by C. Smith, *Phenomenology of Perception* (Humanities Press, New York, 1962/2002).

Phenomenology and the Mental-Automaton Designer

In an attempt to examine phenomenology for its implications in a study of the informational mind, we have presented a very brief view of its perpetrators and their contribution. All four had a deep influence on the course of philosophy and the reader may well wish to pursue this to get a better rounded image. But there are lessons to be learned for those who, like ourselves, are interested in computational models of consciousness. Here we stress those aspects of phenomenology which have inspired our own work on modeling using logic and automata, or which can be clarified through such modeling.

Brentano's analysis that mental states must be *about* something is not a simple notion. In particular, the assertion that a phenomenal mental state is characterized by the 'inexistence' of the target object has caused much discussion among philosophers. Imagining that the organism that has such a mental state is a learning neural network characterized by defined inputs, outputs, states and learned transitions between states for certain inputs, an interpretation of 'aboutness' and 'inexistence' can be attempted. Primarily, Brentano can be interpreted as saying that a thought of a cat, say, is directed at the cat object that only exists in the mind. Yes, we may think of a particular cat that exists in the world, but the fact that it exists in our mind is no indication that this cat exists. But in phenomenology, the presence of the mental state is the starting point of discussion and the fact that they 'come to mind' is the same as saying that the mind has the capacity to be directed toward such objects which, in Brentano's discourse, is the same as saying that the mental objects are intentional and it is their 'aboutness' (i.e., about a cat) that is a starting point for discussing 'being conscious'. Brentano and many of his followers were not concerned with how a mental object comes into being, that is how intentionality might be a dynamical property of mind. We argue below that modeling such acquisition helps to clarify the concept.

Husserl's extension of Brentano's 'intentional act' entailed giving the intentional mental object an enduring existence that transcends the act of bringing the object to mind. In the models below we show that it is possible to formalize the existence of a phenomenal state even if it is not currently in mind. (The basis for this was introduced as 'state structure' in Chapter 4.) That is experience is constantly developing states driven by experience. But these experiences form state structures (one state leading to another), making phenomenal states available to the organism in a variety of ways. Inclusion of this dynamic, we argue below, throws light on Husserl's contention that the phenomenal object needs to be discussed independently of world events — these world events are 'bracketed' to allow discussion of the phenomenal to proceed with clarity. The modeling below also allows us to examine Husserl's thoughts on the temporality and spatial nature of phenomenal states.

Husserl's theories of the human being as a set of states of consciousness did not satisfy Heidegger. He interpreted Husserl as saying that 'being' was defined by the mental states in a version of Descartes' 'thinking implies being' tenet. Heidegger's philosophy centered on existence having a precedence in the order of things ('the primacy of existence'), with mental states occurring as a consequence of 'being'. This allowed him to include aspects of existence that may not be conscious as constituents of a mental life, a facet welcomed by those studying and practicing psychoanalysis. In our modeling work, the 'primacy of existence' is the existence of a neural network. We show, however that this neural network builds up state structure through being exposed to 'the world'. However, this structure has to exist in a fairly specific way before it can be conscious of existing.

The main impact of Merleau-Ponty on the neural automaton modeler is that the automaton must be considered as being embodied. That is, he advocates a model of phenomenal consciousness as being contingent on the organism's use of its 'body' to control the acquisition of input which is then reflected in state structure. It is now time to begin looking at some models and their behaviour.

Iconic Learning

Here we will do something unusual, i.e., to describe a series of experiments designed specifically for these pages to illustrate some of the above notions of phenomenology. First, we use the *weightless neuron* introduced in Chapter 3 in a network of neurons that learns to reflect its input. Then several such networks are used in a system that is capable of actively searching for input.

Iconic Learning: The Beginnings Visual Experience in a Simple Network

In this series of experiments, we take a very simple network of 98 × 98 (9,604) neurons arranged as a square array. We treat this network as an

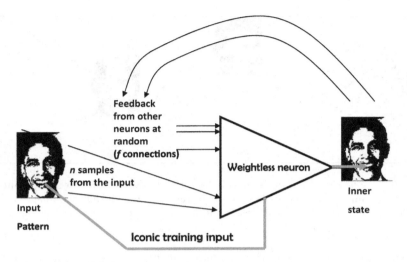

Fig. 5.1.   A weightless neuron as a single stae variable among 98×98 weightless neurons in an array. The process of iconic learning is described in the text.

automaton: so the output of the neurons forms a two-dimensional state. In very loose terms, this will be the 'mind' of our automaton. With the help of Fig. 5.1, we explain how *iconic learning* works.

Figure 5.1 shows one of the 9,604 neurons in the network. It is responsible for generating one of the picture points of the inner state (a portrait of Barak Obama). The neuron has n inputs that come from the input pattern and this number can be determined by the network designer. These inputs sample the input image. However, there is one input which is designed to be different. We have called it the 'iconic learning input' and its function is to cause the neuron to fire according to the colour value of the input picture point to which it is connected.[16]

The iconic training results in a transfer of the input image to the state area of the network. This could be called a 'perceptual' event: the net perceives the input. But now, learning to create a stable state can take place. Once the input image is present at the internal connections of the network,

---

[16]Is such an arrangement biologically plausible? We are not arguing here that it is, since where, when or if mental images occur as patterns in the brain is a controversial matter in current research. However, as we patently experience mental images, the material of this section is a hypothesis of how such mental images come about.

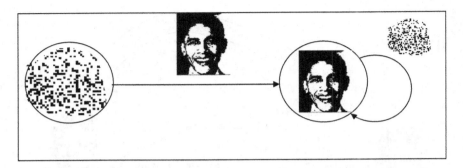

Fig. 5.2.   The state diagram shows circles for states and arrows for state changes caused by input. Further explanation is in the text. Recall that the images close to arrows indicate input patterns, while images inside the states indicate state patterns.

there are f neuron inputs that provide information to the neurons about what other neurons are doing. Further learning will thus create a recurrent internal state. But what happens if the input image changes? There are conditions under which the state is sustained, which is a 'memory' event. This is illustrated as a state diagram in Fig. 5.2.

In Fig. 5.2, the network is shown to start in a random-dot state. The 'memory' training on the Obama picture has taken place, so this picture appearing at the input causes a transition to the memory state. The figure then shows a condition under which the memory image is sustained even if the input is returned to some random dot image. There are other conditions under which the memory can be said to be 'forgotten'. These conditions have a mathematical explanation which we do not deploy here, but illustrate it with experiments which reveal the factors that are at work.

A Note on Where the Mental Images Might Be

Given the above hypothesis of how mental images may be formed in the living brain (from how they *are* formed in our model) would it be the case that a neurosurgeon armed with a suitably accurate brain scanner would be able to focus in on the brain being scanned and 'see' the visual thought of the moment? It needs to be said quite firmly that this would be a misreading of what iconic learning is. Iconic learning does not imply that a neat picture is formed in a neural net. This is because the dominant synapses (iconic training inputs in Fig. 5.1) need not map from the input into the array in an orderly fashion. Indeed, in natural networks, there need not be an array.

So the image is mapped into the network in some arbitrary but consistent way. The neurologist would not know the links in this mapping. But how does the owner of the brain have this access key? The answer lies in the ability of the owner to move and act in the world. This is explained later under the heading of 'depiction'.

Experiments with Iconic Learning

To keep the Obama picture company, the entire world in which the mind-automaton will exist is made up of famous faces as seen in Fig. 5.3.

Experiment 1: Memory and neuron size

Thinking about our own perceptual apparatus, it could be expected from our own experience that the world is perceived and then remembered even if the stimulus has been removed (as suggested by Fig. 5.2). However, whether a mind-automaton actually behaves in this ideal way or not depends on the two major parameters n and f, introduced in Fig. 5.1. First of all, n must be large enough not to allow what are called contradictions, that is the same sample of input met during the learning of two different images which require different outputs from the neuron. If these occur, the neuron, when tested with either of the images will produce an arbitrary output (noise).

Fig. 5.3.   Faces on which the mind-automaton can be trained.

A second reason for the neuron generating noise rather than some meaningful mental state occurs if a neuron input is equally similar to two inputs that have occurred in training but require different outputs. Say the neuron had four inputs and was only trained to output 0 for an input of 0000 and output 1 for an input of 1111, an input of 0101 being equally similar to the two training inputs will output noise. If this happens on the feedback connections (f) the outcome is quite spectacular. Noise is introduced into the state which can destroy its sustainability.

Evidently, these two parameters define the capacity of the automaton's ability to recollect and imagine experiences. As an example, we look at the performance of a net that has sufficient capacity to perceive the eight faces. Here both f and n are set to 30.

Figure 5.4 shows responses for different stimuli shown as 'input' on the left of the figure. In the top line the stimulus is one of the training patterns

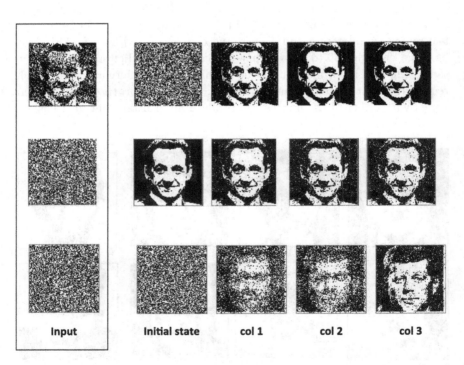

| Input | Initial state | col 1 | col 2 | col 3 |

Fig. 5.4.   States resulting from various stimuli in a net with $f = n = 30$. This is discussed in the text.

distorted by the addition of about 40% noise. Starting in a random-dot state (initial state line 1), the state rapidly changes to a noise-free representation of the training set (col 3). This is an illustration of the way that the net is capable of reconstructing a trained pattern from a distorted one. This is equivalent to remembering what something looks like even if only a glimpse of it was available. In line 2, the input is randomized with the reconstructed state as the initial state. This is like closing one's eyes once the distorted input of line one has been mentally correctly visualized. The vision fades slightly (becomes noisy) but does not vanish. This is due to contradictions in the internal connections as suggested earlier.

The third line leaves the automaton entirely to its own devices. There is a random input, and the net starts in a random internal state. This is a bit like waking from a deep sleep in a dark (no stimulus) room. The net after about 60 steps settles in on one of its possible image states at which point it (obsessively) remains stuck in this state. In-between states are shown in columns 1 and 2.

The experiment is now repeated with reduced values such that $f = n = 10$. Line 1 shows that the capacity of the network to perceive the input has not been much reduced. Yes, there are a few more contradictions but this does not appear to be drastic. The major effect can be seen in line 2. The ability to hold on to a memory has been much reduced and the network falls into a 'mush' composition of the learnt faces. In line 3, it is shown that the mush is ever present if the input and state are random dot patterns.

In the above nets, there is a balance between the amount of influence the input and the internal state have on the selection of the next state. But what if this balance were to be disrupted? Giving more influence to the internal feedback connections (i.e., having more of them) causes the net to get stuck in learned states from which it cannot be shifted by sensory input. Were things the other way around, with the influence biased towards the sensory input, the loss of mental state in the absence of input (as in line 2 of Fig. 5.5) becomes even more strongly pronounced.

Some analysis

In summary, what are we learning from this very simple iconically trained neural net? First, it must be emphasized as strongly as possible that at no point in these experiments is it suggested that the simple net is a model of the brain. The key reason for looking at these examples is to illustrate the kind of informational behaviors that can occur in any dynamic neural

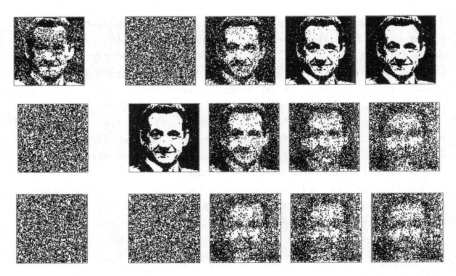

Fig. 5.5.   A repeat of the experiment in Fig. 5.4 but with $n = f = 10$. A discussion is in the text.

network and point out that such behaviors reflect ways that we describe our own mental sensations. For example, we noted that the network 'remembers' a briefly seen state or 'forgets' it if the network is inadequate. This kind of experimentation shows that the amount of remembering a net can do (memory capacity) depends on the size of the neuron. The detail that can be remembered depends on the number of neurons in a system because there are as many pixels as neurons and the detail depends on the number of pixels. This leads to some fascinating conclusions.

It is very likely that the memory capacity depends 'exponentially' on the number of inputs per neuron.[17] So how much experience could a chunk of brain absorb in a lifetime? How long is a lifetime in terms of brain states? This is not easy to answer, but since most delays in neural transmission in the brain are of about 0.1 seconds, let's be generous and say that 10 'thoughts' per second can occur. Being generous again, say that 100 years

---

[17]The limit to capacity stems from the probability of having contradictions, i.e., it depends on the probability of two input patterns in a neuron being the same and the outputs being different. The number of such patterns goes up exponentially (by 2^n for n binary inputs), therefore this allows the number of arbitrarily chosen patterns to go up exponentially before contradictions take place.

is a 'lifetime' then the number of states turns out to be (10 a second ×
60 a minute × 60 an hour × 24 a day × 365 a year × 100 a lifetime)
31,536,000,000. Now we ask what value of n gives us 2^n to be something
like this number, as this will give us some idea of how large neurons should
be to provide a lifetime of thought. The simple inversion which gives us
this is log_2 (31,536,000,000) which, the computer tells us, means that the
number of inputs per neuron in this case is only about 35.

Now, it turns out that brain neurons have between 1,000 and 10,000
input synapses which (allowing that such neurons are less flexible than
those in our simulation) leads to a discussion in the next two chapters about
the size and shape of the state structure required to store lifetime human
experience. We shall see that mental states are 'integrated', that is, each of
the 31.5 billion lifetime states is not arbitrary but is unique and indivisible.
The experience of waking up this morning is quite unique and different from
waking up yesterday or tomorrow. A state is a 'whole' in that it makes no
sense to break down such experiences into sub-events such as the ringing of
an alarm clock and the nature of the weather. It is the close relationship of
all these features that form an integrated mental state. In terms of neural
network engineering, all of life is a perceptual learning experience.

State Structures

To speak in this way of neural automata and mental states has a misleading note to it. In automata theory, a state is something that persists for a
defined period of time. In dynamic systems in general (such as a pendulum
in swing), a state is the instantaneous value of some measurement such as
position or velocity. But when one speaks of a 'mental state', there is no
clear precision. Is it the memory of last night's sunset (as a frame of experience), is it the current thought which guides an interesting conversation
or is it the anticipation of a pleasant event still to come? For a psychologist someone's 'mental state' says something about their mental health, for
a philosopher of mind it could be the belief about something or a 'quale'
such as the taste of a wine. Given this variety of interpretations, it would
be foolish to try to equate a mental state with the single state of a neural automaton. However, using simulated neural automata again, we now
look at some illustrations of the way structures of states might reflect the
various aspects of what is meant by a 'mental state'. We leave the question
of mental health fo0r Chapter 9.

Zones of State Space

Were someone to say 'think of President Obama', much more than a picture of his face comes to mind: he is one of a group of live political leaders, he is American of African extraction, etc. In some way, these features are ever present in a mental state related to a thought of Obama. But then some of these features could belong to other objects as well. For example, at the time of writing, President Sarkozy is alive and is a former political leader.

We illustrate this situation with another simulation where the first step is the broadening of the states to include some known attributes over and above the look of the face. This is shown in Fig. 5.6. Here the images of the faces are extended to include the attributes as indicated. It is very important to understand that these attributes **are not symbols**. They are images produced by the firing and non-firing of neurons, that is, they are in exactly the dimensional domain as the faces themselves. Thinking of them as visualized written words may be helpful.

Figure 5.7 attempts to portray the way in which the commonalities between these states can be expressed as links between them. For example, the figure shows O, Z and M as forming a cycle for Live Politicians, there being cycles for Dead Politicians and Dead Celebrities. We look at an

Fig. 5.6.   VIP faces with attributes added: D means 'dead'; L means 'live'; P means 'politician'; and C means 'celebrity'. See text for a description of these apparent symbols. We also label the faces as (from left to right and top to bottom: L (for Lincoln), C, K, M, Z, O, E and G.)

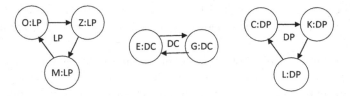

Fig. 5.7.   The faces are shown in sequence to the neural automaton grouped together according to their pairs of descriptors.

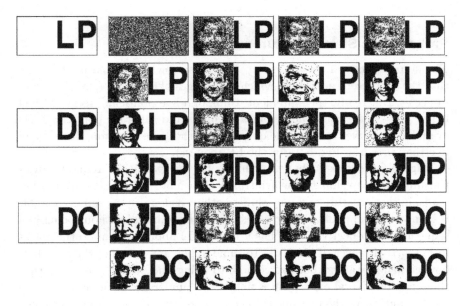

Fig. 5.8.   Results of tests on the net trained on the faces and concept letters. The input attributes are on the left. When the net is in a particular state, and a new attribute is demanded, this particular state is shown first in the sequence, and the first effect of the input demand is shown next.

experiment that indicates how a neural automaton can 'think' about 'concepts' by transiting between states that instantiate the concept. As shown the system is trained to circulate in classes that is, Live Politicians (LP), Dead Politicians (DP) and Dead Celebrities (DC). The full results of what the neural automaton has learned is shown in Fig. 5.8 Here the net is in a random-dot state when the attributes LP are applied. This is like saying: 'Think of the Live Politicians you know'. The net 'falls' into the cycle of 'live politicians' as indicated by the attributes. It can be seen that the net also switches from one cycle to another if the requested attributes are changed.

The key point that is made with this is that knowledge in a brain-like, iconically trained neural net resides in the net as a state structure, that is, concepts create zones of linked states in which not only individual states can have meaning, but so can groupings of such states. It is also possible to have state structures at lower levels of definition such as 'politician', 'live' or 'dead'.

Probabilistic State Structures

The state structures shown in Fig. 5.7 are somewhat special in the sense that they represent a world in which the images of one class (say LP) occur in cycles. But really, the statement 'think of a live politician' feels satisfied if any one of the contenders comes to mind and different politicians feel available in answer to the same question. So the state structure 'feels' more like that shown in Fig. 5.9 (for the LP request).

Figure 5.9 suggests that the 'think of a live politician' request causes the automaton to shift to one arbitrarily chosen of the LP states from other states in the structure and may shift to others as long as the same 'thought' is being accessed. That is, the states can 'come to mind' without being in a sequence. Introspectively this has a better feel about it than do the cycles in Fig. 5.7. However, it gives rise to some important points of theory. First, how can such state structures come into being and second, how is it that there can be several exits from a single state under the same input?

The answer to the first question comes directly from the way that iconic learning works. Say that A is a perceptual event that is to be learned. Then

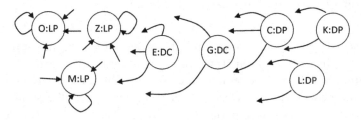

Fig. 5.9.   The states labeled LP form probabilistic attractors as explained in the text.

according to the iconic technique (Fig. 5.1), A is made to occur on the input and the feedback connections to the neurons. Thus, re-entrant states are sometimes called 'attractors' as even with random inputs the net will change state until it enters a re-entrant state. The network then remains 'stuck' in that state in much the way that a fly is attracted to flypaper and gets stuck to it. But say that state and input are random, which attractor will the net fall into? That depends on which attractor is most similar to the random starting state.

The second question is answered below.

The usefulness of noise

So far in this book we have seen noise as the enemy of good communication. But in neural automata, noise can help in the discovery of appropriate attractors. Noise allows automata to jump out of some attractors to find even more attractive ones. In early days of neural networks, Geoffrey Hinton and his colleagues defined a 'Boltzmann Machine'. This used reducing amounts of noise to find the most attractive attractors in a network.[18] In connection with the story in this chapter, given an input to the network such as M:LP, the net is expected to find the attractor state M:LP. But if subsequently merely ..:LP is requested any of the three states with the LP descriptor could be entered. Once this has happened, it could not be argued that the automaton is 'aware' of the *class* of LP objects. A burst of noise serves to find any of the three appropriate states with equal probability. How this works in a simulation is shown in Fig. 5.10. This starts with the state in O:LP with an input demand of 'think of a Dead Celebrity' (..:DC). The stable state is disrupted and falls, after a few steps, into one of the attractors (G:DC). This is where a burst of noise is shown to enter the other (..:DC) state, that is, E:DC.

A 'probabilistic automaton' is then defined as one in which, for a given input/state pair, the next state occurs from a probabilistic distribution of possible states. The mechanism for ensuring this is the use of noise.

---

[18]This was named after Viennese Physicist Ludwig Boltzmann (1844–1906), whose equations of atomic movement in gases led to the identification of temperature-related generation of noise in electrical circuits. In relation to neural networks, see: Ackley D., Hinton G., and Sejnowski T. (1985). A learning algorithm for Boltzmann machines, *Cognitive Sci.* **9**(1), 147–169.

Fig. 5.10.   An input is shown which could lead to one of two attractors. Having reached one, a burst of noise (the random dot pattern) can create a probability that the network falls into either state. Here it is shown falling into the alternative attractor.

In descriptive language, this probabilistic action can cause the automaton 'to be aware of both mental states related to the DC class'. One might even say that it is in this way that the automaton 'becomes aware of the Dead Celebrity concept'.

Do such noise mechanisms help the living brain to achieve some of its consciousness? This is not sure, but the ability to combine mental states might suggest so. Every now and then, one reads articles such as the following:

Science Daily, July 7th, 2008

> Canadian scientists have shown that a noisy brain is a healthy brain. "Brain noise" is a term that has been used by neuroscientists to describe random brain activity that is not important to mental function. ..... But new research from the Rotman Research Institute at Baycrest (Toronto), published in the July 4, 2008 issue of the Public Library of Science — Computational Biology, overturns this notion.

> "What we discovered is that brain maturation not only leads to more stable and accurate behaviour in the performance of a memory task, but correlates with increased brain signal variability," said lead author, Dr. Randy McIntosh, a senior scientist with the Rotman Research Institute at Baycrest. "This doesn't mean the brain is working less efficiently. It's showing greater functional variability, which is indicative of enhanced neural complexity." ... "These findings suggest that the random activity that we think of as noise may actually be a central component of normal brain function."

The Phenomenal Mental State: A Building Brick for Consciousness?

In this chapter, we have done something rather presumptuous. In order to stress the possible importance of automata with phenomenal state structures, we have referred to theoretical analyses in anthropomorphic terms. The automaton 'remembers' .... the automaton 'is aware of' and so on. The only reason for doing this is to argue that the kind of informational processes that takes place in neural automata may provide us with analytic tools and an appropriate language for developing an understanding of properties such as 'remembering' and 'being aware of' in our own brains. This should not be interpreted as a belief that a simple automaton made of a few neurons actually can be aware of anything in exactly the same way as our living brains. It is only an indication that the two may share methods of description and understanding. In the next chapter we examine, again cautiously, some 'information integration' theories which suggest that some network properties, if present, ensure consciousness. We stay sceptical about this strong interpretation, but investigate the intuitions involved to see to what extent that they do lead to a better understanding.

Chapter 6

INFORMATION INTEGRATION: THE KEY TO CONSCIOUSNESS?

... to the extent that a mechanism is capable of generating integrated information, no matter whether it is organic or not, whether it is built of neurons or silicon chips, and independent of its ability to report, it will have consciousness.

Giulio Tononi[1]

Something brewing?

In the above quote, a remarkable claim is made. By the sound of it, the formal basis of consciousness has been tracked down to something called 'integrated' information. Giulio Tononi, a psychiatrist doing research on sleep at the University of Winsconsin, has written a series of papers that have caused the world of the scientific study of consciousness to regard theories of information anew. In 2008, we set out to look more closely at these claims together with colleagues David Gamez and Michael Beaton. The novelty comes from looking beyond information processing as the crunching of data as, say, in the management of an organization but as an organizing process in the brain. We conclude that while Tononi brilliantly directed analysis of information processes toward a study consciousness, many questions remain unanswered. Here we speculate on how they might be answered on the basis of what we have seen in this book so far.

But evidence that something was brewing did not only bubble up in scientific papers. On September 20, 2010, Karl Zimmer, a science essayist

---

[1]Tononi, G. (2008). Consciousness as integrated information: A provisional manifesto. *Biol. Bull.* **215**, 216–242.

with *The New York Times*, surprised his readers with an article ('Sizing Up Consciousness by its Bits') on the way that Giulio Tononi was developing a theory that made consciousness into a measurable quantity. 'Consciousness Meters' were mentioned, as was the ability to measure the amount of consciousness in 'locked-in' patients incapable of communication but possibly fully conscious otherwise. Here we dig into these very important claims to distinguish the potential from the mere hope.

Some intuitions

Here is a personal experience that many, who travel a lot, might have had — waking up in the morning in a somewhat unfamiliar place. 'Where am I' is an expression of a strong feeling of uncertainty. We recall that Shannon's measure of information is based on the resolution of uncertainty. In the 'waking' experience, perceptual input resolves uncertainty: there is a window on the right and a bathroom door on the left. Yesterday's taxi ride comes to mind and then, suddenly, one might become conscious of being in a hotel room in Birmingham, having given a lecture at the University that evening. Put one way, the information is gained through perceptual glimpses which help to construct the appropriate conscious mental state of 'being somewhere'. Put another way the perceptual glimpses are reconstructed by the neural dynamics of the brain in the way that was demonstrated in the last chapter. This is one of the many examples of information integration: the synchronization of the inner state with the external world which could be said to be synonymous with the organism becoming conscious of being in its world. In information integration theories (IIT), such synchronisation needs to occur at the neural level for consciousness to be present.

As a further intuition, a mental experience appears to have two main characteristics: uniqueness and indivisibility. Uniqueness is the feeling that every experience is new (despite its similarity to previous experiences) and indivisibility means that it cannot be broken down into 'sub-experiences'. Becoming conscious of waking up in a hotel in Birmingham cannot be, say, halved and united with the experience of waking up at home. Of course, this could be imagined (with some difficulty) but not experienced. Information integration theory asks what kind of neural network would sustain uniqueness and integration. Such a network would be said to integrate information and such a network can also be linked to having conscious mental states by their being unique and indivisible.

From here we can look at what Tononi developed on the basis of these intuitions, how this appears to succeed and how this might fail to resonate with how we 'feel' our conscious states. But first, a little more about Tononi and the growth of his ideas.

Giulio Tononi

Very much a man of the northern Italian city of Trento, son of its mayor, Giulio Tononi was honored by this city in 2009 as the 'Son of Trento of the Year' for '... his studies of 'soul' and thought which, according to him, are founded in biology' (award citation). A 1985 graduate in medicine of the Sant'Anna University of Pisa, Tononi specialized in study of sleep. In the 1990s, he joined the Neurosciences Institute at La Jolla in California. Here, with the director, Nobel Laureate Gerald Edelman, he started developing theories of integration as the basis of consciousness. Embryonic information integration ideas appeared in a book they co-authored: '*Consciousness: How Matter Becomes Imagination*'. Here the importance of the uniqueness and indivisibility of the mental state was raised. Also raised was the conviction that consciousness depends on the informational characteristics of certain interactions among neurons in the networks of the brain and between the organism and its surroundings and peers. These ideas were not immediately greeted with enthusiasm.

Steven Poole, a highly appreciated book reviewer for *The Guardian* newspaper in the UK, expressed some clear scepticism in his review of the book while at the same time recognizing the potential of the information integration issue:

> *Why does matter arranged in this way, and not others, give rise to minds? This is a question that Gerard Edelman and Giulio Tononi signally fail to answer, despite the grand promise of their subtitle. Hardly surprising, since it is probably the toughest problem known to science. But they do sketch a hypothesis which, if experimentally verified, would go a long way towards answering a smaller but still important question — not how consciousness arises, but what kinds of brain activity are necessary to produce consciousness.*

Tononi, with Edelman and other colleagues Olaf Sporns and David Balduzzi, published a series of papers setting out their developing thoughts on information integration and consciousness. We attempt to summarize this below.

Information integration theories[2] (Contributed by Mike Beaton)

As mentioned earlier, Tononi's theory of integrated information starts from two phenomenological intuitions.[3] The first (previously labeled 'uniqueness') is that any given conscious experience is highly informative. In having the experience, the world seems one particular way rather than any one of an extremely large number of other ways that the world might have appeared. That is, it is informative by virtue of the fact that it resolves the uncertainty. To confirm this intuition, Tononi points out that even an apparently simple experience, as for example that of a uniform pure color, implicitly rules out many other experiences which it might have been (such as looking at a Mondrian painting, seeing a parakeet at the zoo, being in the science museum or at one's desk, etc. almost *ad infinitum*).

Tononi's second intuition (previously called 'Indivisibility') is that the information in experience is integrated — that all the separate distinctions made within one single experience are somehow unified. Again, this intuition seems sound. Experiencing a blue chair, one is not somehow separately aware of the blueness and of the chair, but aware of the combined whole. Indeed, when viewing an entire visual scene, the experience contains a large number of different properties, at different locations, and these various distinctions are, once again, in some sense all integrated: all available to a single subject.

While it is true that both these intuitions can be questioned,[4] our aim here is to explain how they lead to a theoretical perspective. Later we show

---

[2]The material in this section is largely drawn from: Aleksander, I. and Beaton, M. (2011). World-related integrated information: Enactivist and phenomenal perspectives. *AISB Symposium on Machine Consciousness*, York, April.

[3]Tononi, G. (2008). *Consciousness as Integrated Information: A Provisional Manifesto. Biol. Bull.* **215**, 216–242.

[4]For instance some argue [Shear, J. and Jevning R., *Pure Consciousness: Scientific Exploration of Meditation Techniques. J. Conscious. Stud.* 1999. **6**(2–3), p. 189–209.] that a mode of pure experience exists, in which things do not seem to be any specific way at all. This is incompatible with Tononi's claim that every experience at least implicitly contrasts itself with all other possible experiences. As for the second intuition, Metzinger, for one, [Metzinger, T., *Being No One: The Self-Model Theory of Subjectivity.* 2003, Cambridge, MA: MIT Press.] has suggested that the unity of experience consists in the existence of a mental model as of unity, rather than in the existence of anything more fundamental which actually is unified.

that there are important aspects of consciousness which are overlooked in Tononi's predictions of Φ, the symbol given to a measure of information integration.

The photodiode and the camera

To flesh out his two intuitions, Tononi contrasts the case of a conscious human being with the cases of a photodiode and a digital camera. A photodiode can simply detect light above a certain intensity as 'on', and below that intensity as 'off'. This is contrasted with the case of a human. When seeing a blank screen as either light or dark, the human is not just making the light/dark contrast which the photodiode can make, but is also conscious in an implicit way (uniqueness) of the many, many other ways it could have been. This is information gained in the same sense as when a card is dealt from a pack of cards, information is gained by being implicitly aware of the existence of the rest of the pack. This is the very insight that Shannon used in defining the measure of information: getting the result of a tossed coin contains less information (5 bits less to be precise, see Chapter 2) than getting the result of dealing a card from a pack.

Tononi suggests that this highlights a key difference between the photodiode and the human: the number of different states which can be distinguished. This is what he means by saying that consciousness is 'highly informative'.

Tononi then moves on to 'uniqueness' using the case of a digital camera in order to argue that merely 'generating a large amount of information' is not sufficient for consciousness. He considers a camera made from a million photodiodes. Such a camera can distinguish any one from among $2^{1,000,000}$ states, and there is no reason in principle not to scale this design to achieve as large a finite number as desired. Tononi argues that the reason such a camera is still not conscious, is because the information in the camera is not integrated to give unique experiential states — no information is passed between the photodiodes. This communication is essential to distinguish between experienced states, and states that could be created through arbitrary mechanisms such as noise.

Going back to an earlier example of waking up in a Birmingham hotel, were a camera picture to represent that experience, given a slight malfunction in the memory addressing mechanisms of the camera, a picture could be created that is half Birmingham and half home bedroom — a scene that has not been experienced. This is not so easy in the brain since an appropriately dense set of connections exists which delivers this uniqueness. Tononi's additional suggestion, then, is that if a physical system can store a high amount of information *and* if that information is integrated then this may be the direct correlate of the informativeness and integration of conscious experience.

Measures of Φ

Tononi has proposed two major measures of integrated information.[5,6] It should perhaps be emphasized at the outset that neither 'integrated information', nor 'effective information' (which Tononi also defines) is a standard information theoretic measure. Instead, both the concepts and the measures are ones which Tononi and his collaborators define, in order to capture their intuitions about the nature of consciousness. We emphasize this, as it might otherwise be supposed that integrated information and effective information are both well-known and well-defined physical quantities, and that all that is in question is whether these quantities relate to consciousness.

Φ Measure 1 (*Call it* Φ_1)[7]

Tononi's first measure, Φ_1, is a measure of a static property of a neural system.[8] If Tononi is right, it would measure something like the potential for consciousness in a system. It cannot be a measure of the current conscious level of the system, for it is a fixed value for a fixed neural architecture, regardless of the system's current firing rates (for example, in response to inputs or internal dynamics). Tononi's first measure works by considering all the various bi-partitions (splits into two parts) of a neural system:

> 'the capacity to integrate information is called Φ, and is given by the minimum amount of effective information that can be exchanged across a bipartition of a subset'. [see footnote 6]

[5] Tononi, G. and Sporns O. (2003). *Measuring Integrated Information. BMC Neurosci.* **4**(31), 20pp.

[6] Balduzzi, D. and G. Tononi (2008). Integrated information in discrete dynamical systems: motivation and theoretical framework. *PLoS Comput. Biol.* **4**(6), 1–18.

[7] In the papers by Tononi reviewed here, he did not use different symbols for the two versions of **Φ**, but we do.

[8] As with both Tononi's Φ measures, it is also only well defined for a rather limited class of well-behaved systems. Showing that it can be applied more generally would require further work.

That is to say, Tononi's approach requires examining every subset of the system under consideration. And then, for each subset, every bi-partition (split into two non-overlapping parts) is considered. Given a subset, S, and a bipartition into A and B, Tononi defines a measure called effective information (EI). Effective information uses the standard information theoretic measure of mutual information (MI).[9] But rather than the standard mutual information measure which quantifies the information gain from taking account of the connectedness between A and B, Tononi's EI is a measure of the information gain which would accrue if one considered the effect on B when the outputs of A vary randomly across all possible values. The aim is to incorporate some sense of causality:

> 'Since A is substituted by independent noise sources, the entropy that B shares with A is due to causal effects of A on B.'

The logic of this sentence is perhaps not entirely clear,[10] but the general idea is that the effective information from A to B shows the ability of A to affect B. Similarly, the EI from B to A shows the ability of B to affect A. The sum of these two is further defined as the effective information across the bipartition.

Now we can start hunting for Φ_1. First of all, for a given S, we look for the bipartition with the minimum (normalized[11]) EI. Then we define $\Phi(S)$ as the EI of that minimum information bipartition.

But Φ_1 at this point is not yet true integrated information, in Tononi's sense. Next we must look for *complexes* — subparts which are not fully contained in any regions of yet higher Φ_1. According to Tononi, only complexes genuinely integrate information; Φ_1 is a measure of how much information

---

[9]MI(A:B) = H(A) + H(B) − H(AB), where H(. . .) is entropy, a mathematically well defined measure of uncertainty. A decrease in entropy amounts to a gain in information (i.e., a decrease in uncertainty). MI in particular measures the information gain obtained from considering the interactions between A and B, as opposed to ignoring them. If there are no interactions between A and B (if they are independent systems), then the mutual information will be zero, otherwise it will be positive.

[10]After all, what we're really measuring is the mutual information (which is a symmetric measure, MI(A:B) = MI(B:A)) between B and a different system, say A'.

[11]This is an attempt to avoid certain bipartitions being favored for purely mathematical reasons. But see footnote for more on the problems this process introduces.

they integrate, and the Φ_1 value of the *main complex* (the complex of highest Φ_1 in the whole neural system) is the correct value to use for the integrated information of the system as a whole.

The key points to note for now are the following. Φ_1 involves the definition of two novel informational concepts ('effective information' and Φ itself). Φ_1 has an informational interpretation which follows from its definition. It is the reduction in uncertainty which an external observer would gain, if they took account of the interactions between the perturbed version of A and B, as opposed to treating these as separate systems (and vice versa for perturbed-B plus A).

Φ *Measure* 2 (*Call it* Φ_2)

In more recent work, Tononi and collaborators [see footnote 7] have proposed a revised measure of Φ, that is Φ_2. This revised measure has some advantages over the previous measure, in that it can deal with a time varying system, providing a varying, moment to moment measure of Φ_2 (which would correspond to a moment to moment measure of the level of consciousness, if Tononi's approach works as intended).[12]

Φ_2 is also defined in terms of *effective information*, though effective information is now defined quite differently from the version in Φ_1. In this case, effective information is defined by considering a system which evolves in discrete time steps, with a known causal architecture. Take the system at time t_1 and state x_1. Given the architecture of the system, only certain states could possibly lead to x_1. Tononi calls this set of states (with their associated probabilities) the *a posteriori* repertoire. Tononi also requires a measure of the possible states of the system (and their probabilities), in that situation where we do not know the state at time t_1. This he called the *a priori* repertoire. The *a priori* repertoire is calculated by treating the system as if we knew nothing at all about its causal architecture, in which case we must treat all possible activation values of each neuron as equally probable.[13] The *a priori* and *a posteriori* repertoires will each have

---

[12]It has disadvantages too — including apparently allowing the (presumably continuous) stream of consciousness of a given system to be in quite different parts of the system from moment to moment.

[13]In fact, this is not a true measure of our prior knowledge about the state of the system: a given causal architecture may make certain firing patterns simply impossible, in the normal time evolution of the system, whatever the inputs.

a corresponding entropy value (for instance, if the a priori repertoire consists of four equally probable states, and the a posteriori repertoire has two equally probable states, then the entropy values will be two bits and one bits, respectively). This means that, in finding out that the state of the system is x_1 at time t_1, we gain information about the state of the system one time step earlier.

Tononi argues that this is a measure of how much information the system 'generates' in moving into state x_1. Having defined this measure of how much information the system generates, Tononi once again requires a measure of how 'integrated' this information is.

Therefore, he next observes that it is possible to arbitrarily decompose the system into parts. For each part (considered separately) a given current state can only have come from certain possible parent states. Similarly, for the system as a whole, the current state can only have come from certain possible parent states. Therefore we can ask, is there any possible decomposition into parts, such that the information from the system as a whole is no greater than the information from the parts separately? If there is, then we have found a way to decompose the system into totally independent parts.

In the case where the system does *not* decompose into totally independent parts, we can once again look for the decomposition which gives the *lowest* additional information from the whole as opposed to the parts.[14] Tononi calls this the *minimum information partition*. The effective information (the additional information given by the whole, as opposed to the parts) for the minimum information partition is then the Φ_2 value for the system.

Finally, we can do an exhaustive search across all subsystems and all partitions,[15] and once again we can define *complexes*. A complex is a system

---

Even if Tononi's EI were modified to take this into account, however, it would not address the objections to Tononi's interpretation of both Φ_2 and Φ_2 given in the next section.

[14] Once again, a normalization factor is introduced. Otherwise asymmetric partitions will be disfavored, and partitions into multiple parts will be favored, for purely mathematical reasons. Unfortunately, as Barrett A. B. and Seth A. K. (2011). Practical measures of integrated *Information* for time-series data, *PLoS Comput. Biol.* **7**(1):e1001052, doi: 10.1371/journal.pcbi.1001052. point out, this normalization itself introduces undesirable properties into the definition of Φ, and make it implausible that Φ as it stands really corresponds to any fundamental property of the world.

[15] At least in principle; in practice, this may well be far from feasible for neural systems of the scale of a real human brain.

with a given Φ_2 value, which is not contained within any larger system of higher Φ. Similarly, the main complex is the complex with highest Φ_2 in the whole system — and the true measure of Φ_2 (or consciousness) for the system is the Φ_2 of the main complex.

In examining Φ_2, we note that many of the problems with Φ_1 still apply. First, EI and Φ_2 itself are defined in ways which are closely tied to the particular type of system being examined. Although Φ_1, Φ_2 and EI are intended as general purpose concepts, the current mathematics has nothing like the broad range of applicability of standard information theoretic measures. For a further discussion of the shortcomings of information integration theories we refer to Aleksander and Beaton [2011] (see footnote 3). Here we address a major problem with the computational evaluation of either version of Φ and some possible improvements to this and then turn to a further claim of Tononi's that 'qualia' are informationally measurable features within the framework of information integration.

Difficulty in assessments of Φ and how 'liveliness' might improve things

The major flaw of information integration theories is that the calculation of Φ is exhaustive and grows exponentially with the number of neurons. In 2009, using a state-of-the-art computer, David Gamez showed that, using Balduzzi and Tononi's measure 2, it takes 12 hours to calculate the Φ of a 12-neuron network and estimated that a 30-neuron network would take 10^{10} years on the same computer (!).[16] It can be understood therefore that in recent years researchers have attempted to find faster alternative methods. Notable is the contribution by Adam Barrett and Anil Seth,[17] who address Φ_2 and suggest two alternatives, first, Φ_E or an 'empirical' measure of information integration and second, Φ_{AR} which refers to an 'auto-regressive' version of information integration. The reader interested in a full mathematical description of these two methods is advised to read the originating paper. Here we note that these methods cut corners as they consider what happens to the entire panoply of states over time and work

---

[16] Aleksander I. and Gamez D, (2010). Informational theories of consciousness: A review and extension. *Proc. Brain Inspired Cognitive Sys. Conf.* Madrid.

[17] Barrett AB, Seth AK (2011) Practical Measures of Integrated *Information* for Time-Series Data, *PLoS Comput Biol* **7**(1):e1001052. doi:10.1371/journal.pcbi.1001052.

out how information is generated in the series of such possible states. The knowledge of statistical techniques required to understand this methodology is not trivial. Now we do something much simpler.

Liveliness: some history

In 1973, one of the authors (IA) was working on networks of genes rather than neurons. The two are not as far apart as it might seem: genes can be modeled by 2-input binary (weightless) neurons with fixed, but randomly chosen, neuron logic functions (logic functions of neurons are discussed in several parts of Chapter 3).[18] When these networks are started in a randomly selected state, they go from state to state until they return to a previously visited state, at which point a cycle is complete and repeats itself in perpetuity. In this model the states in the cycle are analogous to the chemical changes in the division of a cell, with the number of different cycles involved in a given network being analogous to the number of different cell types of a particular organism that arises from these genes. It was a puzzle to biologists that this seemingly random system produced very few cell types (different cycles) and had short gene replication times (short cycles) which matched what is found in nature. The surprise (first noted in a simulation by Stuart Kauffmann in 1969[19]) is that random networks act in this way without any appeal to evolution. Given a number of genes per cell (i.e., neurons) in a simulation, the resulting replication times and cell types match the species in nature with that number of genes per cell.

One of the authors, IA, with a PhD student, Paul Atlas, set out to discover how to predict the number of cycles and their size distribution. Central to this analysis was the concept of the liveliness of a neuron, which is the probability that a change at the input of a neuron is transmitted to the output. The basis of there being a cycle in the network is that changes must be able to be transmitted around loops in the network and the higher the liveliness, the higher is this probability. When information integration theories came to the fore it seemed that, as the transmission of information across a network was suggested to be the key factor in determining the presence of consciousness, the liveliness methods of 1973 might be applicable.

---

[18] Aleksander I. and Atlas P. (1973). Cyclic activity in nature: Causes of stability. *Int. J. Neurosci.* **6**, 45–50.
[19] Kauffman, S. A. (1969). Metabolic stability and *epigenesis* in randomly constructed genetic nets, *J. Theor. Biol* **22**, 434–467.

In work done with David Gamez (see footnote 17) the concept of liveliness is presented in terms of an arbitrary number of n inputs (rather than $n = 2$ as in the earlier work). Let the binary inputs of a node j be an ordered list of 0's and 1's that form a state or a vector[20]:

$$x_1^j, x_2^j \ldots x_n^j$$

The vectors of the 1 or 0 states of these inputs can be written as

$$X_0^j, X_1^j \ldots X_k^j \ldots X_{2^n-1}^j$$

where the vectors go from 000 ... 0 (i.e. X_0^j) to 111 ... 1 (i.e. $X_{2^n-1}^j$) then, for example, if $n = 3$ and $k = 5$ (both in decimal),

$X_5^j = 101$ (which is 5 in binary)

We now develop some notation which is clarified in Table 6.1. A node is said to **be *lively* on input** x_p^j if its output z_j changes value when x_p^j changes its value. Here $p = 1, 2, \ldots n$ is the order number of the input in question. The liveliness, (x_p^j) of an input p in node j is

$$\lambda(x_p^j) = 1, \text{ if the input is lively, or}$$

$$\lambda(x_p^j) = 0, \text{ if it is not lively}$$

Liveliness can be computed the one particular input p for all of the 2^n possible input vectors.

Table 6.1.   Example function to illustrate the calculation of liveliness.

$x1$	$x2$	$x3$	z	$\lambda(x_1^j)$	$\lambda(x_2^j)$	$\lambda(x_3^j)$
0	0	0	0	1	0	1
0	0	1	1	0	1	0
0	1	0	0	0	0	0
0	1	1	0	0	1	0
1	0	0	1	1	1	0
1	0	1	1	0	1	0
1	1	0	0	0	1	0
1	1	1	0	0	1	0

---

[20]See the appendix at the end of this chapter for a comment on vectors for those unfamiliar with this concept.

Then the liveliness of a node for this input, written as

$$\Lambda(x_p^j)$$

is the number of times for all possible input patterns that the node is lively, divided by the number of input combinations, 2^n. As an example consider the function described in Table 6.1.

The total node liveliness (defined as the average liveliness of all the inputs to a node) for the inputs in Table 6.1 is as follows:

$$\Lambda(x_1^j) = 2/8 \quad \Lambda(x_2^j) = 6/8 \quad \Lambda(x_3^j) = 1/8.$$

As liveliness is a measure of the likelihood of communication across the nodes of a network, this seems to have an affinity with a similar factor found in information integration theories. We take this a little further in the next section.

Relevance to information integration

While a formal link between liveliness and information integration is work in progress at the time of writing, it is possible to identify a heuristic relationship between them. The high liveliness between nodes that are in closer causal contact appears broadly to correspond to the causal interdependence between neurons that is measured by Φ *(the symbol now referring to both versions of the concept)*. For example, the digital camera sensor mentioned earlier exhibits low Φ because there is no causal linking between the elements, and the overall liveliness of this system would be zero as well. However, whilst Φ and liveliness both measure causal interactions, they do not measure exactly the same thing: Φ indicates what information a system provides when it enters a particular state, whereas liveliness identifies the state structures that arise as a result of the causal interactions available to the neurons. Some experiments were carried out on a four-neuron network (A,B,C,D) that was constructed with different functions and connectivity. The Φ of these networks was calculated[21] and these results were compared to the liveliness of each system. The details of results of these experiments may be found in Aleksander and Gamez (2010) (see footnote 17) and they indicate that, very roughly, the trends in loop liveliness of the networks are

---

[21] This was done using David Gamez's software called 'SpikeStream' addressed at http://www.davidgamez.eu/pages/science/spikestream.php.

in the same directions as those of Φ. However, the key result was in the simulation of larger networks which showed that liveliness assessments for a 12-neuron network would take 2 seconds (instead of the 12 hours in the case of Φ) and an estimated 13 seconds for the 100 neuron network (instead of the 10^{10} hours in the case of Φ).

Commentary

It must be stressed that this work on the link between Φ and Λ is highly speculative at this stage. Indeed most of what is said about Φ is only speculative at the moment. But, despite this, Tononi has done something quite innovative and that is to argue that were one to have a well founded science of consciousness, its primary measure might be information and the way it can flow in a neural network. Now we become even more speculative and look at the way this information could have any reference to the world in which the conscious organism operates.

Qualia and information integration

Tononi recognized that information integration theory was much directed toward the capacity of a system to sustain states that can be said to be 'mental'. He described an approach to the quality of such states in his 'manifesto' paper[22] and elaborated this in a paper with Balduzzi specifically directed at qualia.[23] Here we do not provide the details of this work, (leaving this to the reader to discover) but, as we develop an alternative approach in subsequent sections, it is necessary to describe the bare bones of Tononi's outlook.

From capacity to qualia

'Qualia' is a word mostly used by philosophers in order to be able to speak of the quality of an internal experience such as the redness of a rose or the

---

[22]Tononi, G. (2008). Consciousness as integrated information: A provisional manifesto, *Biol. Bull.* **215**, 216–242.
[23]Balduzzi, D., and Tononi G. (2009). Qualia: The geometry of integrated information, *PLoS Comput. Biol.* **5**(8), 1–224.

pain of a mosquito sting. There is no better place to look for explanations than the Stanford Encyclopedia of philosophy[24]:

> ... *Philosophers often use the term 'qualia' (singular 'quale') to refer to the introspectively accessible, phenomenal aspects of our mental lives. In this standard, broad sense of the term, it is difficult to deny that there are qualia. Disagreement typically centers on which mental states have qualia, whether qualia are intrinsic qualities of their bearers, and how qualia relate to the physical world both inside and outside the head. The status of qualia is hotly debated in philosophy largely because it is central to a proper understanding of the nature of consciousness. Qualia are at the very heart of the mind-body problem.*

But how does one look for qualia either in artificial neural networks or in the brain? From the pen of Erwin Schrödinger, Nobel physicist, one of the founders of quantum theory who was deeply interested in the perception of color, we read[25]:

> *The sensation of colour cannot be accounted for by the physicist's objective picture of light-waves. Could the physiologist account for it, if he had fuller knowledge than he has of the processes in the retina and the nervous processes set up by them in the optical nerve bundles and in the brain? I do not think so.*

Tononi claims to have found an informational mechanism for qualia .It is brave of him to state this view in the face of the controversy that surrounds the concept:

> *We take a geometric approach, introducing the notion of a quale as a shape that embodies the entire set of informational relationships generated by interactions in the system. The paper investigates how features of the quale relate to properties of the underlying system and also to basic features of experience, providing the beginnings of a mathematical dictionary relating neurophysiology to the geometry of the quale and the geometry to phenomenology* (see footnote 25).

This is intricate stuff and it is the specific target of the next few pages to unravel some of it, to ask whether the puzzle of qualia has been truly solved

---

[24]Tye M. (2009). Qualia, in E. N. Zalta (Ed.) *The Stanford Encyclopedia of Philosophy*. Available at: http://plato.stanford.edu/archives/sum2009/entries/qualia/.
[25]Schrödinger E. (orig. pub. 1958, 1992). The mystery of sensual qualities, Chapter 6 in <u>*Mind and Matter*</u>, in *What is Life? With Mind and Matter and Autobiographical Sketches* (Cambridge University Press, Canto Edition), p. 154.

through informational theories and to discuss alternatives that come from our own work. To gain some insight into what Tononi presents through some difficult mathematics, we simplify the analysis, still retaining the gist of his narrative. We do use an idea of *vectors* again, the building blocks of the *shapes* in the Tononi quote above, but for those who fear the v-word there is a brief tutorial at the end of this chapter.

Tononi's example of a quale

We use the same circuit as in Balduzzi and Tononi (2009) (see footnote 24), which is reproduced below in Fig. 6.1.

A quale according to Tononi is not the state itself but a compilation of how elementary subsytems within the circuit contribute to the creation of that state by the informational interactions that exist within them. It is suggested that the circuit in Fig. 6.1 can be decomposed into four sub-mechanisms shown in Fig. 6.2.

Now consider just the four units of Fig. 6.1, but assume that no linking mechanisms are present. This means that at any moment there are no constraints on the individual states of the units. This can be annotated as

$$\begin{pmatrix} ? & ? \\ ? & ? \end{pmatrix}$$

The question marks indicate that the preceding state could have had either value (0 or 1), meaning that the units being in state 8 (1000) reveals no information of their previous state, and any one of the possible 16 states might have been present with a probability of 1/16 (0.0625).

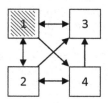

Fig. 6.1.   The nodes all perform the AND function of their inputs. The hashed node indicates that the neuron outputs a logical value of 1 while no hash is a logical 0. So, reading the code of the state in the numerical order shown, the circuit is in state 1000 and this can treated as the binary code for the number 8 in decimal code.

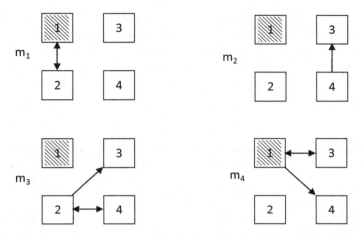

Fig. 6.2. Sub mechanisms of the circuit in Fig. 6.1.

Tononi defines a 'Qualia space' in which each point is represented by a vector (see Appendix at the end of this chapter). The dimensions of this vector are the 16 possible states, and the coordinates are given by the probability with which a state might occur. So, without the knowledge of any of the mechanisms involved, the fact that the previous state could have been any one of the 16 possible choices with a probability of 0.0625 gives us a point in qualia space represented by the vector

$$\mathbf{q}_0 = [(0.0625), \ldots 16 \text{ times}]$$

Now, the mechanism m_1 is brought into play. This involves units 1 and 2 and, according to Tononi, the connections from 3 and 4 must be seen as generating uncertainty at the inputs of 1 and 2. That is, any connections coming into 1 and 2 from 3 and 4 are considered as carrying noise, random 0s and 1s that is. To derive the next qualia vector we must examine all the possible ways for the circuit to enter state 8, and their probabilities. These possibilities arise in the face of uncertainty at the incoming connections to units 1 and 2.

Consider the first four possible states (0–3) of the qualia vector. As all four have the left hand row in common they can be represented by

$$\begin{pmatrix} 0 & ? \\ 0 & ? \end{pmatrix}$$

It is clear (from Fig. 6.1) that no matter how much noise is generated in the right hand column, unit 1 can never enter 1 as required by state 8. So the first four states of the next qualia vector have the coordinate 0. Now consider states 4, 5, 6, and 7, that is, states that can be represented as follows

$$\begin{pmatrix} 0 & ? \\ 1 & ? \end{pmatrix}$$

To discover how these states might lead to state 8, first note that unit 1 needs to become a 1, which will happen with a probability of 0.5 due to the noise in unit 3 (remembering that it is an AND gate and both inputs to node 1 must become a 1 for it to output a 1).

Now, for unit 2 to become 0, this is guaranteed by unit 1 being 0, hence the probability is 1. Finally, the probability of unit 3 and 4 both being 0 is 0.25, as there is complete uncertainty about these two units. Now we take the product of these three probabilities (as they are independent events) to calculate the probability that any one of the states 4,5,6 and 7 should have been the state preceding state 8 and this is 0.125.

But we are not capable of defining the vector q_1 just yet simply because states 12, 13, 14 and 15 also could have been predecessors. They have the form

$$\begin{pmatrix} 1 & ? \\ 1 & ? \end{pmatrix}$$

Using the technique above it can be shown that these four states have a probability of 0.0625 of having been the predecessor. We can now identify q_1

$$q_1 = [0, 0, 0, 0, (0.125), (0.125), (0.125), (0.125), 0, 0, 0, 0, (0.0625), \\ \times (0.0625), (0.0625), (0.0625)]$$

We note that there is a vector in qualia space that goes from q_0 to q_1 and that is the first plank of a complex construction which, Tononi argues, is the quale that is a function of state 8 and the underpinning circuit that causes it. Further planks are added by considering the additional mechanisms. Continuous adding of mechanisms eventually results in the complete circuit, which, in this case indicates state 6 after four steps, that is

$$q_4 = [0, 0, 0, 0, 0, 0, 1, 0, 0, 0, 0, 0, 0, 0, 0, 0]$$

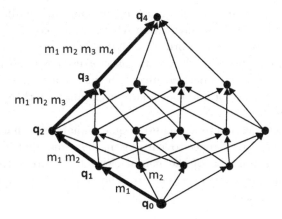

Fig. 6.3. The 'quale' implied by the informational mechanisms that generate state 8 in Fig. 6.1. The path followed in the text is shown in bold.

There are obviously many ways in which the many mechanisms can be brought into play and it is Tononi's contention that the structure compiled from *all* the vectors which result from the progressive addition of the informational function of basic mechanisms is the quale associated with entry into a particular state. A partial quale for the example we have been developing above, is shown in Fig. 6.3.

The justification for this structure seen by Tononi as a representation of qualitative experience is that it not only quantifies the capacity for a network in a particular state to integrate information (the *what* of consciousness) but also shows *how* the various mechanisms cooperate to generate a state.

Criticism of this approach to qualia

There are two criticisms one can make of the above approach. If one believes, as we do, that it makes no sense to talk of consciousness in any way other than as the presence of a phenomenal state (see Chapter 5), then the above structures of progressive informational involvement of mechanisms must be judged in terms of the contribution they make in representing some form of reality for the network. We are fully aware that phenomenology is sometimes addressed without such a representational outlook. Clearly this is what Tononi means when he refers to the entire integrated information approach as being phenomenological. We agree with Tononi as far as this starts with the notion that a mental state must be unique and undifferentiated as a definition of information integration: that may be considered as a first-person specification for a network state that is *felt* and is phenomenological in that sense. But, we argue, the qualia analysis discussed above moves away from the first to the third person through being a mathematical expression of the cooperative action of several sub-mechanisms with no reference to how this might be *felt*.

The second objection to the asserted qualia analysis is that in no part of the theory is there a reference to learning mechanisms: that is, mechanisms that control the function of the neural elements in order to achieve the integration that controls consciousness. The next chapter is motivated by these two objections.

Appendix. A simplification of vectors

Some of us will have met vectors at school being told that a vector is something that has magnitude and direction in three-dimensional space. But there is another way of describing the vector.

Say that point P has the X,Y,Z, coordinates of 1,2,3 and that Q has 2,3,4. Then the, dimensions of the vector PQ may be obtained in the X, Y, Z, space by subtracting the X, Y, Z coordinates of P from the X, Y, Z coordinates of Q. This is (2-1), (3-2), (4-1). That is, the vector PQ has a size, 1,1,1, which would be the coordinates of Q were the P on the origin, that is at the X, Y, Z coordinates (0,0,0,). The point is this, a vector has a modifying property: if PQ is added to a point with coordinates X,Y,Z, the end of the vector will be at (X+1),(Y+1),(Z+1).

As a concrete example, X could stand for 'the number of books on shelf X of a book case, and similarly so for Y and Z. In the above case (P) there

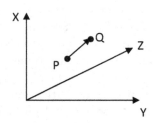

Fig. 6A.1.   A vector PQ in three-dimensional space.

is one book on shelf X, two on Y and three on Z. Adding one book to each shelf is the process of adding vector PQ.

Now there is no reason to have only three shelves: there can be any number of shelves, and vector addition will work. We realize that vector operations are simply ways of working with ordered lists of numbers where each list has the same number of numbers, say n. Then n is the number of dimensions of the vector system. With only three dimensions one has magnitude (length of the arrow) and direction (where is the arrow pointing). With more than three dimensions this meaning disappears, but vector operations remain.

Acknowledgments

The research was supported by the Association of Information Technology Trust and this has made it possible for this chapter to be written.

Chapter 7

THE JOY OF SEEING: GATHERING VISUAL INFORMATION

Yet, it is the very unitary nature of the visual image in the brain, one in which the different attributes of the visual scene — form, color, motion, depth — are seen in precise spatiotemporal registration, that was to conceal the profound division of labor within the visual cortex.

Zeki S. *et al.* (1991)[1]

The divisive brain

Here's a puzzle: as seen in the last chapter, what we experience as our 'mental state' may be described as being unique and indivisible. Looking at a yellow circle on a white piece of paper seems to suggest that somewhere in the brain there is a neural representation of this which distinguishes it from all other visual experiences. That is, as in the 'iconic' ideas expressed in Chapter 5, external stimuli retain their spatial relationships in the inner state. But as is now common knowledge as shown in the quote above, attributes such as color, form, motion and depth stimulate separate and specific areas of the visual cortex. So how can this lead to the world being 'seen in precise spatiotemporal registration'? In what sense can a mental state be unique and indivisible, as it introspectively seems to be, when the activity the stimulus creates is channeled to different parts of the visual cortex? Here we take a brief look of what is known about representation in the visual cortex and how this may be modeled to indicate the transition between this localized registration and the feeling of world-representing coherence.

---

[1]Zeki S., Watson J. D., Lueck C. J., Friston K. J., Kennard, and Frackowiak R. S. (1991). A direct demonstration of functional specialization in human visual cortex, *J. Neurosci.* **11**(3), 641–649.

While a relatively correct view of the early parts (close to the eyes) of the anatomy of the visual system had appeared in science in the 11th century AD,[2] it was only some way into the 20th century that the many different functions of the visual cortex began to be appreciated. Such discoveries rely heavily on measurement methods available to neurologists. The oldest is the study of the effect of lesions, while currently *functional Magnetic Resonance Imaging* (fMRI, see below) is used to measure the activity of neurons largely through the difference in blood flow between active neural areas and passive ones.[3]

As far as the visual system is concerned, it was David Hubel and Torsten Wiesel who first discovered that features of the visual stimulus (e.g., different orientations of lines) activated different parts of the early sections of the visual cortex.[4] This work, for which they were awarded the 1981 Nobel Prize in Medicine, was carried out by the methodical insertion of fine electrodes in the axons of visual neurons in cats and monkeys. Careful experimentation of this kind allowed Daniel Felleman and David van Essen of the University of Texas at Houston to develop a complex map and wiring diagram representing what was known of the macaque monkey's visual cortex.[5] At the same time, a major step for discovering further action in the visual cortex came from brain scanning techniques. Positron emission tomography (PET) was a helpful technique invented in the early 1950s. This involves injecting a low dose of radioactive material and monitoring the gamma rays generated by enhanced blood flow. As active neural areas do imply greater blood flow, this enabled researchers Semir Zeki and his colleagues at University College, London to demonstrate functional specialization in the *human* visual cortex.[6] More recently PET techniques were replaced by

---

[2] An image of eyes connecting through optical nerves to the brain drawn by Arab physicist Ibn Al-Haitham appears in: Polyak S. (1957). *The Vertebrate Visual System* (University of Chicago Press, Chicago, IL).

[3] A good account of functional measurement methods may be found in: Savoy R.L. (2001). History and future directions of human brain mapping and functional neuroimaging, *Acta Psychologica* **107**, 9–42.

[4] Hubel D. H. and Wiesel T. N. (1959). Receptive fields of single neurones in the cat's striate cortex, *J. Physiol.* **150**, 91–104.

[5] Felleman D. J. and Van Essen D. C. (1991). Distributed hierarchical processing in the primate cerebral cortex, *Cereb. Cortex* **1**(1), 1–47.

[6] Zeki S., Watson J. D., Lueck C. J., Friston K. J., Kennard, and Frackowiak R. S. (1991). A direct demonstration of functional specialization in human visual cortex, *J. Neurosci.* 11(3), 641–649.

functional Magnetic Resonance (fMRI) methods which sense blood flow in minute volumes of the brain and so monitor neural activity and changes of activity as perception tests are performed. Here using radioactive tracers is avoided.[7]

The upshot of these experiments is the discovery that visual perception causes activity in disparate specialized areas of the cortex. As already observed above, this is somewhat in contrast with the notion that our experienced mental state appears to be 'unique, indivisible and world-representing'. We take a closer look at what appears to be known about these areas, before speculating about how they might contribute to our familiar visual experience of the world.

Division of labor in the visual cortex

The visual cortex is a highly modular structure with components that are architecturally different, performing different functions which, together, deliver a visual mental experience.[8] A sketch of the areas is shown in Fig. 7.1. This should not be taken to be a block diagram of the visual cortex. It is merely a device that guides our discussion of the functional parts of this system. In the figure there is an allusion to the alignment and contact between these areas. This is a simplification of what is known, but it should be sufficient to address the question of how a distributed system of this kind might lead to an integrated mental state.

The literature reveals a rapidly developing scene.[9] Here we try to pitch the discussion not so much on the detailed anatomy which is continuously being revised, but on principles that may be emerging.

Looking at the figure, we note that there is a progression from the eyes through the Lateral Geniculate Nucleus or LGN (a relay station) to

---

[7]Engel S. A., Rumelhart D. E., Wandelll B. A., Lee A. T., Glover G. H., Chichilinsky E. J., and Shalden M. N. (1994). fMRI of human visual cortex, *Nature* **369**, 525.

[8]Later in this chapter, under the heading of 'depictive' theory, we develop a hypothesis which links visual mental experience to neural events and to external visual events.

[9]Material in this section is based on a broad cover of the up-to-date results of research in the neurology of vision that may be found on the Internet. However, a very helpful short article may be found at: http://www.lifesci.sussex.ac.uk/home/George_Mather/Linked%20Pages/Physiol/Cortex.html#anchor1708113.

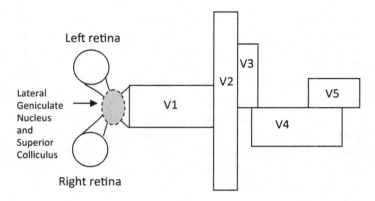

Fig. 7.1.   A schematic guide to the structure of the visual cortex.

areas V1 to V5 in some sort of order. V1 (and sometimes part of V2) are called the *striate* cortex (as striations are seen under a microscope) the rest being the *extrastriate* cortex. We now discuss the sequence of visual areas in an approximate progressive order of their connections starting with the effective input transducers, the eyes.

The eyes and their probing retina

Children's books on how we see often describe the eyes as spherical cameras with lenses and a photo-sensitive plate at the back wall. Yes, maybe, but taking pictures of unfolding visual experience and storing them in the memory of a computer could not be further from what the visual cortex, which gives us visual experience, is doing. The eyes are sophisticated search devices that *saccade over* (jump rapidly around) the visual scene. From this, one must suggest how the unique and indivisible conscious sensation we call a 'mental state' (visual in this case) might come into being.

The primary function of the eyes, is to *explore* the visual world of the observer, whose brain then becomes responsible for the reconstruction of the results of the exploration. True, the eyeballs are very much like the lens of the camera, and the retina is a bit like the photo-sensitive layer of a digital camera, full of light-sensitive 'receptor' cells. These receive light and produce spiky signals for the brain to interpret. There are two kinds of receptors in the retina, rods and cones (so called according to their shapes).

The rods sense light levels and produce spiking signals largely at low light levels, that is, they give us night vision. But it is the cones that give us our sharpest sense of vision. Where the rods cover the approximate 200° of vision each eye can muster, the cones are concentrated in a 10° area, the *fovea*, sometimes called 'a dimple in the middle of the retina'. This dimple is packed with 30,000 cones of which 64% fire strongly if the light falling on them is red, 32% for green and 4% for blue. To see more than just a colorful patch, that is, to see the vivid, colorful world in which we live, the eye must move around and the brain must reconstruct the visual data as it is gathered by the fovea. But there are no pre-planned scans, no random search strategies, the movement of the eye is subtly controlled by the brain which plays a central role in the creation of our visual mental states.

Between eye and V1

We now go on to describe what is known of the parts of the visual system, but we do this with a word of caution. While much has been discovered of how neurons in various areas relate to their projections from the retina, much remains to be discovered about the feedback connections within the system and the dynamic behavior that results from such feedback. One simply assumes that feedback must exist as we are able to sustain or recall imagery with our eyes closed.

The axons of all the retinal neurons form a cable that exits the eyeball through a hole in the eyeball, forming the *optic nerve*. This hole is the celebrated 'blind spot' in the field of vision which does not bother us as it does not affect the foveal region and is unseen due to eye movement. The optic nerve leads to the Lateral Geniculate Nucleus (LGN). This is a relay station which gathers the output of the optic nerve. It helpfully interleaves the fibres of the two eyes so that, as many authors enjoy describing, there is a line through the LGN along which, if a pin could be inserted, it would hit the same spot in the visual field 6 times as it penetrates the six layers of the LGN. Alongside the LGN is the Superior Colliculus (SC). This tiny but crucial brain area controls the saccadic movement of the eyes. This is a network that fires according to retinal content. It issues signals to the eye muscles to centre the eyes on areas of strong firing. This is quite a sophisticated organ, as not only does it receive inputs from vision but also from the auditory part of the brain. This causes the eyes to move towards a sudden sound.

Stepping aside

Before entering a deeper discussion of the main areas of the visual cortex two asides are necessary. First, the SC is not the only organ that causes eye movement. Centrally sited in the brain, the *Frontal Eye Fields* (FEF) also control eye movement, but in a more purposeful way.[10] The FEF receive inputs from processed vision and planning areas, so can move the eyes to pursue a moving target or to resolve unclear visual stimuli. The words 'smooth pursuit' and 'voluntary eye movement' are used to describe what the FEF do. In addition, the FEF are involved in other movement resulting from vision, As, for example, the pointing oaf a finger at a seen object.

The second point is that there are two visual pathways: the so-called *ventral* (i.e., belly side or lower side of the brain) pathway which is where conscious vision is thought to occur, and the *dorsal* pathway (i.e., back or upper side) which is thought to be functional without coming into consciousness. David Milner (now at Durham University) and Mel Goodale (now at the University of Western Ontario) argued that the dorsal pathway, previously thought to be concerned with 'where' information, was actually a guiding pathway for action.[11] One of their celebrated experiments showed that participants blind due to damage in the ventral path could position their hands according to the orientation of a slot into which they would place their open hand. They might even duck were a football thrown at them at head height. The participants report these events as guesswork. In this chapter we examine conditions that may be necessary for the creation of conscious mental states leading to hypotheses that these conditions do not pertain to the dorsal pathway but do in the ventral area. We must stress that this is just a speculation.

V1 — The striate primary visual cortex

V1 is a sorting area for the content of the transmission from the LGN. Small clusters of axons within it react to events in small parts of the retina. Therefore, V1 is said to be *retinotopic*, that is, it retains the spatial relationships of light features projected on to the retina. But this happens in a

---

[10] A useful site is http://brainmind.com/FrontalEyeFieldsArea8.html.
[11] Milner D. and Goodale M. (2006). *The Visual Brain in Action.* 2nd edn. (Oxford Psychology, Oxford).

most uneven way. Remembering that the fovea covers only 10 conic degrees out of the approximately available 200 of the retina, it comes as a surprise that *half* of V1 receives input from the fovea 'pimple'. To appreciate this, think that a top-of-the range digital camera produces about 170 pixels (picture points) per sq. mm, while the foveal projection in area V1 receives the output of about 10,000 cone neurons per sq. mm. Even allowing that three cones may act as one pixel (to express color combinations), the acuity of the pimple is impressive. Of course it has not been forgotten that we still need to explain how we see so much more than the pimple and with a high acuity.

The key functional task that V1 is thought to perform (on the basis of a vast number of neurological measurments) is to present in one position on its surface, an analysis of features that occur on a specific spot of the retina. By 'analysis', it is meant that neurons are 'tuned' to features so that a change in that feature is represented by a change in which neuron fires within the same small area that represents the same visual spot in the world. In particular, one such feature that was intensely studied by Hubel and Wiesel (see footnote 3) was the tuning to the orientation of edges in what are called simple V1 cells. Complex V1 cells can be found that are tuned to fire for the combination of such features. Other cells in these small areas are tuned to color and to movement and within one patch the same spot from both eyes is represented.

What use is all this? To answer this, one recalls that the object of the visual system, and, we suggest, any other part of our perceptual apparatus, is to give us a sense of 'being there' in a world of well — or poorly — defined objects. But it is important not to misunderstand this. The brain is not an object recognition machine that produces inventories of what there is in the world and where it might be found. The path we are following is that the brain has an integrated sensation of being somewhere and the somewhere is made up of objects rather than pixels or their equivalents in other senses. An evolutionary reason for this is that we survive by virtue of our ability to react to and control what objects do rather than the minutiae of what constitutes the objects. The server in a tennis match strikes a ball with a racket and not the molecules that make up either of these. Nor would a player be helped by knowing all about the representations in V1. Every time she throws the ball in the air to strike it, this is a new experience that requires a new unleashing of the muscles that score the desired ace.

We now need to ask how subsequent (extrastriate) areas of the vision system act to move towards these ambitious goals.

The extrastriate visual cortex

Areas V3, V4 and V5, are generally referred to as the 'extrastriate' visual cortex while V2 is sometimes called the 'pre-striate' cortex. However, these labels are anatomical and related to the striated appearence of the primary visual cortex and not so much to what it does. V2 appears to collect features detected in V1 in more complex formations. One may find 'corner detectors' at the junction of two lines and so on. Also color and motion stimulations cause retinotopic stimulation in V2 sometimes based on combinations of retinotopic features.

There is also some recent research showing that it is not only that V1 sends projections to V2, but V2 returns the favor and sends projections back to V1. This means feedback, and feedback means sustainable states and sustainable states mean memory. Indeed, in 2009, a group of researchers at the University of Malaga unequivocally showed that V2 was involved in object recognition memory.[12] Such experiments on rats show that their responses are modified when they have seen certain objects before. Of course, this does not indicate the presence of a mental state, it could simply be a retention of an enhancement between the visual stimulus and the action response. As with much else which concerns brain dynamics due to feedback in networks, V2 will be a subject of continued scrutiny for some time to come.

Textbooks and websites[13] report the functions of the extrastriate cortex roughly as follows. V3 cells do not stand out clearly, but appear to be tuned to motion and depth. V4 contains many color-sensitive cells but is also sensitive to complex spatial and orientation features. It also appears to take part in spatial awareness, i.e., the position of the experiencing entity in the world. V5 (or MT – middle temporal) has cells strongly sensitive to motion, and the area is active if the target image is in motion.

So, in the greater scheme of discovering world-representing mental states that are unique and indivisible, what we learn about representations in the extrastriate cortex is a little disappointing because it is not clear how the integration of responses in different parts of the visual system might take place. Now we approach an hypothetical example of integration through a simple simulated model.

---

[12]Lopez-Aranda M. F. *et al.* (2009). Role of layer 6 of V2 visual cortex in object-recognition memory, *Science* **325**(5936), 87–89.
[13]Some websites are very clear as, for example, http://www.lifesci.sussex.ac.uk/home/George_Mather/Linked%20Pages/Physiol/Cortex.html.

Discovering integration in the visual cortex

In this context 'integration' refers as Zeki says (initial quote in the chapter) to our ability to see more than the foveal content but with the 'precise spatio-temporal registration' of the fovea. In his influential book on the visual system, Zeki devotes the last 5 chapters out of 32 to the difficulty of discovering the mechanisms of integration through expert neurological experimentation.[14] From this we learn that Karl Lashley (encountered in Chapter 4 of this book) was hugely opposed to the discovery of specialized areas in the brain. This is hardly surprising as in his experimental life he showed repeatedly that local lesions had only a small global effect on cognition. Were cognition dependent on localization, this would not be so. Much of Zeki's quest is centered on measuring how the receptive field of neurons is expanded in successive layers of ever more complex neurons. He also speculates on the finding of circuits that oscillate in relation to larger visual fields. We and, indeed, Zeki, are aware of the shortcomings of such quests. Even if the receptive field of the neurons in some area of the brain were to extend to the entire retina, this would be limited to the visual field of the eyes in a fixed position.

It does not need great experimentation to convince ourselves that our sense of visual consciousness extends way beyond the retinal limit. All one needs to do look around and note that we are conscious of a room we are in, a street in which we are standing or the panorama afforded by being at the top of a hill. Doing this, however, we note that there is a great deal of movement in our bodies to 'capture' these visual feelings: the eyes, the head, the body and even our legs may be moving. Visual integration would be a rum thing were it not aided by the work of some muscles.

Our own work on visual integration was strongly influenced as a result of reading Zeki's *Vision of the Brain,* where he reports on a strikingly significant discovery in 1989 by Claudio Galletti and Pier Paolo Battaglini of the University of Bologna.[15] They found that in visual area V3 of an awake, behaving monkey, there were cells that responded to a flash of light if the monkey was looking in one direction but not if the eyes were pointing elsewhere. Over the years, many areas of the visual cortex were found to be influenced by muscular activity not only from eye movement but also from a variety of other muscular action such as the neck, arms and legs.

---

[14]Zeki S. (1993). *A Vision of the Brain* (Blackwell Science, Oxford).
[15]Galletti C. and Battaglini P. P. (1989). Gaze-dependent visual neurons in area V3A of monkey prestriate cortex, *J. Neurosci.* **9**, 1112–1125.

In later years, Zeki and his colleagues developed a model of consciousness based on his discoveries (and those of others) of specialization in different areas of the visual system. He called it the micro-consciousness theory of consciousness.[16] This maintains that the sensitivity to external features in different parts of the visual cortex are unified merely by their asynchronous but near-coexistent occurrence. This triggered some work with colleague Barry Dunmall to complete Zeki's idea with the notion of a muscular referent which would provide a sensation of where things are in the external world and thus extend the integration to beyond the limits of a fixed retinal image. We take a look at this development below.

A Depictive theory

The Crick and Koch stimulus

Two of our publications[17,18] encompass a theory of consciousness that was suggested not only by the work of Zeki discussed above, but also by a seminal paper by Francis Crick and Christof Koch[19] (and a visit by the authors of this book to the Koch Lab at the California Institute of Technology — Cal Tech). We take a brief look at their paper below, but suffice it to say that this led in 1998 to a stimulation of new work on discovering the NCC, the Neural Correlates of Consciousness. Part of this new stimulus was the foundation of the Association for the Scientific Study of Consciousness which, at the time of writing, is heading for its 16th annual conference.

The paper concentrates on the visual modality as this is an area of expertise at the Koch laboratory at Cal Tech. Its first conclusion is that contrary to received wisdom, visual representation in V1 does not correlate with what is seen. This concurs with our view based on the retinotopic function of V1 which cannot be corrected for various forms of movement.

---

[16]Zeki S. and Bartels A. (1998). The asynchrony of consciousness, *Proc. R. Soc. Lond. B* **265**, 1583–1585.

[17]Aleksander I. and Dunmall B. (2000). An extension to the hypothesis of the asynchrony of visual consciousness, *Proc. Royal Soc. B Biol. Sci.* **267**(1439), 197–200.

[18]Aleksander I. and Dunmall B. (2003). Axioms and tests for the presence of minimal consciousness in agents, in O. Holland (Ed.), *Machine Consciousness* (Imprint Academic, Exeter).

[19]Crick F. and Koch C. (1998). Consciousness and neuroscience, *Cereb. Cortex* **8**, 97–107.

There is a suggestion that extrastriate areas being closer to the frontal lobes are likely to be better candidates for ego-centered world-replicating representations which are needed for the planning work of the frontal lobes. Again we concur with this but for an additional reason. The frontal lobes are also responsible for movement and, as a hypothesis, re-entry into the visual areas might account for movement compensation and consequent integration. We expand on this in the material which follows.

A necessary world referent

In '*An extension to the hypothesis of the asynchrony of visual consciousness*' (see footnote 16) we take a 'design' stance in the question of the creation of neural support for an integrated visual experience. That is, we ask how would one design a system that has the necessary powers of reconstruction of the product of a moving fovea (that is, provide 'neural support' for the visual experience). The 'extension' is to that of a theory by Zeki and Bartels (see footnote 15) where the integration of the activity in specialist areas is described as just being coincidental. Here are some of the strands of a logic which, to us, seems inescapable and which removes the coincidental element and replaces it by a binding referent labeled j.

- *Neural support is in complete register with the experience.* To be in complete register means that a minimal event, such as a small speck appearing in the world in view, must correspond to a minimal neural event. Putting this the other way around, there is a minimal change in neural firing which defines what we mean by a minimal visual event. That is, were the speck smaller, it would not lead to any change in neural firing at all. This does not mean that there is an exact image in the neural structure, it could be distributed across the specialist areas of the cortex.
- *Foveal information is composed of minimal neural events.*
- *At every moment in time, foveal information is linked to the information about the muscular action which controls the position of the fovea.* This muscular activity is called the 'attentional referent' j and has the coordinates of the amount by which, and the direction, that the eyeball is displaced from its central 'look-straight-ahead' position. That is, if a spot of light is seen at a particular value of j and the same light having moved, is then seen at j' the two events imply that different neurons will react to the same light information. All the minimal events in the foveal patch have the same indexing information.

The key steps that define the neural support of a visual experience are then the following.

- *The neural support for a minimal event of visual consciousness is the state of a group neurons in different specialist areas but with the same j.* That is, given that the visual system distributes visual information to capture the features of the event in the 'out-there' world, it is the j referent that brings these together as an element of the support and, consequently, the experience.

- *The whole neural support requires a persistence of a sequence of the support of minimal events.* The experience and its support are a continually changing state constructed from a trail of 'fading' minimal events in the support. In this way the integrated and indivisible visual state is better described as a sequence where two states in a sequence have a great deal in common but do not transgress the 'uniqueness' property.

- *Visual memory implies that the neural support has memory, that is, it is an automaton in which the j referent can be internally controlled from another part of the brain.* It is quite possible to imagine a landscape, say, and describe what is on the left and what is on the right. This means that the state of the support automaton retains the j referent as part of the states in its state structure (more of this later in this chapter).

The spirit of the paper (in line with the spirit of the Zeki and Bartels contribution) is that it highlights a list of requirements from neural machinery which appear to satisfy the introspection of what a visual state actually feels like. This led us to attempt to incorporate these insights into a functional computer model, a description of which continues the story here.

An experiment in artificial visual awareness

The material in this section describes what has been done with a simulation (called NRM — neural representation modeler) developed in 2000 at Imperial College by Barry Dunmall. It is intended to illustrate how the iconically trained networks (as discussed in Chapter 5, particularly Figs. 5.1 and 5.2) may form part of a mechanism that has some of the characteristics of the visual system discussed in this chapter. This helps us to conclude the chapter with a discussion of what it is to have a unique and indivisible mental state in as a distributed a set of mechanisms as appears to exist in the brain.

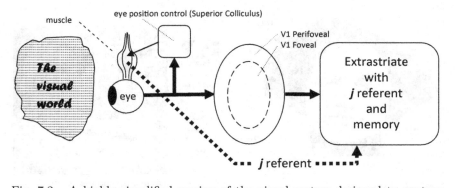

Fig. 7.2. A highly simplified version of the visual system designed to capture some of the dynamics of the mechanisms that lead to a world-representing visual state.

Figure 7.2 shows the structure that was implemented in NRM. It is designed to study the dynamics that lead to a reconstruction of a visual mental state through a searching action of the fovea. The eye position control system plays the role of the superior colliuilus and receives a retinotopic low-resolution mapping which identifies the position of firing areas in the overall visual field. This causes the eye 'muscle' to act and move the fovea to these firing areas. The muscle also generates the j referent which is used to 'gaze-lock' cells in the high-acuity network that plays the role of the extrastriate cortex. In the original model this received color signals from the high resolution network that plays the role of a fovea (see Fig. 7.3). The extrastriate model has a variable number of re-entrant connections which determine the long term memory for representations in this area. The perifoveal (outside the fovea) model is shown to indicate the points of firing which also stimulate the superior colliculus model. The display for this system and some of the network parameters are shown in Fig. 7.3.

We now report on some experiments that illustrate some of the properties of this structure which has been called the VISAW (VISual AWereness) model.

Experiment 1: iconic memory

Iconic learning in the system takes place in concert with the j-referent. This referent selects the area of the extrastriate model according to the eye position and uses the foveal content as an input to that area. Then iconic

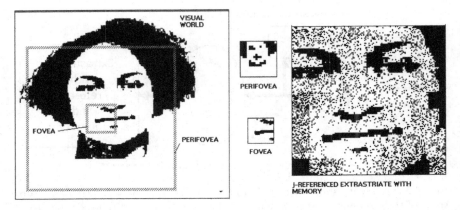

Fig. 7.3.   Display of the simulation of the scheme of Fig. 7.2. The **visual world** is simulated as an 8-color frame of 272×272 (73,948) 3-bit pixels. The **perifovea** is has a resolution of only 17×17 (289) 3-bit pixels while the **fovea** has 48×48 (2,304) 3-bit pixels. Each pixel is the 3-bit output of a weightless neuron with 32, 3-bit inputs and 32, 3-bit re-entrant connections (enabling iconic memory creation). For technical reasons, the fovea cannot visit the entire visual world as the perifovea hits the edges hence the area shown as the 'extrastriate with memory' is restricted.

learning takes place in the sense that the foveal input image is transferred to the selected patch and made stable as a result of re-entrant connections (see Chapter 6 for the single-net case). This is a process which keeps going as the eye moves, eventually covering the entire extrastriate area. Experiment 1 is designed to illustrate that a coherent stable memory state is created (an attractor, indeed) in the state space of the extrastriate model. Figure 7.4 shows the results of a test carried out after the system had learned six-face images under the eye-movement regime.

In a very vague sense, one could describe this experiment as being related to the case of a person waking up in a darkened room and becoming aware (in a noisy sort of way) of a memory. In technological fact, however, all that this experiment shows is that the j-referent machinery had successfully achieved iconic learning over an area much greater than that covered by the foveal patch. The noisy nature of the remembered image results from black input from the foveal area. What happens if VISAW is now exposed to one of the visual inputs used in its training?

Experiment 2: from memory to awareness

Starting with the extrastriate memory state shown in step 50 of Fig. 7.4, the system is faced with visual input as shown in step 1 of Fig. 7.5.

As seen in the rest of Fig. 7.5, a stimulus is built up in the extrastriate model which, after about 20 steps, has altered sufficient 'patches' for the entire model to fall into the appropriate attractor state which is the 'remembered' visualisation of the input.

Here we again stress that this is not meant to be a close analog of what occurs in the living brain. It is a demonstration that the dynamic properties of a neural network with re-entrant connections can switch from being in remembered world-representing states to a perceptual representation. That is, as the system is building a percept from the j-referenced saccading foveal image, previous iconcally learned percepts can be reconstructed. It is interesting to note that such relatively complex mechanisms could be at work in the living brain in order to resolve the problem of awareness of more than the foveal patch. This kind of modeling is just a (slightly naïve) beginning. We consider below what future directions this might take, taking particular account of the uniqueness and indivisibility demanded of a state for it to qualify as a *mental* state.

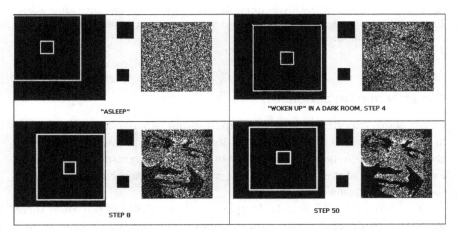

Fig. 7.4. A memory test on the VIAW model. Top left shows an 'asleep' state with the j-referent mechanism paralysed. The rest shows the emergence of one of the face images out of the noise in the extrastriate model under conditions of no visual input.

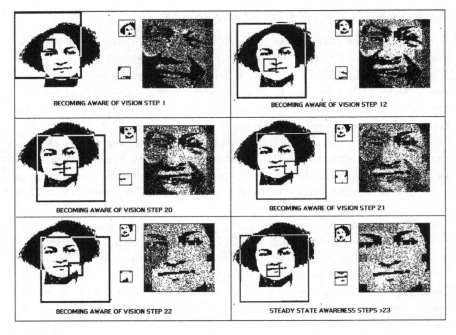

Fig. 7.5. Introducing visual input while VISAW is in a memory state. Areas of the state are altered by the foveal input driven by the j-referent until after about 20 steps the state switches into a reconstruction of what is remembered of the previously seen input image.

The stream of experience

In the above experiments the build-up of visual experience in the VISAW model was based on an adaptation of iconic learning to eye movement and the j-referent. We now look at a way in which an organism might develop its structure of states by exploring its world more extensively than merely through eye movement.[20]

If an entity (say, E) is to build up a visual experience of the world there needs to be a division between an exploratory 'perceptual' activity during

---

[20]We introduced this topic in: Aleksander I. and Morton, H. B. (2007). Phenomenology and digital neural architectures, *Neur. Network.* **20**(9), 932–937, 2007.

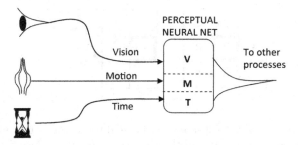

Fig. 7.6. A perceptual dynamic neural net which builds a state structure of experience through iconic learning of vision, motion and time.

which experience is built up and a time when this experience is put to use in what might be called an 'imaginative' activity. The simple system in Fig. 7.6 is used to discuss this. We stress more than ever that the system as shown is *not* intended to be a model of architectures found in the brain, but a suggestion for mechanisms that might be at work in conjunction with much else. So, it may be best to think of E as some form of highly simplified animal or robot.

Perceptual experience: Iconic movement and time

Looking at Fig. 7.6, we assume that part of the perceptual net will be iconically trained (see Chapter 5) to sequence of visual states $v = (v_1, v_2, v_3, \ldots)$. During the lifetime of E it is unlikely that any two such states will recur as precise copies of one another. There could, however, be similarities according to some criterion (such as Hamming distance — see footnote 38 in Chapter 3 for a definition of this measure).

We introduce an m-referent which is a neural state that represents a totality of movement (head movement and body locomotion) which changes the total perceptual input, from what is seen in one position to what is seen in another. (Where the j-referent leads to a reconstruction in space, the m-referent leads to a reconstruction in time. Because directions of movement are items we remember alongside the visual experience gathered during exploration, we suggest that movements are iconically transferred to the perceptual net and informationally integrated (i.e., making indivisible and unique states) with vision. An example will clarify this, but first, what is the nature of the time input?

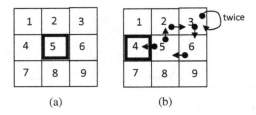

(a)   (b)

Fig. 7.7.   (a) A world of 3×3 squares. The bold frame shows the position of the organism E which moves in this world. (b) The trajectory performed as described in the text.

The inclusion of time as part of the integrated mental state is a tricky move. Despite much research, little is known of the neural basis of time perception.[21] It is sufficient for our purposes to assume that an ever advancing, non-repeating signal reaches the perceptual neural net of Fig. 7.6. Perhaps this signal is a mixture of internal neural activity recording advancing time, taken together with external sensory input, such as seeing watches and calendars, (contributing to the creation of the iconic state). Let these signals be a very large set (limited only by the lifetime of the individual), $t = (t_1, t_2, t_3, \ldots)$. Consider a very simple world consisting of a set of 3×3 square positions as shown in Fig. 7.7. An organism is capable of moving from square to square according to the movement set $m = (n, e, s, w, q)$ (that is, the four cardinal directions and q, a quiescent or non-motion state).

To describe a build-up of state structure, we note that each state has the three components

$$S_j = (v_j m_j t_j)$$

It is also noted that once the three components have occurred at the input and the state is created iconically, the components are no longer independent within the state which is integrated by having the appropriate parameters in the neural net. But what causes the organism to move? In this case we assume that the entity E performs an exploratory trip. For this

[21]Le Poidevin R. (2011). The experience and perception of time, in Edward N. Zalta (Ed.) *The Stanford Encyclopedia of Philosophy.* Fall Edn. See http://plato. stanford.edu/archives/fall2011/entries/time-experience/.

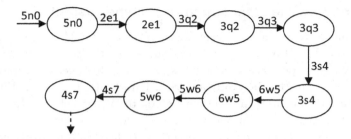

Fig. 7.8. The state diagram learned as a result of applying the movement sequence. We recall that the label on the transition arrows represents the non-integrated input while the label in the states is unique and indivisible.

we assume that there exists unspecified neural machinery which acts on the muscles and that the muscles move E and create the motion signal in Fig. 7.6. For exploration, say that this machinery produces a random set of movements:

$$n, e, q, q, s, w, w$$

This leads to the state structure shown in Fig. 7.8, which is created as follows. E starts at time $t = 0$ in position 5 receiving a muscular signal for moving $n(orth)$. The individual input signals are shown on the arrow leading to the state which is iconically created and integrated as a result of a sufficiently 'integrating' set of interconnections in the network.

We note that the 'halt' in position 3 enters the state structure as two different states distinguished in time. Also at time 6 a state indicating a return to position 5 is found. But this is distinguished from the entry to position 5 at time 0 by the time label and the direction.

The upshot of all this is that a stream of experience is created that extends both in space within a limited perceptual field and in time. This provides an experience of being in an external environment. In the book 'The world in my mind...'[22] this has been called Axiom 1: the sensation of being in an 'out-there' world.

---

[22] Aleksander I. (2005). *The World in my Mind, my Mind in the World Key Mechanisms of Consciousness in People, Animals and Machines* (Imprint Academic, Exeter).

Memory: How the state structure becomes useful

Were someone to ask an experienced user of the London Underground, 'How do you get from Finchley Road Station, to South Kensington Station?' speaking from experience he might answer 'Normally, I get the Jubilee Line and change on to the Piccadilly at Green Park Station, but sometimes the Piccadilly line has problems so then I go on to Westminster on the Jubilee Line and change on to the District and Circle Line'. The memory of the experience he describes relies on properties of the neural network one finds in the example of Figs. 7.7 and 7.8.

Memory means one thing: whatever might be the remembered mental state, it is not driven entirely by its perceptual inputs. Looking at Fig. 7.8, this is like removing the labels on the arrows. Does the automaton still follow the same state path and so recall its past experience? The answer is 'yes' due to the generalization properties of the neurons in the net (see Chapter 3, p. 25). This means that even if a substantial part of the input to the neural net is missing, the net can still follow the learned state sequence. To access the remembered stream, the net needs somehow to be placed into one of its previously experienced states. One possible way for this to happen is for a visual input to be presented for a short time evoking a state within the stream by the net 'falling' into a state in that has the most closely corresponding visual field. Another way to induce a visual state is for some linguistic input to cause an entry into some relevant visual state such as for 'Finchley Road Station'.[23] During the memory act, the network relies on its acquired state structure to 'imagine' the experience of previous train journeys. The important feature of the 'underground' example above, is that the underground user indicates that he is aware of both paths that lead to the end point.

But what does it mean to say 'he is aware of both paths'? The simplest mechanism would require that most mental trajectories are traversed several times. Due to the presence of noise, when a mental state is reached that can lead forward to different paths during different traversals over a period

---

[23]In writing this book we made a conscious decision not to enter the difficult but intriguing topic of the neural correlates of language. So, how the net might enter the visual 'Finchley Road' state for an auditory input is not detailed further. Suffice it to say that audition can be treated as an enlargement of the perceptual state that can be integrated into the states of the stream discussed in the text.

of time, all alternatives will be visited and the result described. But modeling these 'which path shall I choose' moments is, at the time of writing, still a matter of research both in neurology[24] and neural modeling.[25]

From the Foveal patch to a visual mind

The theme of this chapter has been to argue the possible existence of neural mechanisms that are responsible for the creation of a visual mind. What is the secret? It is the integration of movement signals with perceptual ones. At the lowest level it is the integration of eye movement signals with foveal patch information that allows a view of the world wider than that of the foveal patch to be constructed. This relies on a reconstruction of the visual world in the *physical space* of a neural system. Then a similar principle is suggested for the creation of a reconstruction of experience in the *state space* of a dynamic neural system. This makes use not only of movement signals, but also of time. The result is an ordered set of states that is continually extended as the organism 'lives' in its world and gathers information about it.

The significance of information integration becomes clear if we think of 'uniqueness' and 'indivisibility' which are both necessary to create the state structure that holds the experience of the entity. As the structure develops and new perceptions are incorporated, the adjustment of (learning in) the neural net depends on the amount of information that the new percept implies. While this type of theory is part of current research concerns, such information may be related to the likelihood that the percept had been encountered before. In other words, while the state structure consists of distinguishable (i.e., unique) states, incoming percepts have a variable degree of similarity. In Shannonian terms, this is the amount of 'surprise' carried by the new event. In the future, it may be possible to develop an informational model of experience acquisition and retention based on the information carried by these similarities. Outside of any intrinsic interest, this might be useful in diagnosis in a clinical context. It may also be of use

---

[24]Ernst M. and Paulus M. P. (2005). Neurobiology of decision making: A selective review from a neurocognitive and clinical perspective, *Biol. Psych.* **58**(8), 597–604.

[25]Balleine B. W. (2007). The neural basis of choice and decision making, *J. Neurosci.* **27**(31), 8159–8160.

Fig. 7.9. Recalled states for a network trained on the images of Fig. 5.3 with neural connections that are too local and hence lose indivisibility.

to designers of cognitive robots as they might match the size of a necessary neural system to the amount of information contained in the world in which the robot is to behave coherently.

Indivisibility too is essential for simple reasons. First, were the neural system not sufficiently integrated, the mental life may have the characteristics of confused depictions made up of different percepts. Figure 7.8 shows how a network in which causal connections are too localized, creates states that are confusions of the learned patterns. Indivisibility has been lost resulting in states that become of no use in the decision-making process of the entity. Indeed, the structure of connected states is entirely destroyed.

Overall, the ability of a net to integrate is essential to the creation of a mental state structure which reflects experience and, in this way enables the entity to 'live' in its world in an ever more knowledgeable way.

The informational mind hypothesis

In the way of a summary for this chapter, we consider what has been said about the creation of visual mental states and attempt a succinctly worded hypothesis for the informational mind. (The topics in *italics* have been developed earlier in the book).

Informational mind hypothesis (IMH)

The mind of an entity is the *state structure* of specialized parts of a neural brain (living or artificial), created through *iconic learning*. These areas are characterized by two features. First, they are able to create world-representing states by compensating for the muscular action of the body which is used in exploring this world. Second, such specific areas of the brain have interconnections that exhibit sufficiently high values of *information integration* to ensure both that the states of the state structure generate information by being *unique* and that they are capable of representing causal relationships by being *indivisible*.

Corollary: Integrated state structures exist not only in space but also in time. States may group together in sequence to form an integrated state trajectory.

The key feature of this hypothesis is that it 'reduces' mind to an informational state structure. This can be contrasted with the reduction of mind to the physical structure of the brain (as in neurophilosophy) or its reduction to an information processing algorithm as discussed in the next chapter.

Chapter 8

THE INFORMATIONAL MIND: OXYMORON OR NEW SCIENCE?

Not all contemporary thinkers jump with joy at the announcement that a mind might be 'informational'. For example Raymond Tallis, gerontologist and prolific author of philosophical texts, makes the following observation:

> ... 'information' is absolutely pivotal to establishing the conceptual confusions... of much modern thought about the mind and the brain.[1]

Susan Greenfield, pharmacologist at the University of Oxford and commentator on matters relating to the brain has said (as Baroness Greenfield) in an address to the House of Lords bemoaning overexposure to communication:

> I suggest that social networking sites might tap into the basic brain systems for delivering pleasurable experience. However, these experiences are devoid of cohesive narrative and long-term significance. As a consequence, the mid-21st century mind might almost be infantilised, characterised by short attention spans, sensationalism, inability to empathise and a shaky sense of identity ... (House of Lords, February 12, 2009).

One of the founders of the pursuit of the Philosophy of Information, Luciano Floridi, of Oxford and Hertfordshire Universities, concludes one of his seminal papers with:

> The problem is that we still have to agree about what information is exactly.[2]

---

[1]http://www.palgrave-journals.com/jit/journal/v23/n1/full/2000128a.html.
[2]Floridi L. (2011). *The Philosophy of Information* (Oxford University Press, Oxford).

These concerns are not new. Theodore Roszak a historian and cult figure of the 1980s in *The Cult of Information: The Folklore of Computers and the True Art of Thinking* (1986) wrote:

> *The mind thinks with ideas and not information.*[3]

This chapter looks at these attacks and attempts to sharpen the validity of an 'informational mind' through addressing the concerns that these objections represent.

Information: Cutting down on the confusion

Clearly the claim that minds have anything to do with information is controversial. Sadly the controversy comes from advocates and detractors not always thinking of the same thing when the word 'information' is used. One of the objectives of this book is to suggest that looking for informational structures and understanding clearly what is meant by this approach would be a helpful step toward an agreement about what the mind is and what supports it. We believe that the pronouncements quoted above, are not made out of blind antipathy toward 'information', but out of a true concern that using it in conjunction with mind is inappropriate. Here we look at the concerns created by the use of the word and address the most acute among them. We try not to enter into adversarial debates with the info-sceptics, but analyse their points of view in the spirit that a shared understanding of 'information' might be mutually helpful. We therefore set out to explore the objections raised by each of the above four commentators in turn.

Raymond Tallis (1946–)

Described by John Crace of the Guardian as an 'irrepressible geriatrician'[4] Ray Tallis had early ambitions to be a research biochemist and follow the wake of Crick and Watson to 'discover the secrets of life'. He studied medicine as a necessary pre-requisite to biochemistry and discovered that he was a good doctor. The secrets of life took a different meaning when, specializing in gerontology, he saw life and consciousness as being wholly

---

[3]Roszak T. (1986). *The Cult of Information* (Pantheon Books, New York).
[4]Crace J. (2008). *The Guardian*, 3 June.

meaningful to the living and conscious individual. Attempts at scientific analysis, he found, were inadequate to come to grips with the real meaning of what it is to live and be conscious.

Crace tells of Tallis' passion for writing which he did in early mornings while spending the rest of the day working in the hospital. His first book to be accepted for publication was on post-modernist philosophy. Entitled '*Not Sassure*', it was to be followed by a vast number of texts and articles. He describes himself as a humanist, and a staunch defender of the idea that the elements of human life are to be approached through human compassion rather than theory. In conjunction with information and computing, Tallis has focused his suspicion of theoretical analysis on computer scientists who claim to capture 'mind' through informational theories. This is summarized in a little book called '*Why the Mind is Not a Computer*' (WMNC).[5] Tallis' position does not stem from a mistrust of the use of the word 'information' but from a more general suspicion of the appropriateness of available scientific methodology for exploring issues that are fundamentally in the domain of the philosophy of mind, that is in the domain of discussion rather than dissection and formal analysis. He worries about the sidelining of free philosophical argument in deference to the scientific approach. He reacts negatively to attempts to describe consciousness through any form of formal analysis whether this is linguistic theory, neuroscience or the informational sciences, including computing. He thinks that philosophers of the 1950s and 1960s had buckled under the expectation that they should *admire* the scientific method and develop their philosophy accordingly. He questions the work of philosophers Daniel Dennett[6] and Patricia Churchland[7] for having 'emptied' the notion of consciousness of content (for example, beliefs and desires) by having replaced it with computational processes such as 'reactive dispositions' and 'information processing'. The criticism applies both to the logic that might be found in a computing algorithm and to the pattern recognition properties of neural nets.

We find we agree with many of Tallis' concerns. The admiration of computational science found in Dennett's and Churchland's discourses on the

[5]Tallis R. (2004). *Why the Mind is Not a Computer: A Pocket Lexicon of Neuromythology* (Imprint Academic, Exeter).
[6]Dennett D.C. (1991). *Consciousness Explained* (Little, Brown, Boston, MA).
[7]Churchland P. (1986). *Neurophilosophy, Towards a Unified Theory of the Mind/Brain* (MIT Press, Cambridge, MA).

nature of mind do, as Tallis claims, eliminate some important questions of qualia and self. But Tallis goes on to claim that the scientific method in general and the information sciences in particular are inappropriate for such questions. In 2008, Tallis and one of the present authors (IA) had a public debate on whether conventional computational ideas may or may not be helpful in discussions about consciousness.[8] Here we wish to relate this discussion to the points made in this book. Specifically, we argue that informational analysis *is* the appropriate language with which to gain insights into the mind. But informational analysis is not only Shannon's theory of communication, nor is it information processing or artificial intelligence. However, we do argue that 'the informational mind' has more to offer than the 'information processing' metaphor which Tallis finds inappropriate. With contemporary informational theories of networks, far from being ignored, 'qualia' and 'selves' come within their exploratory orbits.[9]

One of Tallis' targets is an attack on 'neurophilosophy', that is, the use of neurophysiology to explore questions in philosophy, particularly the philosophy of mind. He writes (WMNC, p. 23):

> ... *Neurophilosophy cannot accommodate those things that make human beings distinctively human.*

Neurophilosophy is also in the title of Patricia Churchland's influential 1986 book which sows the seeds of a 'mind-is-brain' attitude and the idea that consciousness can be discovered through some neural correlates. Many followed in the wake of this enthusiasm including Francis Crick, Christ of Koch and others in the 'scientific study of consciousness' movement which made seeking the 'neural correlates of consciousness' into a fashionable science. While Tallis would accept that a brain scan might reveal whether a person is awake (conscious) or asleep (not conscious) he would understandably argue that it will not reveal whether when awake she or he is a content or an unhappy individual. While the neural correlates of experiencing pain might be found by experimentation, those of feeling the pain of being rejected by

---

[8]Tallis R. and Aleksander I. (2008). Computer models of the mind are invalid, *J. Inform. Technol.* **23**, 55–62.
[9]Qualia are discussed in Chapter 6 of this book while 'self' is the subject of Axiom 1 of a previous publication: Aleksander I. (2005). *The World In My Mind, My Mind In The World: Key Mechanisms of Consciousness In Humans, Animals and Machines* (Imprint Academic, Exeter). It also features in this chapter.

a lover cannot. It is the latter and many other elements of consciousness like it, which Tallis sees as not being accommodated by neurophilosophy.

Some of these extreme examples actually allow us to highlight what might be a source of confusion: explanations of mechanisms which support thought get confused with explanations of what thought might be about. In neurophilosophy, an 'explanation' of consciousness is an attempt to relate conscious experience to what is known of the physics, chemistry and (micro)biology of the brain. But, as Tallis rightly notes, this fails to provide an account on how thought is *about* something, of how it has a special niche for the *self,* and how it provides an *awareness* that enables the animal (human, if you like) to go about its everyday life. This confusion arises because to 'explain' consciousness or even just aspects of it can mean a variety of things. How anything can be conscious at all needs a very different explanation from how consciousness acquires meaning. Churchland's argument reduces the mental state to the physical state of the brain. According to this all we need do to understand consciousness is to understand the properties of some parts of the brain. Churchland published her book on neurophilosophy at about the time that 'connectionism' (a study of neural networks) became fashionable.[10] She saw connectionist ideas as corroborating her 'mind-is-brain' theme. But most of the work in the connectionist paradigm concentrates on the *recognition* properties of neural nets and the dynamics of neural nets with feedback loops without reference to consciousness.

In this book, we have argued that while a conscious sensation has to have neural correlates, the parts of the brain which are involved have to exhibit some highly specific properties. Looking at the Informational Mind Hypothesis (IMH) at the end of the last chapter, this involves the integration of muscular control signals, iconic learning and a capacity for integration. These conditions directly address the problems of mental content. Iconic learning integrated with muscular control information creates a 'self' that senses its embedding in the 'out-there world'. That is, a model based on this hypothesis would have as part of its state structure the sequence

---

[10]Rumelhart D. E., McClelland J. L., and the PDP Research Group (1986). *Parallel Distributed Processing: Explorations in the Microstructure of Cognition. Volume 1: Foundations* (MIT Press, Cambridge, MA); McClelland J. L., Rumelhart D. E. and the PDP Research Group (1986). *Parallel Distributed Processing: Explorations in the Microstructure of Cognition. Volume 2: Psychological and Biological Models*, Cambridge, MA: MIT Press.

of iconic states which, given language, it would describe as 'I have got to Finchley Road station'. Or, in a memory mode, 'I know what steps it takes to get to Finchley Road station'. We note that the use of the 'I' is not a 'faked' artefact. Any computer could be programmed to output 'I have done this or that'. But this is not the case with the IMH model since it would include a mechanism to represent its own presence in the world as based on the integration of muscular action signals with perceptual ones.[11] In summary, the content of conscious experience exists in two forms. There is the perceptual network, well capable of integration, which is stimulated by the novelty of a perceptual experience. From this develops the second form, the addition of a state to the linear state structure (see Chapter 7), which causes the growth of a structure of states that represent, in an iconic way, a life of meaningful experiences.

So, Tallis' criticisms of neurophilosophy actually encourages us to develop a theory that searches for parts of the neural brain which have the ability to integrate the action of musculature which controls the perception of the world with the perception itself. This is in contrast with blanket beliefs that 'mind is what brain does' as found in traditional neurophilosophy. So, mind is a state structure which is created by an informational integration of action, perception and neural adaptation in very specific areas of the brain. We make no apology for having used the words 'the informational mind': carefully defined, 'information', rather than creating the confusions suggested by Tallis, could be the stuff that a sensible explanation of 'mind' is made of.

Susan Greenfield (1950–)

An Oxford University pharmacologist, Susan Greenfield has become known to the greater public for her spirited and enthusiastic commentaries on brain, mind, consciousness, education, the internet and much else in the media. She does not shun controversy and has recently raised concern of

---

[11]We are not forgetting here the 'mirror neuron' discussion [Rizzolatti G. and Craighero L. (2004). The mirror-neuron system, *Annual Rev. Neurosci.* **27**, 169–192.] where neurons normally used for motor actions respond to an observation of motor actions in others. We find that such single neuron discoveries fit in with the idea of an integrated state of experience and play their part in concert with much other neural activity in other specialized areas of the brain.

the way that children's use of informational technologies may hamper their normal thought processes. In many ways, her pronouncements are not only influential in shaping public opinion in science, but also (in issues other than neuropharmacology in which she is an expert) are representative of a view of science from a commentator's rather than the researcher's point of view. Here we review some of Susan Greenfield'sideas to the extent that they impinge on the 'informational mind'.

Though she is sceptical of the benefits of the internet, an internet search for 'Susan Greenfield' produces a veritable abundance of material with which to make her acquaintance. She grew up in suburban London and, being brilliant at school, slid easily into Oxford University completing her education with a DPhil. in Pharmacology. Then, as a lecturer in synaptic pharmacology she researched Alzheimer's and Parkinson's diseases, founding a pharmaceutical company which addresses these diseases.[12]

Susan Greenfield made her first TV impact in the UK by being the first woman to give the Royal Institution Christmas Lectures in 1994. In 1998, she became the Director of the Royal Institution, an appointment that was to come to an end amid considerable controversy in 2010. In 2001, she was made a member of the House of Lords as Baroness Greenfield of Ot Moor through the then new process of electing 'people's peers'. While her most recent discourse is directed at the doubtful value of information on the internet and the possible detrimental effects this might have on children, we first look at her views on the conscious mind and attempts to understand it. Soon after the publication of her third book on mind and brain (*The Private Mind of the Brain*),[13] Greenfield began to consolidate her views on mind brain and consciousness. In a useful, short position paper, she distinguishes between the words 'brain', 'mind' and 'consciousness' as she wishes them to be used.[14] Brain ('obviously needs no definition'), she suggests, offers little scope for individual personalization. That is, while there are individual differences between the physical structures of individual brains, this does

---

[12]http://www.fortunecity.com/emachines/e11/86/duncan1.html.

[13]Greenfield S. A. (2000). *The Private Life of the Brain* (London, Penguin Books). The other two being Greenfield S. A. (1995). *Journey to the Centers of the Mind: Toward a Science of Consciousness* (W.H. Freeman, San Francisco); Greenfield S. A. (1997). *The Human Brain: A Guided Tour*. Science Masters Series. (Basic Books, New York).

[14]Greenfield S. A. (2002). Mind, brain and consciousness, *Brit. J. Psych.* **181**, 91–93.

not account for the differences in their personalities. So how do personality differences arise? Greenfield has an intuition of what we call integration between specific areas of the brain, noting that such areas do not operate autonomously, but do so in some form of concert. It is in the links between areas, and in the neural structures within them, that differences can occur since they are driven by the acquired experience of an individual which creates the diversity in personalities. That which personalizes the brain is then defined as a 'mind'. Being an expert in the function of synapses,[15] Greenfield finds the mind among them: '[it is] the process whereby connections [the synapses] so exquisitely mirror what happens to us, that I would call the mind.' This is followed by a belief that these changing physical connections 'reflect experience', an idea that must be treated with some care. While it is true that connection strengths between neurons at the synapses change, the time they need to change is much longer (minutes) than the rapidity with which our mental states can change (fractions of a second). There is also a permanent element in these synaptic changes, which would leave the mind much less flexible than it appears to be.

We recall that iconic learning and the involvement of motor activity have the capacity to change synaptic strengths to make the *state structure* (*not* the physical structure) of these networks become the repository of experience (see Chapters 5 and 7). States within this state structure have a direct coding of sensory experience and so become good candidates for the sought-after *phenomenal* 'mental state' or part thereof (see Chapter 5). But having chosen synapses as the parameters of mind leads Greenfield to distinguish 'consciousness' from 'mind', as follows.

For Greenfield, consciousness is a matter of how much the synapses are encouraged into action by so called 'global neurons' which, rather than firing in electrical impulses express their activity by squirting 'neuromodulator' chemicals at the synapses[16] to achieve global regulation of bodily (sometimes emotional) function. Greenfield suggests that consciousness then becomes a variable affair depending on the amount of diffusion of neuromodulators that is taking place (more of neuromodulators in Chapter 9). This enables greater (more diffusion) or smaller assemblies of neurons to

---

[15]Remembering that they are the variable-strength connections between neurons in which learning and adaptation of the brain is thought to occur (see Chapter 3).
[16]Serotonin (digestion regulation primarily), dopamine (motivation, movement and other effects) and noradrenaline (responsiveness and fear).

be 'recruited' in the cause of being conscious. In her view, small assemblies occur in childhood and in dreaming, while overlarge assemblies may be associated with depression since, presumably, there is less sensitivity to external sensory input, and the individual therefore remains dull and feels cut off from the outside world.

In common with similar theories, which Crick and Koch later called 'coalitions of neurons'[17] and Tononi called 'complexes',[18] Greenfield's 'recruitment' (of neurons) model of consciousness is not convincing as a source of phenomenology: 'accessing' synapses is neither clear as a functional mechanism nor does it indicate how such access can lead to being conscious of the details of 'the world out there' as it is now and as it was experienced in the past. Again we suggest that the informational model of the state structure discussed in Chapter 7 resonates a little better with how consciousness feels introspectively. Consciousness does not 'feel' like the waxing and waning of pools of neural activity, even if such waxing and waning may have something to do with how alert we might feel.

We now return to the quote at the top of this chapter: communicating on the internet (specifically through social networking), Greenfield claims, can harm children's brains by destroying curiosity. To dig deeper into this, we took a look at the many interviews that were given by Susan Greenfield both at the time of the above speech in the House of Lords (February 2009), and right up to the moment of writing this chapter (August 2011).[19–22] There are two issues here that impinge on the concept of an 'informational mind': first, is there a distinction to be made between information and knowledge, and second, in what way could brains be affected by any informational interactions so as to result in sub-standard minds?

---

[17]Crick F. and Koch C. (2003). A framework for consciousness, *Nature Neurosci.* **6**(2), 119–126.

[18]Tononi G. (2008). Consciousness as integrated information: A provisional manifesto, *Biol. Bull.* **215**, 216–242.

[19]Wintour P (2009). Facebook and Bebo risk 'infantilising' the human mind', www.guardian.co.uk, 24 February.

[20]Swain F (2011). Susan Greenfield: Living online is changing our brains, *New Scientist*, 3 August.

[21]McVeigh T (2011). Fury as scientist suggests autism link to internet, *The Observer*, 7 August.

[22]Robbins M. (2011). Has Susan Greenfield been represented? www.guardian.co.uk, 8 August.

Using Greenfield'smetaphors of synapse changing and the creation of assemblies of neural activity (pooling), she could be interpreted as saying that a rich and varied interaction between a person's experiences of learning to live in the world and among other people is the best way of ensuring the right amount of synapse changing for the right amount of pooling to take place. The 'right amount' is apparently defined by what people have been doing before getting enmeshed in the internet: reading books, playing, learning to defend themselves in an affray, being intrepid explorers of the world and the universe, listening to their teachers, and so on. Greenfield seems to be saying that the advent of digital communication technology carries the dangers that the real world is being replaced by text, sounds and movies where the effort of having experiences is reduced to the drag of a mouse and the click of a button.

Looking now to the IMH (Informational Mind Hypothesis) of Chapter 7, where conscious states form an informational structure, suggests the following key question. Is true knowledge created through the development of a state structure by the exploration of the real world using purposeful muscular action, whereas discovering things through the internet somehow creates inferior experiential states? In technical terms, it is the movement information part of the iconic state (see Fig. 7.6 in Chapter 7) which is downplayed in internet activity. But the same downplay pertains to a student swatting for his final law or veterinary science finals both of which require much handling of books, the turning of pages and the internalising of text (with no music or movies). With younger children, books still seem pretty popular, and with children who use social network sites the build-up of state structure might actually be enriched by the communication with other individuals. It is not clear how communicating via Facebook, say, is so much worse that communicating face-to-face. To have the possibility of both, only seems to enhance.[23]

Of course, were a child to learn by being spliced to the internet to the exclusion of all else — no school, no sport, no play-dates, no holidays by the seaside, no arguments with sibling and so on — then a very peculiar state structure would be created. But this is not a scenario that is imposed by the presence of the internet. While its presence certainly influences the state structures of the minds of those who use it, it is hard to argue that

---

[23]Families and friends spread around the world find social networking particularly valuable.

alongside the dominant effect of the rest of life, this is necessarily a negative influence. Technically, what do informational models say about how easy access to information will stop children from questioning things and so restrict their gathering of knowledge? In this book, we have not addressed in any depth the drives in a human being that affect the motor actions which determine the development of the iconic state structure. But to get a simple steer on what might happen, consider a general mechanism which needs to choose between action alternatives. Say that the mechanism is in a room with two doors, and what is behind one door is well-known, whereas what lies behind the other is totally uncertain. It seems reasonable to assume that a good move for survival is to select the action that resolves most uncertainty, that is, the action which gains most information.[24] We suggest that the drive to resolve uncertainty is a process that seeks information to create knowledge. That is, the individual's natural drive to develop its state structure will drive it to where it gains most whether this is the internet, libraries or sitting at the knee of a guru.

Luciano Floridi (1964–)

His name is synonymous with the subject of the *philosophy of information*.[25,26] A classically educated philosopher, Floridi was born in Rome where he studied to MA level, before moving to the University of Warwick in the UK to complete his PhD. At the time of writing he holds a post at the University of Hertfordshire and additionally a special post at the University of Oxford. He is not critical of information as a science, on the contrary, he feels that there is still much to be explored by having a clearly defined philosophy in the area.

---

[24]This is reminiscent of the 'choice corollary' in George Kelly's Personal Construct Theory of personality growth [Kelly G. A. (1955). *The Psychology of Personal Constructs*. Vol. I, II [Norton, New York (2nd printing: 1991, Routledge, London, New York)]. The corollary states: 'a person chooses for himself that alternative in a dichotomized construct through which he anticipates the greater possibility for extension and definition of his system.'

[25]Floridi L. (2011). *The Philosophy of Information* (Oxford University Press, Oxford).

[26]Floridi has also published a compact version of his outlook as, Floridi L. (2009). Philosophical theories of information, in Sommaruga G. (Ed.) *Formal Theories of Information, LNCS 5363* (Springer-Verlag, Berlin, Heidelberg), pp. 13–53. It is this shorter publication that was the source for the present paper.

Floridi points to two features of information which attract his attention: first, the word has a polymorphic character — it is used differently in different contexts and hence is philosophically difficult but interesting. Second, while there are theories that address the technicalities of transmission and efficiency, there is still a lack of an information theory which encompasses meaning, that is a *semantic* theory. In reviewing these ideas, philosophical and computational, he attempts to create a set of taxonomic definitions of information designed to include semantics. He suggests a *General Definition of Information* (GDI), where 'information' is defined as a well-structured group of *data*. 'Data' is a term which he defines further. A *datum* can either be (a) something that creates a background/foreground distinction (e.g., a fly, distinguished from its background of a wall), or (b) the state of an object (a large fly compared with a small one), or (c) something that leads to a symbolic distinction with respect to other data (e.g., distinguishing the letter A from letter B in the alphabet gives both A and B a semantic value).

Data can be of different kinds:

- *Primary*, such as a street address stored in a computer database;
- *Secondary*, negative, in the sense that something is missing, as the case when a search for an address in a database returns a nil result;
- *Metadata*, such as 'the address is in a 192.com database';
- *Operational*, the signaled presence of a computer virus may mean that the sought street address may be wrong;
- *Derivative*, meaning that it is gathered from many facts such as various clues in a murder investigation which indicate that the butler did it.

Floridi's philosophy goes on to suggest that for information to exist at all, it must somehow be physically represented. And yet, this physical representation must not be confused with the notion that information *has* physical correlates on which the massage depends. Smoke signals from one hilltop to the next have different physical properties from, say, a mirror made to flash in the sun, but the information they transmit could be exactly the same. That is, to understand the message, one needs to know the agreed code and *not* the physics of smoke or mirrors.

In his discussion, Floridi addresses the age-old question of information that is not generated by a human mind. He calls this *environmental information*, and this includes the possibility of two systems being coupled to one another in some fashion and thus being said to be in informational contact. Many automatic control systems work in this way. An aeroplane on automatic control can be said to fly to its destination using its direction controls which are *informed* by (and reacting appropriately to) the position sensors indicating any discrepancy (due to wind, say) from the desired trajectory. Commenting on Shannon's Mathematical Theory of Communication, Floridi points out that even though it specifically excludes semantics, it still has value in semantic systems as it relates informative content to the degree of surprise carried in the meaning. This is central to theories of integration of information and will be visited again in the last chapter. For now, we still need to get to the heart of Floridi's semantic theory.

He creates a distinction between *instructional* and *factual information*. Factual information is something like 'the television is switched on but there is no picture'. The word 'instructional' is self explanatory — anything we are told about which we do not know already, for example 'for the television to work it needs to be connected to an aerial'. Factual information requires a further classification into whether, while apparently factual, it is true or not. This leads to well-trodden philosophical discussion which need not appear here. Falsehoods can then be seen as unintentional or contrived, leaving true information as being the material from which 'knowledge' can be built up.

In summary, Floridi's data-centered philosophy appears to have two characteristic inspirations: data as it is commonly processed in a computer, and the linguistic representation of world events. This contrasts with our approach which is driven by the way that information creates our minds, and may not be 'well-formed' like the data in a computer and may say something about the minds of living entities that do not use language. However, well-formedness may have an interpretation in a natural, iconic learning context as discussed further in the last section of this chapter.

Theodore Roszak (1933–2011)

Objections to the use of 'information' to describe human thought are not entirely new. In 1986, a sober and appealingly written volume appeared deploring the way information processing in a computer was equated to human thought. The author was Theodore Roszak, and the book was called '*The Cult of Information: The Folklore of Computers and the True Art of*

Thinking'.[27-29] Roszak had much acclaim for his earlier a book published in 1969: 'The Making of a Counter Culture'[30] which showed him to be a 'most articulate, wise, and humane historian'.[31]

This wisdom and the humane concerns are certainly evident in the 'Cult of Information', where Roszak's main concern is that the word *information* was given undue adulation in phrases such as 'Information Technology', 'The Information Society' and 'The Information Economy'. He feared that major decisions that drive the culture and politics of a nation forward would be dependent on algorithms rather than human ideas. He sees Shannon as having done the world a disservice by saying that a transmission line is efficient without knowing what is being transmitted. It could be 'the ballistic missile has been launched to destroy your country' or 'the ballistic missile hasn't been launched to destroy your country'. The noise in the line that could cause the difference between these messages might be considered to be technically minimal, but the implication for mankind might be enormous. So, rather than seeing efficient transmission as being based on the lack of corruption of bits with undefined meaning, Roszak feels that it is the efficient transmission of an *idea* bubbling up in an individual's mind and this being understood by the mind of another individual that is the more crucial.

Roszak suggests that ideas can be ordered in terms of their importance. For example:

'All men are created equal'.

He puts this in the class of *master* ideas, whereas

'Tinker, Taylor ... is a movie worth seeing

is a less masterful idea.

Roszak maintains that no numerical measure of data or information can be used to assess the profundity and value of such ideas. This is true, but

---

[27]Published in 1986 by Pantheon Books, New York.

[28]As we were sketching out this chapter, it was announced that Theodore Roszak had died on July 5, 2011.

[29]An excellent commemorative interview with Theodore Roszak has been posted on YouTube at the time of his death: http://www.youtube.com/watch?v=Y4mzEvqsiuY.

[30]Published in 1969 by Anchor Books.

[31]Alan Watts of the San Francisco Chronicle, reviewing the book in 1969.

to seek the distinction in the 'amount' of information or data that may be
involved is where a misunderstanding occurs. There is another informational
issue, a totally Shannonian one, which does distinguish between the two.
Say that a new President of the USA were to pronounce at her inaugural
address

*I believe that all men can no longer be treated as being equal. The rich are
more valuable to society than the poor and from now on will be given special
privileges at all levels of their existence.*

This would be very surprising, much more so than were someone to say

I didn't like Tinker, Taylor ... very much.

The informational measure comes in at the level of the change in certainty
with which decisions might be taken in the future that might be *caused*
by the pronouncement of an idea. The first statement creates an enormous
amount uncertainty in the beliefs that we might have about our role in
such a future. The second would not threaten our way of life very much. So
the informational impact here is that the existing state structure becomes
far worse at predicting the future in the first case whereas it is hardly
affected in the second. Therefore it is precisely the element of surprise which
determines the level of masterliness of ideas and this has an informational
measure.

While Roszak would accept that there is informational content in the
amount by which ideas might change mental state structure, he makes the
strong point that information does not *create* ideas, though ideas generate information. With respect to the Informational Mind Hypothesis of the
previous chapter, this leads to the question: how, given mind as a structure
of integrated, iconically derived states, are new meaningful states formed?
While the IMH will not provide the answer, it can provide a framework
within which the answer may be couched. For example, taking Arthur
Koestler's theory of creativity,[32] he quotes the example of the case of
Johannes Gutenberg who was struggling with the problem of applying a
controlled amount of pressure to a frame containing the printing characters. Visiting a vineyard, he saw wine being pressed by a screw and plate
arrangement controlled by a transverse beam for turning the screw. That
gave him the idea for doing the same with his frame, and the printing

---

[32]Koestler A. (1964). *The Act of Creation* (Penguin Books, New York), p. 38.

frame was born. This 'bisociation', as Koestler called it, came about by the juxtaposition of what he called *matrices* in the mind. Now, such matrices bear a very close resemblance to the integrated iconic states of the IMH. The 'juxtaposition' then is an integrating state — space link between states which takes place according to the IMH corollary found at the end of Chapter 7. So while an informational theory of the creation of ideas may neither exist nor be necessary, the IMH provides a loose formalisation for suggesting how new ideas may be formed and maintained.

Roszak is sometimes ridiculed for having predicted in 1986 that there was no future for the personal computer. On the other hand, he did see as a positive development the embryonic emergence of groups in California that aimed to use computers to create a 'direct democracy of information' to counteract the concentration of computational power in the defense industry and private corporations. At the time, the technical problems involved in this endeavor were seemingly insurmountable. At present, however, with the internet in place and with access provided for most that live in the Western world, the desire for such communal ownership has become the key driver of social networking phenomena such as Facebook.

The Informational Mind Fights Its Corner

There is common ground among the various attacks on 'information' (or, sometimes just the word 'information' itself). The offending notion is the suggestion that when a computer processes information, this is akin to what a human (or other living entity) does when thinking.

In this book, we stress that the problem lies with the 'computer processing' metaphor which we ourselves totally reject. It masks the 'informational stance' we have taken. In this stance, the *methods of analysis* that apply to engineered information systems apply to the better understanding of the 'brain, mind, and conscious thought' of living beings. But it does not treat brain, mind, and conscious thought as information processing in computers. Of course, Raymond Tallis is right in arguing that 'information' as it appears in computer 'information processing' is a misleading metaphor for the life and thought of a human being. But consider his more general scepticism about the relevance of the scientific method in examining mental function. We can assume that Tallis does not object to the use of scientifically derived and tested medical procedures in physical disabilities such as the re-balance of dopamine for patients with Parkinson's disease or strategies for rehabilitation following a stroke. But when it comes to difficulties that affect mind and thought, why should it be that scientific theories might stop short of being helpful? We have suggested in this book that the natural sciences are not totally appropriate as a starting point for the analysis of mental function. However this does not mean that *informational* sciences are not appropriate. We feel sure that no-one would try to dissuade a keen young medic researching, say, schizophrenia from considering whether a cause might be the failure of a part of the brain to integrate information or a failure in iconic learning mechanisms. In such cases, the physical, biochemical or neurological deficits may not be discernable and the more theoretical notion of information may help.

Susan Greenfield certainly has a point in worrying about young people spending too much time in dragging material from the internet. But parents may be the first line of defense here: in their traditional role they will control excesses as they do for the TV, eating, lying in bed for too long, and so on. It is the 'brain-harming' aspect of her discourse that led us above to draw attention to the way that the informational model of mind needs to include 'curiosity', that is, the mechanisms that leads to the growth of the state structure. Greenfield can be read to say that this is destroyed by too easy an access to information. However there is no mechanism or model proffered which would do this. Certainly, as Greenfield advocates, this issue should be discussed, but it should be discussed with a background of science which includes the modeling of the growth of the state structures of the mind.

The philosophy of information advocated by Luciano Floridi is based on the definition of a well-formed datum and a consequent taxonomy of such data. It is tempting to say that this has nothing to do with the informational mind. But this may be too facile. As a highly speculative step, we recall that one of the characteristics of sustaining an integrated mental state must be that the sustaining mechanism retains the causal relationships within the state in the way they exist in the world. Is this a sign of well-formed-ness? Consider the four images in Fig. 8.1. The top two are easily discernable. That is, one is conscious of the difference between them. Not so for the lower two even if it is revealed that picture point for picture point there is a much greater difference between them. But they are randomly generated dots which do not have causal relationships between them.

So while Floridi's assessment of information is based on some form of well-formedness that clearly suits computing machinery, it may be that our informational minds, by having states that represent the causal relationships of the external world, could be described as being sensitive to a natural kind of well-formedness as well.

Fig. 8.1.   Are we as conscious of the difference between the top two images as we are of the difference between the two bottom ones?

In conclusion, it is important not to fall into one of the traps which underlie Tallis' suspicion of the computing paradigm of mind. Having found a set of rules and taxonomies that describe information using a formally stated philosophy, it would be mistaken to believe that the mind 'knows and uses' such rules to do its informational work. In this book we have suggested that the state structures which we call 'mind' are formed by 'living'. It then seems evident that as such structures grow, the living organism becomes ever more expert at making the further growth specialized and contributory to an individual's personality. The idea that living individuals simply learn to obey the same rules as some massive computational algorithm based on a formal philosophy of information is an informational red herring.

Chapter 9

THE UNCONSCIOUS MIND: FREUD'S INFLUENTIAL VISION

Having advocated that consciousness is a state structure of world-representing states, what do we make of the following?

> *The conscious mind may be compared to a fountain playing in the sun and falling back into the great subterranean pool of the subconscious from which it rises.*
>
> Sigmund Freud, *The Interpretation of Dreams* (1900)[1]

Freud's bold identification of a 'subconscious', or as he preferred to call it, an 'unconscious mind' as the repository of hidden, but problematic mental states lies at the heart of his work. In this chapter, we suggest how our discussions of the 'informational mind' can play a role in an understanding how a 'subterranean pool' can come into being, and how this formal look at the 'unconscious' throws light on what consciousness is.

A Few Definitions

We explore Freud as a person, to understand how his ideas on the 'great subterranean pool of the subconscious' might have arisen. As this subject has a rather specialized vocabulary, it might be helpful to draw attention to this and elucidate its contents from the start.

---

[1]Following Storr (1989) (detailed in footnote 5 in Chapter 5 of this chapter) other quotes from Freud's writings will be referenced according to the *Standard Edition of the Complete Psychological Works of Sigmund Freud* as (SE, vol no, page number).

The subconscious

In every-day language, the word 'subconscious' is used in slightly different ways. More often than not, the word implies thoughts or behaviors for which one cannot immediately identify a conscious cause. For example (many thanks to quotation websites):

> *Most of us harbor a significant amount of subconscious fear about death, and act out of this fear in our daily lives.*

Christy Turlington, fashion model

> *I dream a lot. I do more painting when I'm not painting. It's in the sub-conscious.*

Andrew Wyeth, realist painter

> *Whatever we plant in our subconscious mind and nourish with repetition and emotion will one day become a reality.*

Earl Nightingale, author of '*Think and Grow Rich*'

There is agreement in these samples of usage, that the subconscious is something separate from one's ongoing train of thought. In 1915, Freud regretted having used the word earlier, warning against its continued use[2] as being ambiguous and misleading. Indeed we learn from 'Wikipedia' (quoting psychoanalyst, Charles Rycroft) that it is a word which is 'never used in psychoanalytic writings'. Freud recommends that only one distinction be made, that between the conscious and the unconscious.

The unconscious

Again there are several ways in which this word is used, but here it is useful to focus on the way this was important to Freud. From the perspective of this book, it seems convenient and not too far from a consensus of opinion that 'mind' can be understood to mean the sum total of mental events that

---

[2]Freud S. (1915). *The Unconscious. The Standard Edition of the Complete Psychological Works of Sigmund Freud*, Volume XIV (1914–1916): On the History of the Psycho-Analytic Movement, Papers on Metapsychology and Other Works, 159–215

have occurred in one's life so far. The conscious mind is that collection of mental events that are accessed through the mechanisms of memory and *the unconscious* is a set of mental events that have occurred in the past but cannot be accessed through normal thought processes.

This must be distinguished from other possible uses of the word. For example, we speak of an 'unconscious behavior' when we mean an automatic behavior like a seasoned driver changing gears in a car. But this is more an issue of attention, that is, it occurs when changing gears does not require thought and can become 'automatic' (no pun intended). It should also not be confused with temporarily inaccessible memories like not being able to remember a name upon seeing a face. The key puzzle surrounding the unconscious is how it is that states of mind can exist without coming into consciousness. In what sense do they 'exist'? It is one of the main aims of this chapter to interpret how this might occur by illustrating it with the behavior of some informational automata.

The pre-conscious

In contrast with the unconscious, where certain mental events are seemingly not accessible, a pre-conscious mental event, for Freud, is one which may not be in the current sequence of conscious thought, but is still accessible. For example, one might have made an appointment to have dinner at a friend's house in the evening. In a chat with another friend during the afternoon, the possibility of having a drink together in the evening enters the conversation. At this point, the dinner arrangement is remembered and one 'becomes conscious' of this. In other words the mental state of going to dinner is there, but becomes explicit only as a result of an appropriate trigger.

Repression

It was Freud's difficulty with getting patients to recall certain events of their childhood, unpleasant ones which led him to postulate that a process of repressing such memories was at work. Of course there could have simply been reluctance by the patient to dwell on certain memories. But no, Freud concluded that in some cases the patient was truly incapable of entering certain areas of thought. Repression, then, is a process whereby certain memories and their attendant thoughts are relegated to the unconscious part of the mind. We discuss how this might happen in a state-based system later in this chapter.

Psychoanalysis

The troubles of Freud's patients appeared to stem from seemingly irrational drives, the roots of which they appeared not to understand. Freud postulated that such drives are inexplicable due to their causes being lodged in the unconscious areas of the mind. Psychoanalysis is an endeavor whereby the analyst can piece together the nature of the repressed states in order to work with the analysand to explore these in the safe and caring framework of analysis. In other words, Freud was specifically interested in addressing events which might have been repressed in early childhood. During psychoanalysis the patient is encouraged to free-associate about early experiences in order to attempt to discover and understand the unpleasant events. Freud also encouraged his patients to discuss their dreams as he felt that these provide clues to the repressed memories.

Looking at Freud as a person and some influences that may have led him to develop the methods for which he became known, we then attempt to link these methods to the state structure models of mind we have been discussing in the rest of this book.

Sigmund Freud (1856–1939)

There cannot be many who have not heard of Sigmund Freud. Many will also have a cartoon in their heads of him — an image of a bearded and be-glassed person seated just behind the patient stretched out on a couch. Time Magazine used this vignette of Freud on the cover of their 1999 listing of the 100 most influential people of the 20th century. Freud is of interest here because he adopted the search for the unconscious in his method of therapy, using free-association and the analysis of dreams. While biographies of Freud abound on the net[3] and in book form[4,5] our biographical sequence here focuses on Freud's background in science and the influences on him of other thinkers, in order to discover the possible roots of his formulation of the unconscious.

---

[3]For example http://en.wikipedia.org/wiki/Sigmund_Freud.
[4]Ferris P. (1997). *Dr Freud, A Life* (Random House, London).
[5]Storr A. (1989). *Freud, A Very Short Introduction* (Oxford University Press).

Sigmund Freud was the first born to Jacob and Amelie, Galician Jews of modest means living in rented accommodation above a baker in Příbor, now in the Czech Republic. Sigmund's brother Julius was born only eight months after Sigmund and died six months later. It is said that Sigmund was left with unresolved traces of jealousy and self-reproach as a result of this death. This later led Freud to an interest in 'infantile amnesia' which, in most people, erases all but fragments of memories before the age of five or six. It is also said that this created in Freud a deep interest in retrieving such memories through unconstrained discussions with his patients and the analysis of dreams (see page 16 of Freud's 'The Unconscious' (1915) as referred in footnote 2 of this chapter).

Exceedingly bright at school (described as 'precocious' by Ferris[4]) Freud studied medicine in Vienna. Here he became involved in research at the Physiological Institute led by Ernst Brücke, a formidable exponent of the idea that the explanation of many psychological effects lay in the natural sciences. Freud took well to research in this area, but later abandoned it to be more financially secure when he became engaged to his future wife, Martha Bernays. So in 1885, he went to work at the Pitié-Salpêtrière Hospital in Paris, where he was mentored by 'The Father of Neurology' and director of the hospital, Jean-Martin Charcot. This institution had previously been a prison for the so-called 'criminally insane', the 'mentally deficient' and prostitutes. But by 1885 this institution was well on the way to being one of the world's major centers for treating and attempting to cure sufferers of mental disturbances. Freud became familiar with Charcot's practice of using hypnotism to help patients suffering from what was then called hysteria.

While, in later years, hysteria is mentioned as being the salient affliction presented by Freud's patients, the word needs some qualification. Historically associated with emotional excesses in women (linked to the Greek word □στέρα, *istera* — the uterus) the word is no longer used in the same way in medical practice. Its symptoms would now best be described as a psychological disability resulting from an unmanageable concern with sexual matters or fear of disease. A typical case of what was then considered hysteria was that named the case of Anna O. Her real name was Bertha Pappenheim, and she was not Freud's patient, but that of his colleague Joseph Breuer. Freud, on his return to Vienna in 1886, opened his practice and became intrigued by the history of this particular patient. Bertha Pappenheim had been a bright and active woman when she started suffering severe and frightening hallucinations. Breuer practiced hypnotism to try to recover the memory of the first hallucinations which he traced to the memory of the patient's father who had been severely ill. On exploring this memory with his patient Breuer reported a cure. Freud suspected that there was a suppressed sexual motif in Pappenheim's memory of her father and this led him to look for such a background in his own patients.

The sexual nature of the repressed states made sense as these, particularly if incestuous, would be felt as being at best inappropriate or, at worst, as being evil and therefore candidates for repression. Storr (reference in footnote 4, p. 24) draws attention to a pronouncement made by Freud in 1896 that was to link Freud's philosophy to children and their early sexual experience:

> *I therefore put forward the thesis that at the bottom of every case of hysteria there are one or more occurrences of sexual experience, occurrences which belong to the earliest years of childhood but which can be reproduced through the work of psychoanalysis in spite of the intervening decades.*

He later qualified this view by saying that the experiences need not have been real but the result of phantasies of a wishful kind. It was this belief that led both to accusations by some that Freud had stopped being a scientist as he provided no evidence for his opinion and in contrast, by others, that he was a visionary with a deep understanding of the human mind. Freud never stopped believing that he was a scientist.

There are three elements of the significance of Freud's work which, whether they are scientific or not, certainly deserve a scientific assessment. The first is whether, given some way of modeling world-reflecting mental states, conditions can be found which make some states inaccessible. Such conditions provide a model of repression. The second is whether there are methods of retrieval of such states which make them accessible again. These are *dreams* and *free association*. Whether such methods are helpful or not helpful to the patient is not necessarily a scientific question. Now we look a little more closely at Freud, dreams, free association and Freud's hopes for psychoanalysis.

Dreams and Free Association in Psychoanalysis

Freud saw dreams and their interpretation as '. . . the royal road to a knowledge of the unconscious activities of the mind . . .'. In 1900 he published one of his most influential books: *The Interpretation of Dreams.*[6] He felt that this was an important contribution and called it:

> ... the most valuable of all discoveries it has been my good fortune to make. Insight such as this falls to one's lot but once in a lifetime.

(SE, IV.xxxii)

He believed that dreams were hallucinatory satisfactions of repressed desires, but were disguised so as not to distress the patient. The task for the psychoanalyst is to *interpret* the dreams presented by the client (the *manifest* content) so as to reach their true meaning and enable the patient to come to terms with the repressed content (the *latent* content). A discussion of dreams would normally take place within Freud's 'free association' regime in which he encouraged his reclining patient to allow thoughts to emerge on impulse with the psychoanalyst intervening only in a minimal way, sometimes to encourage a removal of censorship. Dreams would be part of this discussion had a dream recently occurred.

As Storr points out (see p. 46 of Storr (1989) as referred in footnote 5), while Freud's main objective in the interpretation of dreams was to reveal repressed childhood sexual desires, he was aware of the fact that there are dreams that occur due to other lifetime experiences. For example physiological factors such as hunger or an itch can affect a dream. Frightening episodes in the past, such as being in violent battle in a war can emerge in a dream. Also normal sexual desires, such as being attracted to someone at work, could also emerge in a dream. This makes the task of dream interpretation during psychoanalysis a difficult one, as it depends first on the possibility that that markers of the repressed material would show through the disguise and second that the analyst would spot it.

Well known are the stories where the analyst interprets a dream about lighthouses as being phallic in origin or a dream of being swallowed by a whale as having female genital connotations. We bear these features in mind in the theoretical assessment which follows. However, as many commentators remark, it may not be the precise aim of discovering the hidden experience in a dream that was central to the psychoanalysis movement

---

[6]Freud S. (1976). *The Interpretation of Dreams.* Trans. by J. Strachey. (Pelican Books, London). Also SE IV and V.

that Freud engendered, but the process of giving the patient more initiative during the therapy. The free association method becomes more of a cooperation between patient and therapist in addressing troublesome thoughts of greater or lesser accessibility.

The 'inner life' of an automaton

While the process of psychoanalysis[7] and the notion of the unconscious[8] have had detractors who accused Freud of not being a rigorous scientist, in the framework of automata theory and informational analyses it is possible discover some formal descriptions of what may be happening. In the appendix, a basic mechanism is described which develops the state structure of an automaton to represent the experienced world. However, this state structure remains as the 'inner life' of the automaton which not only controls its behavior but also its course of thought and, indeed, this enables us to discuss the unconscious and the process of psychoanalysis. But first we briefly dip into a vast issue in psychology, that of emotions. Without some informational model of emotions, we can go no further.

Emotions and brain chemistry in the informational mind

It may seem odd that we have managed to talk of the informational mind so far in this book without mentioning emotions. In the history of philosophical discussion on the mind, *emotions* have had a clear place. Ronald de Sousa writes convincingly about this in his succinct essay on emotions in the *Stanford Encyclopedia of Philosophy*.[9] The nature of pleasure and distress are discussed by philosophers, including Aristotle (in *Rhetoric*[10]) and Brentano (in *The Origin of Right and Wrong*, 1902[11]). In very broad

---

[7]Masson J. M. (1988). *Against Therapy: Emotional Tyranny and the Myth of Psychological Healing* (Common Courage Press, London).
[8]Watters E. and Ofshe A. (1999). *Therapy's Delusions: The Myth of the Unconscious and the Exploitation of Today's Walking Worried* (Scribner, New York).
[9]de Sousa R. (2010). Emotion,in Zalta E. N. (Ed.) *The Stanford Encyclopedia of Philosophy*. Available at: http://plato.stanford.edu/archives/spr2010/entries/emotion/.
[10]Aristotle: *Rhetoric* II, 1–11
[11]Brentano, F. (1902). *The Origin of Right and Wrong*. Trans. by C. Hague. (Archibald Constable & Co., London).

terms it is clear that emotions influence the direction of thought (avoidance of the distressful and encouragement of the pleasurable). Discoveries in neurology which can be modeled in an informational sense are important here. We have seen in Chapter 3 that Hodgkin and Huxley identified neurons which secrete so-called *neurotransmitters* that can modify the functioning of large neural assemblies. Some of these neurotransmitters exert global effects on the synaptic functions of large neural areas. This is referred to as a neuromodulatory activity and is seen to be triggered in parts of the brain (hypothalamus, amygdala and the pre-frontal cortex) that are known to be involved in emotion.[12] Even more important is research which shows that one particular neuromodulator (noradrenaline) can control the learning properties of the brain, particularly in the key element in learning, the hippocampus.[13] This is particularly important in showing how state structure models of perceptual experience might be modified as a result of their emotional content.

We need to see what this means in the context of the automata-theoretic model of the creation of state structure. Figure 9.1 is a highly simplified version of the world in the Appendix (Fig. A1).

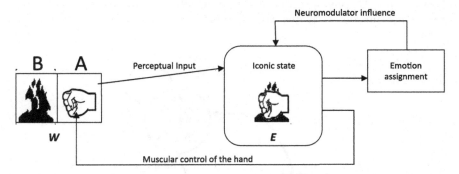

Fig. 9.1. The entity E is an iconic learning automaton which controls the position of its hand (and eye) to be in one of the two positions of world W: A where the hand is comfortable and B where it is in a fire.

[12]Fellous J-M. (1999), The neuromodulatory basis of emotion, *The Neuroscientist* **5**(5), 283–294.
[13]Gelinas J. N. and Nguyen P. V. Neuromodulation of hippocampal synaptic plasticity, learning and memory by noradrenaline, *Cen. Nerv. Syst. Agents Med. Chem.* **7**, 17–33.

The principles of building state structure as detailed in the appendix are summarized here. Initially the entity E causes an exploration of the world W by selecting moves at random. Here the world W has only two places that can be explored: A and B. In B a fire is raging whereas A is neutral and 'comfortable'. The exploration is done by a hand (and an eye if you like) and what the entity E receives through its perceptual channel includes the output of heat sensors in the hand. The muscular controls that E can exert to move the hand are *left, right* and *stay*. Let us assume that these controls are deployed at random, but without incorporating signals that represent *time* (see the appendix for an example including time). Also it is assumed that moves that transgress the boundaries of the world are just not used. And, let us say that E has a switching strategy for attending and not attending to the perceptual input. When not attending, the input is replaced by noise which allows E to explore its state structure internally. These two phases are called the *perceptual* and the *imaginational* phases.

The learned state structure after random exploration is shown in Fig. 9.2.

Conventionally, in the perceptual mode, the automaton would put its hand in the fire, remove it or let it stay in one of the two positions totally at random. But the hand in the fire does not only generate passive heat measurements but also activates pain centers in the main automaton which are

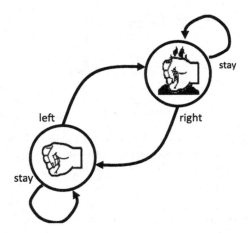

Fig. 9.2.   State structure learned by automaton E. If the input is replaced by noise, this is a probabilistic automaton: there is a division of probabilities for taking a transition out of a state.

evaluated as being negative by the emotions box. Indeed the pain centers are likely to be able to act directly on the musculature to stop damage to the hand. The key role of the emotions box is to evaluate the consequences of actions. As innate reactions, moving the hand from A to B into the fire is labeled as 'bad' while staying in A is labeled as 'good'. The move from B to A would also be labeled as being good. It is here that the neuromodulators are thought to do their work. In technical terms, the neuromodulator strengthens the connections that increase the probability for entering emotionally good states and reduces the probability for entering the bad states.

Specifically, the value of being able to switch away from the perceptual drive into the imaginational one becomes important. There the automaton is able to explore its state structure without risk and even be reinforced for moving toward good states since the emotional evaluator and its neuromodulatory influence are at work even in the imaginational mode.

In summary, we argued that iconically equipped automata not only acquire state structures that reflect the nature of the world but also are capable of evaluating the states of this structure in terms of the the extent to which they lead to further exploration of the world which is to the best advantage of the organism. Emotions and their ability to change the state structure of the automaton through neuromodulatory effects are key to the definition of the informational mind despite the fact that our treatment here can only be described as cursory. We now return to an exploration of the definition of the unconscious.

Repression: A Possible Mechanism?

Commentators on Freud's methods point out that initially he saw repression as one way a thinking system has of forgetting memories of traumatic experiences. The puzzle is that the word 'forgetting' suggests some form of erasure or deletion whereas Freud and the hypnotists who preceded him suggested merely that some process of hiding was in place. Indeed for computer scientists 'forgetting' is synonymous with the irretrievable deletion of a file. However, the mechanisms in the automaton model above actually favor the idea of 'hiding' a mental state. If left entirely in the imaginational mode, the automaton is transiting from state to state according to the current probabilities of transition and is modifying such transitions according to the emotional evaluation of the imagined states. Now, say that there exists the memory of a state that has an unbearably distressing emotional evaluation. As we have seen, Freud considered such traumatic events to be rooted in sexual notions, including both the actual memory of sexual abuse and phantasies of the same kind of event.

This is a useful illustration of Freud's understanding of an unbearably distressing thought. In terms of the mechanisms sketched above, however, it is easy to understand that in the imaginational mode every time the distressing mental state is entered, the strength of the transition to it is reduced until it is made almost totally unlikely. So, glancing at Fig. 9.2, it is as if the imaginational transition from the comfortable state to the painful one were to be removed altogether.

It can now be stressed that the uncomfortable state has not stopped existing: but it cannot be accessed during conscious thinking. Should some form of major noise be briefly applied to the network, there may be a finite probability that the repressed state is entered. We shall return to this, but for now we recognize that *the unconscious* may be considered to be a collection of mental states which have become inaccessible because of their highly charged negative emotional values.

How can repressed states be detrimental?

One outlook on repressed states could be that, having been made inaccessible, they can no longer distress the thinker. But the basis of psychotherapy is that this is precisely not the case. The detrimental nature of repressed states is that they leave the thinker with fears which cannot be resolved as the solution lies in understanding the very states that have repressed. In automata terms, the mental state structure is left with state cycles that are short of entering the repressed cycle but still have some negative emotional values. There is an oft-quoted case study of 'little Hans' (not his real name) and his fear of horses. Hans' father contacted Freud as he was concerned about his son being terrified of going out into the street where there were many horses. According to Freud's (long-distance) analysis, the difficulty started with his mother wanting to punish him (at the age of 3) for playing with his penis. She threatened to call a doctor who would cut it off. Freud noted that the child spent mornings in his parents' bed where he must have noticed his father's penis and its size. In a highly simplified version of the analysis,[14] Freud's opinion was that the repressed thought was Hans'

---

[14]https://www.simplypsychology/little-hans.html (author: Saul Mcleod, 2008)

sexual feelings (involving his penis) for his mother. Hans began to fear his father's anger sometimes expressed during the visits to the parental bed. Now, Freud suggested, that horses with their visible genitals and their facial hairy features elicited thoughts of an exaggerated fear of the angry father, creating fearful emotions that led to the ritual of not wanting to go out into the street, reported as a fear of horses. The real fear was the unthinkable thought of being castrated by his father for desiring his mother.

In theoretical terms the state sequence [horse (large penis)] — [father (large penis)] — [desire for mother] — [castration] was repressed by an emotionally mediated avoidance of the action of looking at horses. While this is an illustration of Freud's early theory that repression is almost always due to sexual desires or experience in early childhood, as Storr points out (footnote 5, p. 23), the importance of this example lies in the general principle that early emotions are the cause of current problems, a notion that still influences the many and varied styles of contemporary psychoanalysis. But what can be said of the process of psychoanalysis itself?

Psychoanalysis: A Possible Model?

Given that repressed states can cause difficulties for the represser, and having suggested in what sense that the process of psychoanalysis is intended to be effective in redressing such distress, here we ask whether with the emotion and neuromodulation model it can be seen that the negative effects of repression can be counteracted. Freud's contention is that the process of psychoanalysis aids the patient distressed by the effect of repressed states, by revealing these states and understanding what caused them to be repressed. That is, the analyst encourages the patient to follow freely the association of his own ideas for which the analyst provides an interested and sympathetic ear. This puts the analyst in a position of trust that enables the analysand to feel safe in following thought paths which would be hard to follow in environments outside the therapy room. In terms of Fig. 9.1, one needs to ask whether is it possible to produce thought patterns that are akin to the repressed states, but in which the emotional responses are toned down by being in the safe hands of the therapist. Freud's contention is true that many (if not most) repressed states are due to sexual desires or experiences in childhood which create a sense shame that the child cannot bear. In the therapy room, the patient may no longer be a child, and he or she is in the presence of a sympathetic listener. In the literature on psychotherapy much is said about the role of *transference* in the process of analysis. A few paragraphs about this major and controversial subject in the context of our modeling story may be useful to the reader.

Transference

Transference is defined as the direction of emotional sentiments that affect a patient's existence toward the psychotherapist. Love, hate and fear could be the emotions involved. Freud originally felt that transference got in the way of an objective relationship between therapist and patient. However, with time, he recognized that that this effect could be helpful toward a successful therapy. Contemporary psychotherapists still discuss the value or otherwise of this effect. From Fig. 9.1 it would seem that transference during an analysis session would be couched in the *perceptual* mode of the automaton. But say that a cause of distress in the patient is an inappropriate feeling toward a parent. Transference toward a therapist may provide the perceptual input that is similar enough to that which led to repressed states. The result of bringing such into conscious thought during the therapy may lead to a neuromodulatory action which retains and examines the repressed state in consciousness.

We stress that this suggestion is pure speculation, but such speculation may lead those in a position to research the question to develop the idea further.

Like mending a broken leg?

In summary, we have suggested in theoretical terms that psychotherapy may be able to mend the *broken state structure* which constitutes the mind. This is the informational version of mending a broken leg or providing a chemical cure for cancer in physical material. It may be possible to enrich this suggestion through an in-depth modeling of case histories. Now we use the model of Fig. 9.1 in order to examine Freud's contention that an analysis of *dreams* is the 'royal road' toward a healing process in psychotherapy.

Dream Analysis as a feature of Psychoanalysis

As seen earlier, Freud saw his work on the analysis of dreams as '. . . the most valuable of all discoveries . . .'. By coincidence, the authors, while gathering the material on Freud's work on dreams, visited the Asklepion, a historical site named after Asklepius, a healing god of Greek mythology. Found near

Pergamon in what is now western Turkey,[15] this was a sanatorium for those with mental disturbances and was at the height its prominence in the 3rd Century AD. The Asklepion was one of many such Romano-Greek centers where people who were distressed in a way that would now be described as being mentally disturbed traveled long distances to apply for admission. The therapists were priests who believed in prayer to Asklepius and worked with a prescribed sequence of rituals. The central ritual was an 'incubation' (relating to the Latin word, *incubus* — nightmare), that is, a place where a person could dream, sleep and report their *incubi* to the trusted therapist. Indeed it is likely that such sleep periods may have been induced through drugs.

While dreaming, the patient may be awakened and asked to recall the dream. From these reports the therapists were understood to judge how far towards a cure the healing had progressed. Exactly how this was done is not clear except that dreams of a snake or a dog (the symbols of Asklepius) were taken as signs that the cure was complete. It is known that the celebrated Greco-Roman physician Galen, born in Pergamon, (encountered briefly in Chapter 3) was first a patient and then a therapist at the Asklepion. Following Aristotle,[16] Galen believed that dreams could be an indication of the state of health of a person and could direct the therapist toward a plan for a cure.

Freud was well aware of the importance of the analysis of dreams in antiquity in alleviation of mental diseases (SE IV, 58-63), but argued that this did not provide him with a cohesive progression of knowledge on which to base a theory. So Freud invites us to look for formalisms that treat dreams as more than the folk idea of them as erroneous replays of daily experience. Now we take a closer look.

Freud's use of dreams (see footnote 6).

Primarily, Freud believed that dreams that relate to repressed unconscious states are not direct manifestations of such states. He regarded them as disguised, less traumatic states which are nonetheless related to the offending memory. He dubbed the content of the repressed state as *latent* and

---

[15]There are many references to the Asklepion on tourist sites, here is an example: http://www.spiritualtravels.info/articles-2/asia/turkey/pergamumbergama/the-asklepion-healing-center-at-pergamum/.

[16]See http://classics.mit.edu/Aristotle/dreams.html.

its explicit manifestation in the dream, as *manifest*. That which makes the task of the analyst difficult is that the manifest version is not a neat mapping of the latent content with just some of the parameters changed. For example, a childhood fear of male castration for having had sexual desires related to the child's mother will not appear as a neat dream of, say, (as a caricature) losing one's finger while cutting a loaf of bread stolen from the father. Freud warns that dreams may contain a mundane object that emerges from a much richer meaning in the latent version. In our own terminology, a latent meaning may be an entire state structure such as that created during an emotionally charged period of one's life as a child. For example, the latent content may be of being repeatedly reprimanded at a particular address which involved an unwelcome journey such as in a carriage with a scary horse. What is available to the analyst may be an uneventful dream of walking the dog within the same town but being inexplicably anxious when recalling that dream.

Here, what Freud calls *condensation*, is at work: one of the mechanisms that protects the thinker from the emotions aroused by repressed states. A total of four such mechanisms can be involved. The second is *displacement*, where an object with a strong emotional effect is detached from the context in which the emotion arises and attached to a less poignant situation. For example, a dream of nailing a wooden panel to the house of acquaintance F may hide a repressed desire to bludgeon F to death with a hammer. The third hiding mechanism is *representation*, where Freud speaks of the fact that some linguistic complexities of thought such as 'if', 'although', 'unless'and so on are hard to represent as a largely visual dream state. The therapist, he argues, has to work with projections of complex structures into a visual form which hides some of the original impact of the thought. For example, a traumatic encounter with a pack of dogs on the one occasion when mother was being unfaithful with a visitor might not easily emerge in a dream if during other of his visits there were no dogs. The therapist has to work with representations of animals, home, mother and visitors as separate vignettes in order to piece together the nature of the traumatic event.

Similarly, a tendency for dream mechanisms to resort to protection through *symbolism* creates another difficulty for the analyst. This is the often quoted set of mental euphemisms for genitals. For example, in the case of 'Little Hans' cited above, Hans' father reported that the boy had had a vivid dream involving a robust giraffe and a crumpled one and that he had been upset by the father sitting on and removing the crumpled one. Freud saw the crumpled giraffe as a symbol for the mother and the robust giraffe rather obviously as the classical phallic symbol seen in conjunction with a powerful father distancing the mother from the boy when he visited their bedroom.

Finally, Freud saw as misleading attempts by the analysand to make sense of a dream, the elements of which do not necessarily cohere. It is here that the concept of a free association encourages the patient to express the fragments of the dream without attempting to fit them into a rational story.

Some Hand-Waving Informational Theory

The model of the informational mind outlined in the appendix is a state structure which has two aspects: the perceptual and the imaginational. Freud's concern with the unconscious and its effect on possible sequences of thought has drawn attention to emotion as an important operator on the imaginational aspect of state structure. The effect of emotion has the power to alter the probability of state transitions in the imaginational mode. We illustrate this transformation in Fig. 9.3. The state structure on the left represents the imaginational version with no effect from the emotionally induced neuromodulatory action. The group on the right represents a possible effect of the emotional changes. Thick arrows represent increased probabilities of transition and missing arrows represent much reduced probabilities.

The key points to note are:

1) The group (j, k, l) represent the repressed 'thought' arising from an emotion-driven degrading of the probability of transitions into this group. As a result, there is no access to the regressed thought in this mode.
2) In the 'emotion' state structure only the salient transitions are shown, there could be many more transitions in the non-repressed version of the state structure as the automaton is probabilistic.

Dreams and State Structure

In an earlier book, (*The World in my Mind* — TWIMM),[17] one of the authors considered the way in which a neural automaton could represent

---

[17]Aleksander I. (2005). *The World in My Mind, My Mind in the World*, Chapter 3. (Imprint Academic, Exeter).

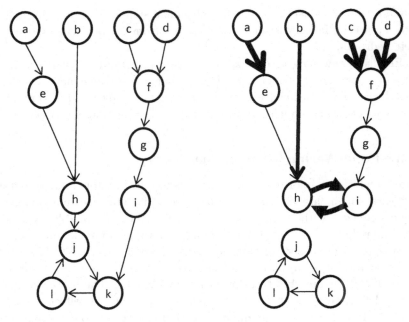

Fig. 9.3.   Illustration of the transition from no emotional neuromodulation (left) to altered transition probabilities (right) due to the effect of emotions.

the process of sleeping and dreaming. Here we sketch the essence of this argument and then use it to return to look at what might occur in the context of psychotherapy.

Dreaming occurs during a conjunction of physiological factors which lead to phases of sleep referred to as REM-sleep (REM stands for Rapid Eye Movements). While the sleeper is mainly paralyzed in terms of muscular action and perceptual input, the brain cycles across different depths of sleep which at the deepest level allow the muscles of the body to relax and the firing activity in the brain generally to use less energy. This satisfies the function of sleep: the need to rest (reduce energy consumption) in both the chemical and electrical activities of the brain and so to achieve a small amount of regeneration to counteract daily wear. REM sleep occurs in the shallowest level of sleep, just below the level that is associated with being awake.

In the deeper, non-REM conditions of sleep, the firing activity of the brain is so subdued that if a participant in a sleep experiment is woken up she will on most occasions not report having had a dream.

Not so in REM-sleep. If the participant is awakened then, a dream is often reported. All of this begs the question 'what is REM sleep and dreaming for?' Some,[18] being influenced by computer mechanics, suggest that dreaming helps to fit the states laid down during a day into some memory system which already contains remembered data. That is, they identify dreaming with storage optimisation routines on a digital computer. In our analyses, we are compelled not to use such processing models as they clash with our informational theories which are based on the emergent dynamics of a neural system rather than the skills of a programmer.

Others, such as Nobel Laureate Francis Crick and his colleague Graeme Mitchison, suggest that, rather than accommodating new daytime experiences, dreaming clears out unwanted ones.[19] While this idea addresses the dynamics of a neural net and needs an emotional evaluation of states, it sees the states entered in dreams as being spurious and 'spring-cleaned' out of the system. In TWIMM, the conclusion is reached that entering REM sleep is an inevitable step for the brain as it cycles across the various phases of neural activity that achieve the necessary physical relaxation, before eventually waking in the morning. It is suggested that in REM sleep the brain enters states within the structure of existing iconically learned states and state sequences which are now consistently without input. That is, the automaton becomes wholly autonomous. This contrasts with the waking experience where there are continuous attentive switches between perceptual and imaginational modes. This keeps the automaton within control and thought is driven by references to actuality. It appears that in REM sleep and hence dreaming, waves called ponto-geniculate-occipital (PGO) arise. These waves activate the visual system. In TWIMM it was tentatively suggested that these waves introduce a 'shaking-up' of the automaton which prevents it from getting stuck in a state or a state cycle. Also, the involvement of visual parts of the brain in the PGO activity may explain the fact that *visual* events are reported when woken during a REM period and this leads to the *representational* limitations defined by Freud and mentioned above.

---

[18]Breger L. (1969). Dream function: an information-processing model, in L. Breger (Ed.) *Clinical Cognitive Psychology* (Prentice Hall, New Jersey).
[19]Crick F. and Mitchison G. (1986). REM sleep and neural nets, *J. Mind Behav.* **7**, 229–250.

Back to repressed states and dreaming

We now summarize the observations made above.

a) Sleep is a process of physical relaxation which prepares the brain for another period of awake activity.
b) This involves a cycling across several patterns of neural activity (or inactivity), one of which (REM) reinstates the state structure that has been described as 'mind'. The involvement of the visual system in PGO waves underscores that the salient modality in dreaming is visual.
c) State transitions in REM sleep are governed by probabilistic values and allow transitions between states not directly linked during perceptual interactions experienced in the world. This may explain the occurrence of bizarre juxtapositions which are sometimes found in dreams.
d) Consequently attractors and repressed states such as shown for the emotionally influenced part of Fig. 9.3 describe the function of the automaton during REM sleep leading to the following argument.

Looking again at the two state structures in Fig. 9.3 we note that before repression, states h and i lead into the 'root' (j, k, l). We recall that in a probabilistic automaton a link between two states arises from some causal affinity between the states due to a similarity between them. As a result of the repression, we have suggested that it is possible for h and i to form a cycle that stands in relation to the repressed cycle similarly to the way that Freud sees a *manifest* dream to stand in respect to the repressed *latent* thought. While this is an interesting hypothesis, a neural simulation that incorporates emotions might be effective as a demonstration of the way that repression leaves a manifest trace in consciousness.

A Perspective on the Unconscious

The motivation that drove this chapter is that recognizing the unconscious is a way of obtaining a purchase on what it is to be conscious. This is not an entirely original ambition. Bernard Baars' in his computational Global Workspace model of consciousness identifies conscious mechanisms in contrast to unconscious ones in his model[20] as does Murray Shanahan in a

---

[20]Baars B. (1998). *A Cognitive Theory of Consciousness* (Cambridge University Press, London), p. 198.

recent book.[21] To be precise, the models of Baars and Shanahan are based on where in a stylized model of the conscious brain (the Global Workspace model) consciousness may occur, and how this is supported by brain activity that is not conscious. We have attempted to do something different and look at the question of how some mental states can be unconscious when others, *occurring in the same physical space* may not be. This brought us to a study of Freud's psychoanalysis which is specifically concerned with the fact that unconscious states can have a bearing on the conscious life.

The formal argument sees emotions as having a re-structuring effect on the state structure of imaginational thought. Within this, pleasurable thought is favored over distressing thought and mechanisms exist which render highly traumatic events inaccessible or (in the language of psychoanalysis) repressed. Such states constitute the unconscious. In agreement with Freud, formal descriptions show that in disconnecting traumatic states, other state groupings are created that 'represent' the unthinkable states. This allows the therapist to develop skills which allow her to attempt to understand the nature of the hidden states. This is a classical informational process. Partial clues continually reduce the lack of knowledge the therapist has of the repressed state. It is also her skill which, with no formal model at all, provides a comfortable ambience in which the patient can come to terms with the power of the gradual discovery of the content of the unconscious states.

---

[21]Shanahan M. (2010). *Embodiment and the Inner Life. Cognition and Consciousness in the Space of Possible Minds* (Oxford University Press, London).

Chapter 10
ARISTOTLE'S LIVING SOUL

To attain any assured knowledge about the soul is one of the most diffi-
cult things in the world.

Aristotle, *De Anima* 1,1,2[1]

We agree. But in this chapter, by way of a conclusion to the arguments set
out in this book, we look at Aristotle's own writings in *De Anima* on the
mental nature of a living being. Much of the perceived difficulty persists to
the present day and this leads us to ask whether what Aristotle describes
as 'one of the most difficult things in the world' might have been made
easier had he been able to include informational structures in his analytical
armory. Predictably, we would answer 'yes'. Now we overview *De Anima*,
commenting on where informational issues seem to be important.

De Anima or 'On The Soul'

It is thought that Aristotle wrote *de Anima* in the last 10 of his 62 years.
Commentators stress that the 'difficult' task was undertaken by the philosopher armed with the maturity of the years that made him one of the principal creators of Western philosophy. For Aristotle, the soul is that which

---

[1]Most of the quotations are from 'De Anima', cited as (book,part,paragraph)
referring to the translation by J. A. Smith for the MIT Classics series:
http://classics.mit.edu/Aristotle/soul.mb.txt. We have also used Christopher
Shields' essay 'Aristotle's Psychology' in the Stanford Dictionary of Philosophy: Shields C. (2011). Aristotle's psychology, in *The Stanford Encyclopedia of
Philosophy* (Ed.) E. N. Zalta. Available at: http://plato.stanford.edu/archives/
spr2011/entries/aristotle-psychology/.

defines life through the ability to grow and procreate. In a human being, the soul is that which distinguishes the corpse from the living being. It is for this reason that in later theology and religious philosophy the soul was easily seen as 'leaving' the body at the moment when the living body becomes reduced to the corpse. In contrast to this, for Aristotle the soul is the essence of a living organism which, by definition, is lost with death. When a light is switched off we do not believe that the light has gone somewhere else.

But 'mind' ('*νουσ*', that is, *'nous' in Greek*) is a property of the soul — a different kind of element from emotions such as fear, anger or joy which Aristotle saw as being enmeshed with the body. From our own work (in Chapter 9) we would agree with him that, had one to decide whether emotions are objects of thought or objects of the body, we would primarily opt for the body, but would allow that thought could have emotional content. Emotions affect thought in the sense that they are capable of changing the structures of the elements (states) of thought,[2] which requires bodily chemistry (i.e., neuromodulators). Aristotle sees emotions as being couched in the complex of body *and* soul while 'mind', as the thinking part of the soul, appears less tied to bodily matters. So to what end could explanations of mind by a natural scientist serve? The natural scientist is an expert in matters of the body, and, while thought cannot exist without the body, it cannot be understood through the functioning of a body any more than the function of a computer can be understood from the knowledge that its components contain silicon.

Does this sound familiar? Indeed, Aristotle's perplexity on this issue projects through history to the current time through the enduring ghost of dualism between mind and body. If we attempt to explain the mind in terms of the molecules of the body we fail. Equally, if we assume that mind can only be explained by using the mind, that is, purely through a philosophical argument, this fails to explain how distortions of the physical lead to distortions of the mental. Aristotle keeps the discussion at the abstract level by questioning how the mind as part of the *form* of the body (i.e., part of the soul) can interact with the *form* of world objects that are to become the objects of thought.

---

[2]Kelly G. A. (1955). *The Psychology of Personal Constructs* (Norton, New York). It was psychologist George Kelly, seeing thought as a collection of inter-related constructs used to evaluate perception of the world, who defined anxiety as the realisation that one's system of constructs would have to be changed.

Aristotle's Hylomorphism

As Christopher Shields (see footnote 1) points out, to understand Aristotle's description of the relationship of body to soul, one needs to understand his use of *Hylomorphism*.[3] A combination of the word ὕλο (*hylo*) meaning matter (like wood) and μορφή (*morphē*) meaning form, the term refers to a very general method that Aristotle applied to his explanations of the causes of things in the world. Using the example of a bronze statue of Hermes, Shields points out that such an explanation relies on being clear about the *material* of which an object is made; the *formal* structure which defines (say) that this is a statue of Hermes and not Zeus; the need for an *effective* agent who has the knowledge for creating the statue (the sculptor) and the *final* goal that the object is to achieve (e.g. to honor Hermes or to help to hold up the corner of a temple).

Now, Aristotle needs to establish the distinctiveness of the soul where he will be looking for the power of 'understanding' the *form* of objects in the world:

> ... *we can wholly dismiss as unnecessary the question whether the soul and the body are one: it is as meaningless as to ask whether the wax and the shape given to it by the stamp are one, or generally the matter of a thing and that of which it is the matter....* [2,1,6]

Given that, according to Aristotle's hylomorphism, the body is the 'matter' and the soul is the *form* that defines the 'livingness' of the animal, the question arises as to how the two together form a unity. To this Aristotle has the robust reply of the stamp and the wax. In the informational domain, a similar question often occurs: if it is neural activity which causes mind, mind must be equated to the neural structure of the brain. We fight against this blatant form of materialism by showing that, like the stamp and the resulting wax object, the neural network and its informational learning, while causing the mind or the state structure, are distinct phenomena with distinct properties. It is the informational analysis that allows us to relate the one to the other. That is, the state structure has a subtle but scientifically analysable relationship to the network in the same way as the shape given to the wax by the stamp has a scientifically analyzable relationship (pressure, temperature, malleability, etc.) to the stamp.

---

[3]Note that the word is used in recursive functions in computer science. This is not related to what is being discussed here.

Properties of the soul

The ability to think, that is, the possession of a mind, is treated by Aristotle as one of the properties of the soul. The other salient ones are perception and nutrition. Nutrition is essential to life: lack of nutrition will cause a collapse of the form of life and the soul will collapse with the collapse of the body. In informational worlds this is paralleled by the recognition that no informational activity is possible without some source of energy. But nutrition in a living animal requires that the animal be capable of finding food and gathering it, which, as Aristotle notes, requires perception. But what is perception? Aristotle's first premise is that perceiving implies *a change* in the perceiver. But this is a special type of change, a type of change applicable to some objects and not others. A mushroom cannot perceive even though an object (a rock falling on the mushroom) can create a change in the mushroom. Living objects have a perceptual substance that can be changed by what is impinging on the five senses, a substance which a plant does not have. Aristotle left it at that: the changing substance must be central in what it is that defines the soul.

Here, we glimpse at how this relates to some of our own work.[4] In a world of events that can be perceived, we suggested that there is a minimally perceivable event and that this event is defined by having just enough energy to a change the value of one state variable in whatever might be the current internal perceptual state. In this model of a link between outer change and inner change there is a trace of Aristotelian influence across the best part of 2,500 years.

For an event E to be perceived by agent A, Aristotle requires the satisfaction of the following relationships (as presented by Christopher Shields):

i) A has the capacity for receiving the *sensible* form of E
ii) E acts upon that capacity by *enforming* it; and, as a result,
iii) A's relevant capacity becomes *isomorphic* with that form.

As Shields points out, (i) makes A into an 'active' receiver rather than a passive one like the mushroom struck by a rock. In the theory of the systems examined in this book, it is the integrated neural structure that has been said to have this active property. It is often questioned whether Aristotle's use of 'enforming' and 'isomorphic' is absolutely clear. Shields

---

[4]Aleksander I. and Dunmall B. (2003). *J. Conscious. Stu.* **10**(4–5), 7–18.

suggests that the best interpretation is like that of a blueprint of a house being isomorphic to the house itself. In our work, it is the iconic learning that causes the 'enforming' and the iconic states of the state structure that are isomorphic with the form of the event E. This needs some qualification.

In our interpretation (i) means that A must have a capacity to absorb whatever the senses can reveal about the *form* of E. From the point of view of not only iconic learning but also the general notion of soul, mind and consciousness, it is controversial to say that such properties can be internally 'enformed' through the senses. This would be tantamount to saying that one person can perceive the soul of another. Consequently, Shields suggests that, because the 'blueprint' representation is the only isomorphism that is possible, Aristotle's 'analysis of perception hangs in the balance'.

This leads us to elaborate the nature of iconically learned state structures and Aristotle's 'enforment'. With most objects in the world, the enforment is transmitted through the senses: two snakes may look much the same, but to the expert eye noticing a slight difference, the form of the one as being poisonous is distinguishable from the other as not poisonous and the isomorphism leads A to take the appropriate care. However, were the snake still, the doubt whether the snake is alive (i.e. soul-full) or dead (soul-less) does not come from the current sensory state. In this sense any instantaneous isomorphism becomes ambiguous. The fault is with the model of the 'blueprint' which is a passive isomorphism. In contrast, an iconically created state structure would be active in the sense that the *possibility* of the snake moving would have been 'enformed' into A as a state trajectory *triggered* by the sensory input and therefore perceived correctly (through a sustained isomorphism) as a potentially live snake. At this point it becomes interesting to look at how Aristotle distinguishes mind from perception.

The mind according to Aristotle

Aristotle supposes that there is a functional affinity between perception and thought:

> ... *If thinking is like perceiving, it must be either a process in which the soul is acted upon by what is capable of being thought, or a process different from but analogous to that. The thinking part of the soul must therefore be, while impassible, capable of receiving the form of an object; that is, must be potentially identical in character with its object without*

being the object. Mind must be related to what is thinkable, as sense is
to what is sensible. [3,4,2]

This leads to a sequence of assertions similar to those of perception. To define that an event E is *thought* by agent A, Aristotle requires satisfaction of the following relationships (again as presented by Christopher Shields):

i) A has the capacity for receiving the *intelligible* form of E
ii) E acts upon that capacity by enforming it; and, as a result,
iii) A's relevant capacity becomes isomorphic with that form.

Now, (i) refers to the form of E that can be thought about even when E is not being perceived. In this sense, it becomes tempting for us to draw a parallel between our state-structure formulation of the relation between perception and thought. In Chapter 9, we introduced the difference between a *perceptual* state structure and an *imaginational* one. We suggest that the intelligible form of E is the state sub-structure triggered by a 'chain of thought'. Taking the snake example above, a chain of thought may be that of setting off on a walk in an area where snakes are often encountered. In the imaginational mode, the system may enter a sequence of states in which the imagined view of the poisonous snake and the non-poisonous one are entered in some sort of state cycle. Then (i) means that the set of states in the imaginational mode may not be the same as that in the perceptual mode. Clearly, certain perceptions may simply not be salient enough to have altered the state structure. So in (ii) in order for E to be intelligible it must exist in the imaginational state structure. That is, it exists in the sense that its state sub-structure is that of the form or lack thereof of E. So there are states for both the snake being potentially alive or potentially dead. This complies with the *enformed* requirement of (ii). Then for (iii) A's capacity for thought includes whatever may be thought of as the *form* of the objects in the world. That is, one can think of honoring Hermes when the statue is seen, but not when any lump of bronze is seen.

Despite treating the soul with mind as one of its constituent parts, Aristotle, as the result of a philosophical deduction, laid down a challenge for those who wish to treat it as a scientific question. They will have to explain what, given that mind is *enformed* in terms of the *forms* of the objects of the world and given the hypothesis that there is an isomorphism or resonance between mind and such external forms, are the mechanisms that might bring this coherence about? In what way is the inner mind *like* the enforming exteral forms? How is it that mind appears to be nothing before it starts thinking? What is the basis of desire?

It has been our thesis in this book that, armed with a concrete set of models of systems which have information as their life-blood, we can approach some of Aristotle's challenges. These are the issues that have lurked behind the choice of material throughout this book which we feel can be briefly summarized in the light of Aristotle's challenge.

Aristotle and the informational mind

The science

Imagine the state of science as Aristotle left it. In his reasoning, a thinker has a scientifically un-defined mind — part of the *form* of a living human[5] — where the most likely organ to possess such a property was to be the human heart (Chapter 3). It took the likes of Claudius Galen in the first century AD to put the mind back in the head while still maintaining an undiminished respect for Aristotle's philosophy of the function of mind. However, in addition to Aristotle's rational isomorphic *form* of mind, belief in a spiritual character of the phenomenon survived through various interpretations and surfaced in the ventricles of Descartes pineal gland dualism. Here the philosopher and the mathematician/scientist embodied in the one person of Descartes parted company, as there was no scientific basis for Descartes supposedly functional, famously dual, model of the mind. Aristotle might have noted an 'isomorphism' between a thought of intending something as a spiritual object in the ventricles and the execution of the action as mediated by the pineal gland, but might have questioned how the thought came to be resonant with the perceived world in the first place.

We saw that the first glimmerings of science were the discoveries in the 17th century by Willis, who saw that the dissected brain of the mentally ill contained a different mix of chemicals from that found in those thought be normal. No longer could one blame mysterious spirits for such misfortunes. But it took scientists (called *neurologists* after Willis) the best part of 200 years to discover the cellular structure of the brain (Schleiden, Purkinje, Golgi, Cajal, Sherrington, then Hodgkin and Huxley) and conclude that

---

[5] Aristotle maintained that only human minds have the ability to 'understand' the form of the objects of the world. Animals have a soul that requires nourishment and the satisfaction of desires, but display no understanding in their behavior.

the brain was riddled with informational exchanges among neurons that could be modified by the excretions (now called neuromodulators as seen in Chapter 9) that Willis had discovered. But as yet there was no sign of Aristotelian isomorphisms.

Boston

Thank goodness for the Boston academic institutions. Between the 1940s and the end of the 1950s not only did Shannon (while at MIT) suggest a science to quantify informational transactions (Chapter 2) but also he discovered logical tools that could be used to assess the function of nodes in networks where information flows. MIT was also the eventual academic home of Warren McCulloch and Walter Pitts, who ran with the idea that such logical descriptions could be applied to the neurons of the brain. Not only this, but the discoveries of Sherrington that synapses could vary transmission between neurons made this logical model of a neuron into a device the logic of which could be changed. The result of this realization was good and bad. The 'good' was that the brain could be seen as having a vast number of learned behaviors mediated by neuron plasticity. The 'bad' was that this led to stimulus-response behavioral models of the mind which left out the possibility of deliberation and hence also left out any space for the Aristotelian isomorphism. Despite this, engineers in the 1960s began to think of variable stimulus/response networks as a way of designing practical systems that could learn to recognize patterns. We saw that this enthusiasm died about 1968 as a result of the publication the Minsky and Papert criticism of the lack of functionality of networks vis-à-vis the general purpose computer.

Reverberations

A move toward deliberation took place in the 1940s as a result of the distaste that psychologist Karl Lashley had for the idea of the stimulus/response mind. There was no scope here for *any* kind of sustained thought between the stimulus and the response, never mind Aristotelian isomorphic behavior. We saw in Chapter 4 how the work of Lashley and his student Donald Hebb, addressed the masses of re-entrant connections in the brain. Such feedback leads to the possibility of internal 'reverberations' in networks which mediate between stimulus and response and create a space in the network for some form of 'deliberation'. It also gave an impetus much later, in the early 1980s, to a second wave of interest in neural networks with internal states. This brought to the fore some of the giants of the neural network field: Hopfield, Kohonen, Werbos, Grossberg and Carpenter and many others.

State structures

In such 'recursive' networks we discovered (Chapters 4 and 5) another tool that is central to our own formalizations of mind: the state machine or 'automaton'. This is a way of being aware that reverberations are complex and have a *structure* of states. For example, such a structure could be a set of internal states that represents the way one makes a cup of tea. But, with the possible exception of Kohonen, Grossberg and ourselves, there was very little known on how these recursive or dynamic networks could hold reasonable representations of reality, that is be the basis of Aristotelian isomorphisms. We called our efforts 'iconic learning' where the internal state of the dynamic network was directly forced from an external event. In Chapter 5, we examined this under the heading of phenomenology. This asks not how the external and the internal can be isomorphic, but in what sense the internal is, indeed, *about* the external. We now see iconic learning as having been (despite having been defined early, in the late 1960s) a step in the right direction towards creating isomorphic mental states. But more is needed in order to have isomorphisms that involve the exploratory motion of the organism and the control of motion — a function of much importance to Aristotle.

Aristotelian form as integrated information

In Chapter 6, we described a step which links the physical and the mental in a way that uses what we know about neural networks but leans heavily on an introspection of how mental states 'feel'. This is the Integrated Information Theory of Giulio Tononi which leads to an answer to the question 'what is a mental state like?' 'It is unique and indivisible' is the answer which somewhat pleasingly leads to prescriptions for how networks that reverberate need to be constructed in order to carry states that relate to, or, perhaps even are isomorphic with, the uniqueness and indivisibility of events in the world. Here we speculate that uniqueness and indivisibility are precisely the properties of the *form* of events rather than the matter. Indivisibility, we have shown, is the ability to represent the causal relationships extant in world events and these are to do with *form*. A spoon has certain causal relationships among its elements that make it a spoon rather than a fork or a lump of metal. What this says is that one can prescribe the structure of networks that, in their reverberations, have a capacity to represent form.

What is missing in this theory, despite some attempts we have discussed and criticized, is how the body can be energized into movement so that it can search out the *form* of an external event. We argue that this activation is necessary for the internal isomorphism to have a personal feeling. Such personal activities are *qualia*.

Vision

In Chapter 7 we have looked at isomorphisms that occur particularly in the visual modality and examine the machinery of the visual areas of the brain. This is amenable to simulation which explains how eye movement is necessary and utilized to provide isomorphisms that are much more comprehensive than the limited view that is generated by the fovea of the eye. This is reminiscent of the questions that Aristotle was asking about the role that the body plays by being able to move and explore the world. But it is here that Aristotle might have been pleased with the power of the laptop due to its capacity for simulation and the ability to do exploratory science (as one might do in biology) in this artificial domain. In Chapter 7 the isomorphism between world and mind, as mediated by movement (of the eye only in this case), can be observed on the visual screen emerging as a virtual object in a simulated neural network.

Detractors

Were there none, a certain level of quality control would be missing from the kinds of arguments presented in this book (Chapter 8). Here we meet Raymond Tallis, who feels that informational explanations cause confusion in any discourse about mind; Susan Greenfield, who fears that information is a poor substitute for knowledge; Luciano Floridi, who feels that 'data' is a clearer philosophical object than 'information', and, finally, we noted the late Theodore Roszak's fears that an information society' could be hijacked by media moguls. In perspective, most of these worries stem from the association of the word *information* with *information processing* in a computer. In our own use of the word we stress the importance of information as a Shannonian object which causes a change in our structures of thought and not as the description of what a computer does. To explain, for us, information is that which changes the structure (i.e., linking) of states which constitutes the informational mind. It is a formal description of the way in which we gather our experience. Studying mind without information is like trying to explain the nature of a flame without physics or chemistry.

But this is precisely the position of scientists and philosophers from Aristotle to the 20th century. It is indeed admirable that Aristotle was able to ponder:

> *Thus that in the soul which is called mind (by mind I mean that whereby the soul thinks and judges) is, before it thinks, not actually any real thing. For this reason it cannot reasonably be regarded as blended with the body* [3,4,3]

Here we have shown, in the language of information, that the 'blending' of mind and body is the interdependence of state and physical structure. In addition, to be *thought*, a state has to be unique and representative of the causal relationships that exist in the world and which influence the senses. Whether this is right or wrong, without the language of information, the discussion cannot take place. The detractors may have their weapons pointed at the wrong meaning of the word 'information'.

Emotion

In Chapter 9 we examine Sigmund Freud's ideas of the unconscious. For this impressive and influential figure, emotion is that which both creates the unconscious and the problems it creates. This gave us the opportunity to speculate on the way that state structures of the mind might go through changes largely in the *imaginational* mode as defined in Chapter 7. Our original model was based on the creation of a stream of states during perception. This stream breaks up and forms a different linked structure of states when one 'imagines' or 'remembers' one's experience. But introducing emotions as internal evaluations and using the findings that emotions are closely linked to neuromodulators leads to the possibility that the state structure of the mind can *reconfigure*. Even in common language we say things like 'I was so disgusted with the way that John was mean to his wife that I changed my mind about liking him'. Freud's belief that events in childhood (such as misplaced incestuous desires and fears of consequent punishment, even mutilation, by adults) provided us with a vehicle for showing how the variation of state structures can lead to inaccessible or *unconscious* states.

Then Freud's method of revealing the unconscious in dreams or free association again leads us to ask how this might happen in state structures. Here it is of some interest to recognize Aristotle's consideration of dreams. He notes that emotions are involved first in the creation of mental 'impressions'[6]:

> ... *even when the external object of perception has departed, the impressions it made persist and are themselves the objects of perception: and [let us assume], besides, that we are easily deceived when we are excited by emotions .... according to different emotions ... for example the coward excited by fear, the amorous person excited by desire ... the former thinks he sees his foes approaching, the latter, that he sees the object of his desire; and the more deeply one is under the influence of the emotion the less similarity is required to give rise to these illusory impressions.* ... [2,7]

He argues that such impressions (whether accurate or not) become the material for dreams and, possibly, deliria. Here he writes how such impressions can come into consciousness:

> ... *The residuary movements <mental objects> are like these: they are within the soul potentially, but actualize themselves only when the impediment to their doing so has been relaxed; and according to as they are thus set free ... they possess verisimilitude after the manner of cloud shapes which in their metamorphoses one compares now to human beings and a moment afterwards to centaurs.* [3,1] (The words indicated in< > have been added by the authors).

Aristotle's insight into the importance of emotion in creating 'residual' states, the need for a relaxed atmosphere to retrieve them and the importance of having someone to interpret them would have pleased Freud (he makes no direct reference to Aristotle in 'The interpretation of dreams'). From the point of view of this book, we read with some feeling Aristotle's work on dreams recognising how difficult he finds it to express mental events in terms of 'movement of the blood' where we now have

---

[6]Here the quotes are from '*De Insomniis*' (*On Dreams*) published by eBooks, Adelaide, 2007, and translated by J. I. Beare. The paragraph notation is the same as for *De Anima*, earlier in this chapter, except that they refer to [part.paragraph] only as there is only one book.

informational states as the building bricks for discussing both the conscious and the unconscious mind.

Finally: Aristotle and his laptop

We (IA and HM) imagine ourselves on a visit to Chalkis on the Greek island of Euboea (also Evia). This is Aristotle's last residence and the place of his death from a stomach complaint in 322 BC.

> **Igor:** Thank you very much for agreeing to see us. We work in an academy in a different land and at a time in the future. We know that this sounds strange, but just think of it as an illusion. We have written a book which makes frequent reference to your teachings, particularly on the nature of intellect that may be found within the soul.
>
> **Helen:** We will not try to explain where we have come from, but have brought you a present: it is called a 'laptop computer'. In our land these boxes are common — they were originally constructed to perform many calculations very fast, but now it is claimed that they can be used to model those mechanisms that give to a human an understanding of the world.
>
> **Aristotle:** I have a choice to believe that you are charlatans, but, as you do not have very much to gain by visiting me, I will hear you out and thank you for the 'present'. Perhaps I can ask you some questions. The first is, if it has a mind, how does it move, eat and forage in an intelligent way?
>
> **Igor:** This box does not move eat and forage, but it is sometimes given a mechanical body which can move: it is then called a robot.
>
> **Helen:** But the robot does not need to forage. We come from a place where energy can be stored inside a machine.
>
> **Aristotle:** Ah! '$E\nu$ $\varepsilon\rho\gamma\alpha\iota\alpha$'. This means 'at work' and these are words which I used to indicate that, through work, one's resources are used up and the energy has to be replenished. This is what the cycle of living and resting does in living creatures. So how does your $\lambda\alpha\pi\tau o\pi$ go about replenishing its energy if it does not forage?
>
> **Helen:** In our world, energy is generated centrally. It is called electricity and distributed to dwellings, so we can 'charge' the laptop when

its energy wanes. Electricity will only be discovered in about 2,000 years' time.

Aristotle: How strange! But this robot with the laptop inside it, you say it moves, but where does it go? What controls it?

Igor: The robot can have an artificial eye which sends little impulses of energy to the laptop which inform the laptop of what it is that is being sensed by the eye.

Aristotle: You use the word 'inform' but how? Does the artificial eye speak?

Helen: In a way, yes. Think of a mosaic and imagine sweeping across it with your finger, each time a little lower. For every stone encountered you speak its color. If the sweeping movement is repeated inside the robot, the image seen by the eye can be reproduced. In fact, it turns out that the sequence of color values is also done by little impulses of electricity.

Igor: Early robots to be built by a man called Grey Walter were able to wander about and find sources of energy.

Aristotle: You seem to be suggesting that these robots are somehow comparable to living animals, or even humans, by virtue of the fact that they move in a purposeful way. One of my observations is that the form that distinguishes animals requires procreation. How do your robots procreate?

Helen: They don't: but they are built so that we can study whether a human-made machine can contain a mind-like substance which is sensitive to the form of things in the world.

Aristotle: But all you have made is a child's toy. How could it possibly have a mind without having any needs and desires that come from its biology?

Igor: We are not arguing that the robot is alive. But its motions in the world and their control are not just those of an inanimate object being struck by another as you discuss in *Physics*.

Helen: The robot not only has an internal source of energy, but it also has a source of knowledge about how to control this energy. So, in a sense, it can have needs such as avoiding bumping into trees.

Aristotle: But where does it get this 'knowledge'?

Helen: It is built into it by a knowledgeable person.

Aristotle: Its '*nous*' can therefore only partly be compared to the *nous* of a living creature. It also assumes that this knowledgeable person should be an outstanding biologist who understands those movements of the body that are responsible for the *nous*.

Igor: This is precisely why we are here. You see, we think that what makes the laptop and the robot do useful things is a non-palpable substance which informs them both. Therefore it is called *information*.

Aristotle: You mean that the essence of *nous* in a living entity is this thing you call *information*?

Helen: Yes, but the *nous* of a living entity is much more complex and sophisticated than that of a robot. The important thing is that by studying how this informational *nous* works in the robot we might understand better how it works in living entities.

Igor: To cut a long story short, what is known now is that the *matter* important to the soul is made of little cells (which, by the way, are in the head and not the heart) and these cells, by sending electrical pulses of information one to another can represent the causal relationships that make up the form of the objects in the world. This creates the sensation of awareness of objects outside ourselves.

Aristotle: Yes, yes dear people, what you say seems to be very significant, but I recognize that you are part of my delirium due to this stomach ache. I find that you are telling me more than I can understand in my current state. But when I recover, I will attend to your gift. For now let me just say that it pleases me that in that far-off land whence you come, that land in the future, you still think of me and that I may have played a part in your ideas. Mine are getting a bit hazy so I must ask you to leave.

Helen and Igor as we fade from Aristotle's delirium: We wish you well and hope your stomach ache soon recedes.

Appendix
THE INFORMATIONAL MIND: A FORMAL PORTRAIT

In the rest of this book, some brief descriptions have been given of the way the state structure of some neural automaton builds up. This state structure *is* the informational mind of an automaton. Here we try to be less vague about how this scheme works and follow through an example of how the structure builds up. This model can then be considered as a bead bracelet from which we can reflect back on the book to see how this bracelet can string the topics (beads) of other chapters together.

A World and the automaton

The world in which the way an automaton might develop a mind is shown in Fig. A1. This is about the simplest structure in which we can discuss the creation of a mind. It bears a resemblance to the example seen in Chapter 7 (Fig. 7.6) but here the argument is more general and taken further. There are two major players here, an entity E which 'observes' the world through a constrained window on the world W. E can choose to move the window in a finite number of ways by using an action signal a_t. The aim here is to define some conditions under which one can begin to ask whether E is becoming conscious of W. Central to this is an exploratory behavior of E in W from which E develops a state structure that is to become its 'informational mind' of E.

The World

W is an automaton in the sense that it receives an input which changes the position of a window in response to an action signal from the entity. The state of the window is determined by its position in the world. The window

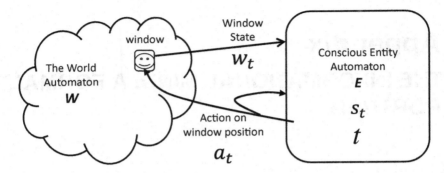

Fig. A1.   A closed system with which the question can be asked: how does learning entity **E** become conscious of some world **W** and its existence in that world? It is the state structure of **E** that is its 'informational mind'.

also represents the position of the entity **E** in the world. In loose language it can be said that **E** 'looks' at a fixed pattern determined by the position of the window. This pattern is the current (at time t) state of the world: w_j. The world receives an action input from **E** which we call a_t.

The formulation for **W** is a triplet:

$$\boldsymbol{W} :< A, W, p >$$

where, $A = \{a_1, a_2 \ldots a_{/A/}\}$, is the set of action inputs and $/A/$ is the number of elements in the set.

Also, using similar notation, $W = \{w_1 w_2 \ldots w_{/W/}\}$, each element of this set is the content of a window. All such window states are assumed to be unique and indivisible thus according with the tenets of Information integration theories. However, it is possible to define a similarity function $H(w_i * w_j)$ which results from a comparison between the two states and can be required to have a value in the interval $(0 \rightarrow 1)$ with 0 meaning orthogonality and 1 meaning total similarity. The exact function of the comparison (e.g., Hamming Distance in the case of binary windows) need not be stated at this moment.

In the triplet for **W** above, p is a mapping from the current window state to the next as mediated by an action state a_t transmitted from **E**, that is:

$$W \times A \overset{p}{\to} W' \tag{1}$$

this indicates that the set of all (w_j, a_t) pairs maps according to a specification p into the *next* occurring window state, w'_j. This is the model of a fixed world which is explored by $\boldsymbol{E}$ which is formalized next.

The entity

$\boldsymbol{E}$ the Entity is a learning automaton. It is defined by a 5-tuple

$$\boldsymbol{E} :< W, S, A, q, r >$$

where A is as defined for $\boldsymbol{W}$, that is a set of actions generated by $\boldsymbol{E}$ and W is the set of all possible window states in $\boldsymbol{W}$, as defined above. Also, $S = \{s_1, s_2 \ldots s_{/S/}\}$ is the set of internal states of $\boldsymbol{E}$, where:

$$S \times W \overset{q}{\to} S'$$

this indicates that the set of all (s_j, w_k) pairs maps according to a specification q into the *next* occurring entity state, s'_j. Note, the process of learning is a process of building q.

Also the action of $\boldsymbol{E}$ on $\boldsymbol{W}$ is defined by

$$s \overset{r}{\to} A$$

(using the expression conventions used above)

That is, all the (s_j) elements of S map into the set of actions A according to some specification r. How r is developed is also discussed under the heading of behavior. There are many possible learning modes that represent different ways of dealing with time and action learning. We formalize some below.

Learning method 1: Closed random walk

Let the window state at time t be w_t where $w_t \in W$. Let this be the first step of learning and let the network be in some previous state s_{t-1}.

Learning then proceeds as follows. The net is trained to execute the following:

$$(w_t, s_{t-1}) \overset{q}{\to} s_t$$

That is, the input of the net receives the window state and internal state and forces the iconic representation of the window state, s_t as the state at time t. This forms an entry in some truth table which implements q.

It should be noted that $s_a \cong w_a$, that is, the iconic representation is very much like the corresponding input, but the separate notation is used to respect the provenance of where these patterns are found.

A further element of learning is the determination of the action associated with entity states. While this can be done in many ways, one particular method is selected here to illustrate how the system in Fig. A1 might behave.

The method consists of assigning an *arbitrarily* chosen $a_t \in A$ to state s_t, making,

$$s_t \xrightarrow{r} a_t$$

The arbitrariness makes the exploratory action of $\boldsymbol{E}$ random. This forms an entry in some truth table which implements r. This is like saying that having entered a state which closely represents the current window state $\boldsymbol{E}$ moves the window to w_{t+1} by taking the arbitrary action a_t as follows (according to the relationship (1)):

$$(w_t, a_t) \xrightarrow{r} w_{t+1}$$

With this, the learning process can be repeated for window content, w_{t+1}, and so on as time progresses.

Learning behavior

We now go through the above as a time sequence to show how state structure builds up.

- $\boldsymbol{E}$ 'sees' the world through a window which is in state w_t, that is, w_t is an input to automaton $\boldsymbol{E}$. In the example model, w_t is specified as an image of $q \times q$ binary picture points for the purposes of illustration.
- It is assumed that $\boldsymbol{E}$ is time sensitive, that is, the automaton also receives an input t (where $t = 1, 2, 3, \ldots$).
- $\boldsymbol{E}$ receives three signals (w_t, t, a_t) where a_t is the action signal generated at time t which moved the window to a position where in $\boldsymbol{W}$ where its state is w_t. t is a time signal internally generated in $\boldsymbol{E}$.
- Iconic training means that $\boldsymbol{E}$ is forced to enter state (s_t, t, a_t) where s_t is the inner iconic representation of w_t.
- We note that (s_t, t, a_t) is *unique* because that particular value of t has never occurred before. At this point a_{t+1} is arbitrarily chosen.

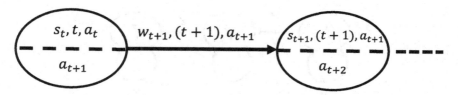

Fig. A2. Two steps in the iconic learning of state structure in E. Each oval is a state with the elements of the state above the dotted line and the action output below the line. The input is on the transition arrow.

- This leads to a new world input w_{t+1} and the new learned state $(s_{t+1}, (t+1), a_{t+1})$ which again arbitrarily generates an output a_{t+2} and so on. We can now draw a picture.

Figure A2 shows that a linear state structure builds up in E that faithfully represents the exploratory actions of E in W.

The imaginative mode

This is defined by E being 'inattentive' to input. In practical terms we see this as *dis-integrating* the information at the input, that is, replacing it by noise. The result of this is that the state structure built up through experience loses its linear structure and becomes a probabilistic automaton where transitions occur according to the similarity between states in the state structure. To clarify this, we introduce a slightly different learning mode during exploration.

Learning to make attractors in the state structure

A criticism one can make of the learning method seen above is that the states created have a fleeting character, whereas much of what was said about state structures in this book refers to *attractors* (see Chapter 5). A training scheme that iconically creates attractors due to progressively experienced states X, Y, and Z is shown in Fig. A3. Here we initially do not include the time inputs and comment on this later.

To analyse this, consider the following table which indicates the training that is involved in creating the state structure of Fig. A3. The iconic nature of this results from the learned next state being the same as the input.

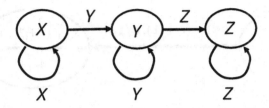

Fig. A3.   The creation of attractors for states for X, Y and Z in sequence.

Table 1.   Training which leads to Figure A3.

Line No.	Input	State	Next State	
1	X	X	X	*Makes X re-entrant*
2	Y	X	Y	*Creates transition from X to Y*
3	Y	Y	Y	*Makes Y re-entrant*
4	Z	Y	Z	*Creates transition from Y to Z*
5	Z	Z	Z	*Makes Z re-entrant*

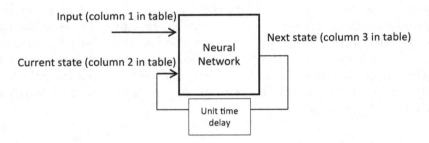

Fig. A4.   Network arrangement to be read in conjunction with Table 1.

Now consider what happens in this state structure were it to be in state X and were the input to be a frame of random noise. We assume that this noise input (say N) has the following similarities to the three training sets (measured, say, as a percentage of point-to-point similarity) Nx, Ny and Nz. Each of these measures has an equal probability of being anywhere in the interval $(0 \rightarrow 1)$. It might be worth drawing a picture:

Given the noise pattern N and looking at Table 1, one needs to establish which input/state pair in the training set is the most similar to the current pair. Say that total similarity scores 1 and that the similarity between any two training patterns is 50%. Now taking line 1 of the table the similarity score is $(Nx+1)$ because the net is currently in state X and the input is Nx similar to input X which is indicated in this line. Note that the maximum is 2 scored by an input/state pair which is one of the training pairs. Now the complete set of similarities for the whole table can be enunciated:

Line 1: $(Nx + 1)$ (The state is X adding 1 to whatever the input score is with respect to X)

Line 2: $(Ny + 1)$ (The state is X adding 1 to whatever the input score with respect to Yi

Line 3: $(Ny + 0.5)$ (due to the 50% similarity between states X and Y).

Line 4: $(Nz + 0.5)$ (due to the 50% similarity between states X and Y).

Line 5: $(Nz + 0.5)$ (due to the 50% similarity between states X and Z).

We look first for what values of Nz, will make line 4 (the condition is the same for 5) score the highest of all the lines, causing the next state to be Z. Noticing that line 2 is always of lesser value than line 3, the condition for line 4 to win is

$(Nz + 0.5) > (Nx + 1)$ with respect to line 1 (that is, $(Nz > (Nx + 5))$

and

$(Nz + 0.5) > (Ny + 1)$ with respect to line 2 (that is, $(Nz > (Ny + 0.5))$

A picture might help to illustrate the first of these conditions:

As all values of Nz and Ny are equally probable, the area shown in grey within the total area of the unit square shows that the probability

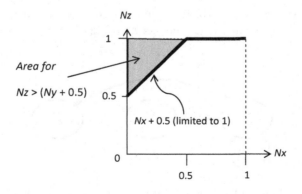

Fig. A5. Shows the area that satisfies $Nz > (Ny + 0.5)$.

of $Nz > (Ny + 0.5)$ is $1/8$. This is also true of $Nz > (Ny + 0.5)$. So if the next state is to be Z it is the conjunction of these two events that must ensue, and therefore the probability of the next state being Z is $1/64$ ($0.015625 = P$, say).

Otherwise it is merely a question of whether $Nx > Ny$ in which case the next state w ill be X while if $Nx < Ny$ the next state will be Y. If the two are equal, X or Y occur with equal probability. This probability will be

$$\frac{\left(1 - \frac{1}{64}\right)}{2} = 0.492188 = Q \text{ (say)}$$

Therefore it is clear that the network is behaving in a probabilistic way and the onward transitions from state X are shown in Fig. A6.

The principle being represented here is that while the automaton has a high probability of following the 'experienced' set of states, it can be 'distracted' to another state in its memory.

Commentary

In the earlier part of this formal discussion we suggested that *time* was an important part of a state which supported its uniqueness. Without going into details we suggest that the time information does not alter significantly the behavior in the imaginative mode as all transitions in one state that progress with time can be treated in the same way as the transition from X to Y in the above discussion. In other words, not only are attractors discovered by the net in response to perceptual input, but also durations and points in history of certain experiences are encoded. They may be retrieved by the occurrence at an arbitrary tim of some perceptual experience, or even by accidental transitions (such as P in Fig. A6).

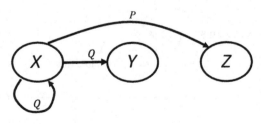

Fig. A6.   Probabilistic automaton resulting from the introduction of noise at the input.

The statistical assessments above point to the fact that the larger the state structure (i.e., the more states like Z that there might be) the less likely will the automaton be to follow learned state trajectories. However, this can be offset by the input being replaced by noise even when learning is taking place. More detailed assessments of this are beyond the scope of this book (not to mention the statistical abilities of the authors!)

Author Index

Subject Index